Some Versions of Cary Grant

Some Versions of Cary Grant

JAMES NAREMORE

OXFORD

UNIVERSITY PRESS

OXFORD
UNIVERSITY PRESS

Oxford University Press is a department of the University of Oxford. It furthers the University's objective of excellence in research, scholarship, and education by publishing worldwide. Oxford is a registered trade mark of Oxford University Press in the UK and certain other countries.

Published in the United States of America by Oxford University Press 198 Madison Avenue, New York, NY 10016, United States of America.

© Oxford University Press 2022

Library of Congress Cataloging-in-Publication Data
Names: Naremore, James, author.
Title: Some versions of Cary Grant / James Naremore.
Description: New York, NY : Oxford University Press, [2022] |
Includes bibliographical references and index.
Identifiers: LCCN 2021052835 (print) | LCCN 2021052836 (ebook) |
ISBN 9780197566381 (paperback) | ISBN 9780197566374 (hardback) |
ISBN 9780197566404 (epub) | ISBN 9780197566411
Subjects: LCSH: Grant, Cary, 1904-1986—Performances. |
Grant, Cary, 1904-1986—Criticism and interpretation. | Motion picture acting. |
Motion pictures—United States—History—20th century. |
Motion picture actors and actresses—United States—Biography. |
Motion picture actors and actresses—Great Britain—Biography.
Classification: LCC PN2287.G675 N37 2022 (print) |
LCC PN2287.G675 (ebook) | DDC 791.4302/8092—dc23/eng/20211110
LC record available at https://lccn.loc.gov/2021052835
LC ebook record available at https://lccn.loc.gov/2021052836

DOI: 10.1093/oso/9780197566374.001.0001

1 3 5 7 9 8 6 4 2

Paperback printed by Marquis, Canada
Hardback printed by Bridgeport National Bindery, Inc., United States of America

For Darlene

Contents

Acknowledgments

I owe special thanks to Professor Charlotte Crofts of the University of the West of England, Bristol, who invited me to give a talk for the biannual Cary Grant festival in the city of Grant's birth and indirectly gave me the idea for this book. Mark Glancy, Grant's outstanding biographer, read the manuscript, corrected many of my errors, and made important suggestions for improvement (any surviving errors are mine, not his). I was also given helpful suggestions from film scholars David Bordwell, Joseph McBride, Dana Polan, and Robert B. Ray, who encouraged me from the start. My editor, Norman Hirschy, was unfailingly helpful and supportive, repeatedly offering good advice. A grant-in-aid from Indiana University provided financial assistance, and Carmel Curtis of the Indiana University Moving Image Archive gave me expert help in preparing the illustrations. Above all, literary and film historian Darlene Sadlier, who happens to be my wife, read the book as it was being written and, as always, made it better.

1

Introduction to Methods and a Brief History of a Star

Everyone wants to be Cary Grant. Even I want to be Cary Grant.

—Cary Grant

I.

This book isn't a biography of Cary Grant, though I've benefited from the research of Grant's biographers, especially from Nancy Nelson's *Evenings with
Cary Grant* (2012, first published 1991), Scott Eyman's *Cary Grant: A Brilliant
Disguise* (2020), and Mark Glancy's *Cary Grant: The Making of a Hollywood
Legend* (2020). My interest here is in Grant's art rather than his life. Several
readers may recognize that my title, *Some Versions of Cary Grant*, alludes to
the British poet and critic William Empson's *Some Versions of Pastoral* (1935),
a classic study of pastoral themes in the history of English literature.[1] His
subject was very different from mine, but like him I want to show surprising
variations within a familiar topic. I also want to apply techniques of close
reading roughly analogous to the ones that made Empson's criticism vital.

Empson was dealing with the language of literature, but I'm dealing with
film performance, which involves language and many other things, some difficult to convey. Robin Wood, in writing about one of Cary Grant's films, has
remarked, "no matter after how many viewings, the spectator is delighted by
small touches of comic business often beyond the critic's reach, since they
defy verbal description: matters of gesture, expression, intonation."[2] Wood
may be right, but I plan to test the limits of critical reach. I write not as a
practitioner of the actor's art, but as a viewer in the audience who admires

---

[1] A scholarly edition of William Empson's *Some Versions of Pastoral*, edited by Seamus Perry, has
recently been published by Oxford University Press (2020).
[2] Robin Wood, *Howard Hawks* (London: British Film Institute, 1983), 68.

Some Versions of Cary Grant. James Naremore, Oxford University Press. © Oxford University Press 2022.
DOI: 10.1093/oso/9780197566374.003.0001

an actor's skill. Because I can't quote from performances in the way literary critics quote from poetry, I depend on what ancient Greek rhetoricians called *ekphrasis*, or detailed description. I'm aided by frame enlargements from Grant's films, but even they can't always suggest the quality of his movements.

Was Cary Grant, as David Thomson has argued, "the best and most important actor in the history of the cinema"?[3] Thomson's writings, like my own, are mainly Anglocentric and devoted to Hollywood, but leaving aside world cinema and speaking only of both male and female English-speaking actors in Grant's day, was Grant actually a better actor than Robert Mitchum, Agnes Moorehead, Geraldine Page, Mickey Rooney, Barbara Stanwyck, or (shocking as the suggestion might seem) Bobby Darin? Was he better than Laurence Olivier, who in *The Beggar's Opera* (1953) carries a beautiful woman in his arms as he climbs a high ladder and sings a love song? (Whatever the case, I wish Grant rather than Olivier had played Archie Rice in *The Entertainer* [1960].) Was he better than dozens of recent English-language movie actors one could name, among them Cate Blanchett, Kevin Kline, Tilda Swinton, and Denzel Washington? I think not, but I'm convinced that in the era of the classic Hollywood studios, nobody was more technically adept and gifted, and nobody more important as a movie star.

Any study of a performance by a star needs to deal with the relationship between an actor (a performer with a range of physical traits and technical skills, some inherent, others developed, which result in a personal style), a role (a fictional character with physical and personality traits the actor must embody), and a kind of aura or star image (an intertextual phenomenon determined by publicity and performances, influencing the kinds of roles the actor plays).[4] Besides all this, the star is a social subject whose life history can become public, affecting the performances, roles, and image.

Consider Grant, whose image at the height of his fame represented the epitome of urbane masculine glamour. Tall, dark, and handsome, he was a former acrobat and vaudeville performer who on screen moved with catlike grace and energy. Even though he was a skilled horseman, he never played a cowboy like Gary Cooper (except for a 16mm home movie he made with Betsy Drake) and was never a swordsman in tights like Errol Flynn. His star image—which, like all such images, is an oversimplification based on

---

[3] David Thomson, *A Biographical Dictionary of Film*, 3rd ed. (New York: Alfred A. Knopf, 1994), 300.

[4] For an important discussion of the "star image," see Richard Dyer, *Stars* (London: British Film Institute, 1979).

his physical qualities and a limited set of roles—is chiefly that of a debonair man in a drawing room, sometimes with a hand in his pocket and shoulders slightly hunched, who wears clothes beautifully but behaves with unpretentious casualness and deft comic timing.

Grant's smile was highly expressive, capable of many inflections, and he spoke with a unique mid-Atlantic accent that made him a success not only in movies but also on radio. It's the voice of an educated Englishman who wants to sound American, or maybe an American who wants to sound British. Mark Glancy has described it as a mixture of Bristol (where Grant was born), Brixton (the south London variant of Cockney), and Broadway (which accounts for Grant's staccato clarity).[5] For American ears especially, it connotes upper classness. Tony Curtis, who co-starred with Grant in *Operation Petticoat* (1959), gave a memorably funny impersonation of it in *Some Like It Hot* (1959), in which Curtis plays a fake yachtsman out to seduce Marilyn Monroe. At one point in the film, Jack Lemmon says to him, "Where did you get that silly accent? Nobody talks like that!"

The impersonation has partly to do with Grant's habit of crisply enunciating words and putting cadenced stress on them—as in *North by Northwest* (1959), when he complains that he shouldn't be confused with a fellow named George Kaplan: "I've been in his *hotel*! I've tried on his *clothes*! He's

---

[5] Mark Glancy, *Cary Grant: The Making of a Hollywood Legend* (New York: Oxford, 2020), 58.

got *short sleeves* and *dandruff*!" In the 1960s, the comic Larry Storch impersonated Grant by saying "*Ju*-day, *Ju*-day, *Ju*-day," a line Grant had never spoken, which nevertheless became associated with him. According to Peter Bogdanovich, Jack and Bobby Kennedy once called Grant on the phone because they wanted to hear him speak. "My *secretary* told me the *President* was on the *line*," Grant told Bogdanovich, "so naturally I was curious why he was *calling* and picked right up."[6]

Grant's stardom was mainly the product of pictures he made between the late 1930s and the mid-1960s. During the 1930s, when movie stars were kept busy churning out product, he made twenty-eight films, many of them forgettable, before Leo McCarey's *The Awful Truth* (1937) helped create what would become the popular notion of Grant-ness—an image that was given other dimensions over the next decade and made even more popular in wide-screen, color films such as *To Catch a Thief* (1955), *An Affair to Remember* (1957), *Indiscreet* (1958), and *North by Northwest*, in all of which he was tanned, understated, and aged like a fine wine. For most of his career, Quigley Publications in Hollywood published a poll of movie exhibitors listing the top-ten stars of the year, based on box-office returns; the poll was unreliable in many ways, often dependent on how many films a star made in a given year, but it reflects Grant's late-period success. He made the list in 1944, 1948, 1949, and every year from 1959 to 1966.

Grant was unimpressive in costume pictures such as *The Howards of Virginia* (1940) and *The Pride and the Passion* (1957), and he tended to avoid action genres. When he played a military character, usually it was a well-tailored naval officer. Many of his films conformed to a wandering-versus-settling structure common to male leads in Hollywood, but he developed a special quality as a romantic leading man—he seldom pursued women, they pursued him. Andrew Britton describes his style as "a male heterosexuality which is so different in tone from that of the action hero, and which is arrived at through a different kind of relationship with women—a relationship in which the woman appears so often as the educator of the male, and of his pleasure."[7] That ended with his last movie, *Walk, Don't Run* (1966), in which he played a matchmaker for Jim Hutton and Paula Prentiss; he was sixty-two at the time and thought he no longer had romantic appeal as a leading man. He had already turned down *Man's Favorite Sport?* (1964), a movie Howard

---

[6] Quoted in Peter Bogdanovich, *Who the Hell's in It?* (New York: Alfred A. Knopf, 2004), 97.
[7] Andrew Britton, *Cary Grant: Comedy and Male Desire* (Newcastle upon Tyne: Tyneside Cinema, 1983), 17.

Hawks developed for him, similar to *Bringing Up Baby* (1938) and very much about the woman as "educator of the male, and of his pleasure," which eventually starred Rock Hudson.

Like all major stars, Grant was the topic of publicity, gossip, and biographical writing. He was born Archibald Alexander Leach in 1904 and never tried to conceal his birth name. In *His Girl Friday* (1939), when he's told by another character that he's finished, he snarls, "The last person who called me *that* was *Archie Leach*, the day before they *cut* his *throat!*" The name became so well known that in *A Fish Called Wanda* (1988), John Cleese could joke about it by playing a hapless London barrister named Archie Leach. The real Archie's home, however, was Bristol. According to biographers, his mother, Elsie, was refined, strict, and possessive; his father, Elias, was handsome, an alcoholic, and a philanderer who may have dreamed of a theatrical career but made his living as a presser in a tailoring factory. Archie came home one day to find his mother gone. He thought she had abandoned him but was eventually told by his father that she had died. Many years later, he discovered she was alive and committed to a mental institution for "mania."

At age fourteen, under the nominal care of his father, the athletically and musically talented Archie was expelled from school, probably because he wanted to be. Fascinated by the theatrical productions at the Bristol Hippodrome, he soon found work as a member of Bob Pender's troupe of comic acrobats. He sang, danced, played piano, walked on stilts, turned somersaults, and helped perform knockabout skits that earned the Pender troupe a 1920 tour in America. When the troupe returned to Britain, Archie remained in the US, getting occasional work as a stilt walker and street hawker of handmade ties. In 1927, he made the first of his Broadway theatrical appearances in operettas and musicals; in 1931, he signed a five-year Hollywood contract with Paramount; and in 1942, he became an American citizen, legally changing his name to Cary Grant.

There were aspects of Grant's life that might have damaged his star image, but somehow never did. He was married five times, and in the 1950s experimented with LSD, praising its psychologically therapeutic powers. (In 2021, the unorthodox musical *Flying Over Sunset* premiered on Broadway, depicting three famous people who were early advocates of LSD: Cary Grant, Aldous Huxley, and Clare Boothe Luce.) For a brief moment in 1947, right-wing watchdogs labeled several of his films communist propaganda. (There were times when he seemed liberal, as when he came to the defense of Charles Chaplin and Ingrid Bergman, who had been ostracized in America, or when he broadcast a radio appeal for gun control after the assassination of Bobby Kennedy; but there were other times when he seemed conservative.) Far more potentially dangerous to his stardom were his early relationships with men. He lived several years with the effeminate costume designer Orry-Kelly, who helped his young career in New York and Hollywood. A more lasting relationship was with fellow movie star Randolph Scott. The two met when they acted in the pre-Code drama *Hot Saturday* (1932) and soon began living together in a rented Santa Monica beach house. There was nothing unique about this arrangement—at roughly the same time, David Niven and Errol Flynn shared a house they called "Cirrhosis-by-the-Sea." But when a gay photographer took publicity photos of Grant and Scott working out together they became subject of rumors (they also once dressed for Halloween in drag). Paramount dubbed the beach house "Bachelor Hall" and commissioned magazine stories to assure readers that Cary and Randy were regular guys. They co-starred only once more, in the screwball comedy *My Favorite Wife* (1940), playing rivals for Irene Dunne and providing innuendo for those in the know. It was Grant who had suggested casting Scott.

In the 1960s, Peter Bogdanovich asked Howard Hawks if there was any truth to the stories that Grant was gay, and Hawks derisively snorted that the idea was "ridiculous" because "every time I see him, he's got a younger girl on his arm."[8] It was Hawks, however, who exploited Grant's talent for broad comedy by dressing him as a woman in *Bringing Up Baby* and *I Was a Male War Bride* (1949). The rumors about the Grant-Scott relationship didn't become widely known until 1975, after Grant's career ended, with the publication of Kenneth Anger's *Hollywood Babylon*, a gossipy, sometimes mean-spirited book that was prone to error or exaggeration. In a 1970s TV interview, the comic Chevy Chase jokingly called Grant a "homo," and Grant filed a lawsuit that was amicably settled out of court. Grant said he had nothing against homosexuals, but wasn't one.

Grant well knew that his stardom depended on his good looks, urbanity, and appeal to women. When he played a scruffy character in *Father Goose* (1964), movie audiences were disappointed; they wanted him to be Cary Grant. "You know what's wrong with you?" Audrey Hepburn famously asked him in *Charade* (1963), and swooningly answered her own question: "Nothing." This perfection, however, was slow to develop. In his early Paramount films he seems stiff and his face looks as if he still has baby fat.

[8] Quoted in Bogdanovich, 117.

He initially attracted attention as a shady but glamourous lover of Marlene Dietrich in *Blonde Venus* (1931), in which Joseph von Sternberg taught him to part his hair on the right, and as eye-candy for Mae West in *She Done Him Wrong* (1933) and *I'm No Angel* (1933). In the first of the West films, she asked him, "Why don't you come up sometime and see me?" It went over so well that in the second one she changed it from interrogative to imperative: "Come up and see me sometime."

In the 1930s and 1940s, Grant sometimes smoked and drank too much, but in later life he became a health advocate, preserving his looks throughout his career. His impeccable taste in clothing was probably influenced by his father's work in a tailoring factory (his father insisted that if Archie had only one suit and pair of shoes they should be good ones), his early admiration of Douglas Fairbanks, Sr. and his friendship with Cole Porter. He often supervised his film wardrobe, although he occasionally skipped bespoke suits, dressing down or wearing off-the-rack items from Brooks Brothers. (There is an unintentionally hilarious promotional video on YouTube entitled "How to Dress Like Cary Grant," in which a young salesman for *The Gentleman's Gazette* gives an illustrated lecture on Grant's style, then dresses supposedly like him with unfortunate effect.) Despite his sartorial glamour, he seems never to have been a true social butterfly and may have bored some of his wives because as he grew older his chief enjoyments were baseball and watching TV.

Grant managed his own career to a remarkable degree. A frugal and canny businessman, after retiring from movies he joined the board of directors of Fabergé cosmetics and was elected to the board of directors of M.G.M. Much earlier, at the height of the studio system, when actors were completely under control of management contracts, he was one of the first stars to become a freelancer. Resentful because Paramount paid him less than Gary Cooper and refused to loan him to M.G.M. as Gable's co-star in *Mutiny on the Bounty* (1935), he left the studio after his initial five-year contract, announced that he wouldn't sign exclusively with anyone, and temporarily resigned from the then-powerful Motion Picture Academy.

Grant never won an Oscar and had to wait until 1970 to receive an Honorary Award for his life's work, but his decision to freelance was a good one. He became not only a financial success but also a kind of auteur, perfecting his image. According to many people who worked with him, he was an unusually well-prepared actor who made contributions beyond his own performance. Garson Kanin remembered: "Almost more than any other quality was his seriousness about his work . . . He related very well to the other players. He not only took his own part seriously; he took the whole picture seriously. He'd come and look at the rushes every evening . . . In reality he was an extremely serious man, an exceptionally concentrated man. And extremely intelligent, too."[9] As a freelancer he was usually able to pick his writers and directors, and in later life he produced several of his films. He also gave Delmer Daves, Clifford Odets, Richard Brooks, and Blake Edwards their first opportunity to direct.

Always aware of his looks on screen, Grant instructed photographers to favor his right profile, perhaps because he had a mole on the left cheek. He didn't always make good decisions about films: *Dream Wife* (1953) exhibits all his comic skills but seems painfully silly and somewhat misogynistic, and the less said about *The Pride and the Passion* the better. He turned down an amazing number of plum roles, among them James Bond (he was probably an influence on Ian Fleming's character, but *North by Northwest*, which in some ways foreshadowed the Bond pictures, is better than any of them); Linus Larrabee in Wilder's *Sabrina* (1954); Norman Maine in Cukor's remake of *A Star Is Born* (1954); and Humbert Humbert in Kubrick's *Lolita* (1962). James Mason was cast in two of these films and as Grant's dark double in *North by Northwest*, a picture on which Grant made even more money than Hitchcock.

As I've indicated, the star's image is always an oversimplification. Moreover, it can obscure the talent needed for its creation. In Grant's case the image was so powerful that he was sometimes treated with condescension, as if he were simply a charming fellow who always played the same thing. Katharine Hepburn said that Grant was "a personality functioning . . . He can't play a serious part or, let me say, the public isn't interested in him that way . . . But he has a lovely sense of timing, an amusing face and a lovely voice."[10] Pauline Kael wrote that Grant was "a wonderful object of contemplation," who "might have become a great actor" if he had "taken more risks."[11] Remarks such as these, based on the fallacious assumption that the star's image requires no work and that Grant's performances in a gallery of great films lacked variety or seriousness, should be dismissed out of hand. Hepburn was correct that Grant was a "personality functioning" (so was she), but this simply means that he was expert at what in an earlier era was called "personality acting," or the creation of attractive or distinguishing traits that can recur across roles.

[9] Quoted in Nancy Nelson, *Evenings with Cary Grant: A Biography* (Lanham, MD: Applause Books, 2012), 115.

[10] Quoted in David Shipman, *The Great Movie Stars* (London: Hamlyn, 1970), 254.

[11] Pauline Kael, *When the Lights Go Down* (New York: Holt, Rinehart & Winston, 1977), 25–26.

At a specialized or meta level, Grant was a supremely successful example of something we all do in everyday life, which is why the metaphor of life as theater is so common, and why some people may have thought Grant wasn't acting. The situation for him, and in a less complicated way for everyone, has been well described by Robert Ezra Park:

> It is probably no mere historical accident that the word person, in its first meaning, is a mask. It is rather a recognition of the fact that everyone is always and everywhere, more or less consciously, playing a role . . . In a sense, and in so far as this mask represents the conception we have formed of ourselves—the role we are striving to live up to—this mask is our truer self, the self we would like to be . . . our role becomes second nature, an integral part of our personality. We come into the world as individuals, achieve character, and become persons.[12]

We might say that Grant came into the world as Archie Leach, created a movie-star image named Cary Grant, and strove to live up to that person. "I guess to a certain extent I did eventually become the characters I was playing," he once said. "I played at being someone I wanted to be until I became that person. Or he became me."[13]

II.

Look closer, and things become complicated. We can offer a more accurate description of Grant's art if we make a series of smaller generalizations based on the range of performing skills required for his films; there were not only different genres in which he worked but also different versions of Cary Grant, involving more versatility than commonly recognized. These different Grants can mingle or combine, but in a given film they're usually dominated by the Grant who is appropriate for a particular role. In the chapters that follow, I discuss five of them:

1. *Farceur Cary*. Farce, a comic form practiced by Plautus, Shakespeare, and countless others, is typically associated with stock characters, exaggerated

---

[12] Quoted in Erving Goffman, *The Presentation of Self in Everyday Life* (Garden City, NY: Doubleday, 1959), 19.
[13] Quoted in Nelson, 68–69.

performance, awkward sex situations, confusions of identity, fast-paced action, rapid entrances and exits, and acrobatic clowning. In Grant's childhood, elements of farce were woven into British music-hall entertainment, which featured bawdy comics, slapstick clowns, drag acts, magicians, and every sort of popular singing and dancing. London's East End had large, working-class music halls that gave a Cockney accent to farce, and Charlie Chaplin, an important influence on young Grant, developed his comedy near that environment. (There are interesting parallels between Chaplin and Grant: both were left-handed, both were British, both were comic acrobats, and both had difficult childhoods with institutionalized mothers; in his own way, Grant was as important a comic actor as Chaplin.)

Grant began his career in the farce-related comedy of the Pender troupe, an all-boy variety act that featured juggling, stilt walking, animal imitations, eccentric dancing, singing, mime, and comic slapstick. This was the basis of Grant's theatrical training, and one reason he became a great movie star is that he could imbue a variety of films, including sophisticated romantic comedy and dark drama, with elements of lowbrow farce. In *Charade*, for example, he amuses Audrey Hepburn by taking a shower with his clothes on.

In *Holiday* (1938), a comedy of manners emphasizing "play" as an antidote to stuffy, high-bourgeois repression, he not only does a back flip but also supports Katharine Hepburn when she stands on his shoulders for a tumbling act. In *The Philadelphia Story* (1940), another comedy of manners, he and Hepburn play a battling married couple and collaborate in a physical pantomime indebted to the silent comics: exasperated when she deliberately breaks his golf club over her knee, he exits his house, turns, and shoves her in the chin, whereupon she falls backward stiff as a board through the open door. Director George Cukor's framing of the shot is crucial, but perhaps only Grant and Hepburn could have made this sort of pantomimic violence against a woman seem amusing.

In *North by Northwest*, the suspense is infused with farce: see Grant's close-ups when he drunkenly tries to keep the sports car he's driving from going over a cliff, or notice his reaction when he finds himself in the crowded UN building, standing over a dead man and holding a knife as photographers snap his picture. In scenes of this kind he's highly expressive, but he was also a superb straight man, capable of getting a laugh with subtle reactions. In his early days in New York, he knew and closely studied one of the best comic straight men, George Burns. An obvious example of what he learned is the moment in *To Catch a Thief* when he turns and looks slyly toward the camera after Grace Kelly gives him a long, sultry kiss.

The truly farcical Grant pictures belong to a cycle known in the 1930s and early 1940s as "screwball comedy," and his ability to make clowning glamourous was first noticed in two of these films of 1937: he's a wealthy, tuxedoed ghost in the hugely successful but today only mildly amusing *Topper*; and, more importantly, a wayward husband in *The Awful Truth*. These were soon followed by Howard Hawks's *Bringing Up Baby* and *His Girl Friday*. Later in the decade, Frank Capra's adaptation of *Arsenic and Old Lace* (1944) was one of Grant's most popular pictures, although as Grant himself later said, it's overstated and semi-hysterical, lacking comic variation. Farce has a more effective recrudescence in Grant's post–World War II comedies. In *The Bachelor and the Bobby-Soxer* (1947), he's a man-about-town who relaxes elegantly in his bachelor apartment with a drink and a book, hears police sirens, and discovers an underage girl sleeping on his couch; in *I Was a Male War Bride* (1949), he's a French military officer who has to dress as a female; and in *Monkey Business* (1952), after drinking a youth serum, he does a one-handed cartwheel, has fun with Marilyn Monroe, and regresses to childhood.

2. *Dark Cary*. The antithesis of the farces were the noir-like films Grant made chiefly with Hitchcock, who repeatedly cast him as a man with sinister or unsympathetic traits. Some of Grant's comic, romantic, or adventure roles give a hint of this darkness, especially his wealthy manipulator of Dietrich in *Blonde Venus*, his crook and con man in *Sylvia Scarlett* (1935), his unscrupulous newspaper editor in *His Girl Friday*, and his gambler/draft dodger in *Mr. Lucky* (1943). See also his role as the jilted, embittered boss of a God-forsaken airline in *Only Angels Have Wings* (1939); for that film, he invented the scene in which he dumps ice water on the drunken Rita Hayworth's head.

But Hitchcock gave us the genuinely disturbing Grant, just as he later did with James Stewart in *Vertigo* (1958). The two major examples are *Suspicion* (1941), the story of a woman's passionate, masochistic love for a man who may be planning to kill her; and *Notorious* (1946), the story of a man whose sexual insecurity and egoism almost causes the death of a woman he loves. Grant also has unattractive traits in *North by Northwest*, but they tend to be treated in comic/satiric terms. Probably Hitchcock's most psychologically dark use of Grant would have been in a picture that unfortunately was never made: a modernized version of *Hamlet*, to which Grant gave tentative approval in 1946.

Grant was an ideal actor for Hitchcock not only because audiences liked and identified with him but also because he could give rough shadings to an otherwise polished character. Pauline Kael may have been wrong about the range of his talent, but she was right to observe that his "romantic elegance" was "wrapped around the resilient, tough core of a mutt."[14] Even more important, he was adept at registering small, understated actions and facial expressions in a crisp, lucidly readable style. Again and again he demonstrated control over degrees of expression, unobtrusively aiding Hitchcock's editing and emphasis on subjective point of view. He could look off-screen right or left and perform normal movements with a precisely calibrated effect. He was the kind of actor that a theorist like Lev Kuleshov, from whom Hitchcock seems to have learned a great deal, would have appreciated.

3. *Romantic Cary.* Most Hollywood movies of the classic studio era were "romantic" in the sense that, at some level, they were love stories with boy-meets-girl plots. *Notorious*, with its celebrated long-take kissing scene between Grant and Bergman, is both a suspense film and a romantic film, but its romance is subtly perverse. Hollywood's purely romantic films tended to be musicals, which treated love in utopian fashion, or "weepies," which were centered on the suffering and sacrifices of women. Apart from the dreadful Cole Porter biopic *Night and Day* (1946), Grant avoided musicals (he sang a romantic tune in *Kiss and Make Up* [1934]), and his male-centered romantic melodrama *In Name Only* (1939) is disappointing. His two best films in the romantic vein are Leo McCarey's *An Affair to Remember* (1957) and Stanley Donen's *Indiscreet* (1958), both of which employ the formula of boy meets girl, boy loses girl, boy gets girl.

An Affair to Remember, co-starring Deborah Kerr, is a wide-screen, color remake of McCarey's *Love Affair* (1939), which starred Charles Boyer and Irene Dunne. Although it uses virtually the same script as the original, it became something of a cult film, in which Grant's performance is both more

---

[14] Kael, 27.

comic and more darkly shaded than Boyer's had been. *Indiscreet*, one of four films Grant made in partnership with Donen, was shot in London and was Grant's reunion with Ingrid Bergman. One key to his charm in both of these films is that he's grown older. Remarkably well preserved, he acts in a relaxed fashion and approaches love scenes with a mature, attractive discretion or reticence. Here as elsewhere in his late career, he creates a low-key sophistication and romantic glamour built from reactions to the other players and clever manipulation of small objects. Unlike other romantic leading men of his generation—Boyer, for example—he improved with age, and this had as much to do with his performance skill as with his handsomeness.

4. *Domestic Cary*. In several of Grant's films, he plays a happily married, middle-class husband or a settled professional man who becomes married. Mostly light comedies, these films have never been given the close critical attention they deserve, probably because they lack the broadly farcical gags, dark suspense, and sleek romance of his more celebrated work.

The comedies in the category are different from the screwball pictures of the 1930s not only because they lack strong farcical elements but also because the best screwballs don't involve children or the theme of children. (Qualified exceptions are *My Favorite Wife*, one of the umpteen movie adaptations of *Enoch Arden*, in which the children are sentimentalized props, and *Monkey Business*, in which Grant himself becomes childlike.) In the domestic films, offspring have more importance, and Grant is unusually good at playing scenes with them, in part because he seems to have liked children. The opposite of W. C. Fields, who sometimes made fun of America's sentimentality about childhood, he's expressively witty, interacting with young people in realistic fashion and without condescension.

The only non-comic film of the domestic group, George Stevens's 1941 tear-jerker *Penny Serenade*, won Grant an Oscar nomination for his portrayal of a character who suffers a series of calamities: his wife loses her unborn child in a Tokyo earthquake; he and the wife move to California and struggle through economic disaster while trying to adopt a child; his successfully adopted child dies from an illness after only a few years; and he sinks into a psychological depression that almost costs him his marriage. This isn't one of Grant's best films, but it's one of his most eventful and emotional, showing what he could do in moments when he expresses an anguished need. The comic pictures, in contrast, are more satisfying as wholes. They include *Mr. Blandings Builds His Dream House* (1948), in which Grant plays a Madison Avenue ad man who lives in a crowded New York apartment with his wife and two preteen daughters and dreams of becoming a country gentleman; and *Every Girl Should be Married* (1948), the first of Grant's appearances with his third wife, Betsy Drake, and a picture he partly wrote without credit, in which he's a pediatrician pursued by a young woman who wants to marry him and have his baby. At one point Grant does a dead-on imitation of Drake's character, who was in some ways modeled on Hepburn in *Bringing Up Baby*.

In *Room for One More* (1951), Grant's second film with Betsy Drake, he's an engineer with three children whose wife arranges for the adoption of a thirteen-year-old girl and a boy with a disability. It's an unusual case of a domestic picture with a social purpose. The less comic, less purely domestic *People Will Talk* (1951) also has social purpose, serving as writer/director Joseph L. Mankiewicz's veiled commentary on the McCarthy era. Grant, who later said he disliked the film, plays a wise, unorthodox doctor who lives with a mysterious male friend; in the course of events, he gives advice to an apparently pregnant single woman and eventually marries her. *People Will Talk* is filled with Mankiewicz's intelligent dialogue, which Grant performs beautifully, in part because he had the rare ability to convey quiet, unassuming intelligence (a quality equally important in the thriller *Crisis* [1950], in which he plays a US surgeon forced to operate on a Latin American dictator). His more amusing moments in the film, such as his love of electric trains and joy in conducting an amateur orchestra, also convey his essentially childlike sense of fun.

5. *Cockney Cary*. Grant wasn't a Cockney. Bristol is very far from London, where such authentic Cockneys as Claude Rains and Michael Caine were born. But Grant loved old-fashioned Cockney entertainment and played a Cockney in several films. In *Gunga Din* (1938), a hymn to British imperialism co-starring Sam Jaffe in blackface, he's a tough, bulked-up Cockney soldier with a burr haircut who engages in comic roughhouse and battles a violent Indian rebellion alongside his pals Victor McLaughlin and Douglas Fairbanks, Jr. And in *Mr. Lucky*, he teaches Cockney rhyming slang to Laraine Day (he calls it "Australian slang," which was the term American gangsters gave to the slang that originated in London).

Two of Grant's Cockney roles are especially important, and together comprise the most unusual films of his career. *Sylvia Scarlett*, in which he's a combination thief and song-and-dance man, was the first film that earned him critical praise for his acting. Unfortunately, it was a major box-office flop, perhaps because creative talent associated with the film—George Cukor, Katharine Hepburn, and Compton Mackenzie, who wrote the novel that was the source of the screenplay—were either gay or bisexual, and they gave an unorthodox sexual tone to the film. It took many years for the culture to change enough to provide an environment that could appreciate *Sylvia Scarlett*. Grant's performance, however, has always been admired for its toughness, air of danger, and flair as a clown-costumed, piano-playing entertainer.

The second film, *None But the Lonely Heart* (1944), based on a 1943 novel by Richard Llewellyn, was dear to Grant's heart and a project of which he was justifiably proud. When he received his 1970 lifetime achievement Oscar at the 42nd annual ceremony, it was the only film he requested should be included in the Academy's montage of clips from his work. Not without flaws, it's a brave undertaking made with relatively few compromises and has long been underrated by critics (including me). It's one of Grant's most effective performances, and not just because he adopts an accent and plays a character different from his usual persona. The furthest thing from a method-style actor, he nevertheless has the ability to render subtext. Again and again, this film shows him subtly conveying a feeling of embittered alienation and deep loneliness beneath the surface of Ernie Mott's cheery bravado and tramp-like rebellion.

III.

I don't claim that the aforementioned generalizations about Grant's "versions" are the only way of categorizing his work; they nevertheless have heuristic value and help us appreciate his range. To gain a full understanding of the kind of work he does, however, we need still closer examination of his behavior in the context of individual films. That's the aim of the next five chapters, which are arranged in the order of the versions just described. Each chapter focuses on only two or three films because Grant made so many it would be counterproductive to discuss all of them. Some readers may regret that I haven't chosen several of his best. I've given detailed commentary on *Holiday* and *North by Northwest* in a previous book,[15] and neither *The Philadelphia Story* nor *Only Angels Have Wings* were especially necessary for my purposes. My chief concern has been to treat a reasonable number of representative films as wholes. Although the focus is always on Grant, his work was guided or supplemented by other important talents, and his performances should be seen in relation to the narratives that support them. The point is to comment on his excellence and on the excellence of the films. Before moving to that task, however, a few generalizations having to do with the poetics of film performance are worth keeping in mind because they figure in subsequent chapters.[16]

1. *Stage versus Screen.* A common way of distinguishing between theatrical acting and movie acting is to say that actors in film don't "project" as they do on stage. But while cameras and microphones can give us quiet or understated performances, good movie acting isn't always subdued—think of Robert Mitchum's crazed preacher in *Night of the Hunter* (1955). Orson Welles insisted that film acting could be just as big as stage acting; the major difference, he pointed out, is that performance on stage is aimed at the many eyes across an auditorium, and performance in movies is aimed at the single eye of a camera. Hence in analyzing film performance, we need to think about the actor's physical relation to the camera and the degrees of ostensiveness or "showiness" required by certain genres, films, or scenes. Musicals and comedies, for example, are ostensive genres, in which actors tend to use a slightly exaggerated style to express surprise, delight, confusion, alarm, and so forth.

A more important difference between movie acting and stage acting is that movie close-ups make much greater use of the expressions in a player's

---

[15] James Naremore, *Acting in the Cinema* (Berkeley: University of California Press, 1988), 174–92, 213–35.

[16] Matters discussed in the next four paragraphs are treated in much greater detail in Naremore, 27–96.

eyes. Grant's large, dark eyes are highly expressive and one reason for his success. They communicate with the camera and can be sly, thoughtful, amused, joyful, threatening, and sad. Consider the scene in *Only Angels Have Wings* when he looks down at the dying Thomas Mitchell. It's a film in which men show more love for one another than for women; Grant plays a tough, stoic character, but his eyes become deliquescent.

2. *Expressive technique.* Movie scenes can involve two people seated at a table or multiple characters and complex blocking. Sometimes the floor of a set is marked with gaffers' tape indicating the spots where crossing movements should end and characters should stand. The movement of camera and players in the longer takes results in a sort of choreography, guided by a need to keep the actors' expressions and gestures visible.

The expressions themselves can be more or less conventional. Theatrical performance in the past two hundred years originates with what historians call a "mimetic" or "pantomime" tradition of codified expressions and gestures, which actors learned to imitate; but in the twentieth century, except in the avant-garde, it moved increasingly toward improvisation, realism, and naturalism. (Improvisation on the stage is, of course, different from improvisation in movies because film scenes can be reshot.) In the late nineteenth century, playwright William Archer's *Masks or Faces* argued that actors should never imitate emotions: "We weep our own tears, we laugh our own laughter."[17] Be that as it may, Hollywood movie actors in the interwar years were still using fairly conventional (if less flamboyant) poses and facial expressions to indicate grief, joy, puzzlement, fear, confusion, and so on. The best of these actors, however, developed a physical and emotional idiolect. In Grant's comedies, for example, we encounter not only the distinctive Grant enunciation but also the Grant mumble, the Grant whinny, the Grant crouch, the Grant double-take, the Grant tendency to bite his lower lip in teasing fashion after making a joke, and the Grant habit of rubbing his hands together in satisfaction.

3. *Expressive coherence and performance within performance.* Actors often play characters who are acting for other characters. As in everyday social life, the people in movies tell lies, engage in deception, adopt masks of propriety, or put on public shows. Often we know when they're performing an act for others because the plot tells us, but in most cases professional actors need to let their characters' masks slip a little, suggesting an expressive incoherence, an underlying shadow of deceit or unease that we see but the other characters

---

[17] Quoted in Toby Cole and Helen Krich Chinoy, eds., *Actors on Acting* (New York: Crown, 1970), 365.

don't. This is one of movie acting's more subtle and complex tasks. It operates somewhat differently in comedy and drama because comedy tends to emphasize or exaggerate incoherence and social failures. Grant is equally good at comically failed performance, as when he tries to conceal Hepburn's ripped dress in *Bringing Up Baby*, and at dramatic suppression of emotion, as when he conceals his feelings from Bergman in *Notorious*.

4. *Wardrobe and objects.* Actors express emotion or create personality not only with their faces, movements, and gestures but also with their clothing and things they handle. Women toy with jewelry, smooth scarves, and handle purses; men adjust ties, light cigarettes, and tip hats. Grant took care with his wardrobe so that he could easily put a hand in a pocket at the right moment and was expert at using objects in a scene. In *Room for One More*, for example, he makes a cake while talking with three children and has a conversation with his wife while washing dishes. In *The Awful Truth* he chats with his guests while dispensing eggnog, and in *Every Girl Should be Married* he has a conversation with an athletic trainer while demonstrating his skill on a speed bag. Very early in his career he had observed Jack Benny and George Burns on stage and noticed that Benny never played the violin: "He probably held it for the same reason George holds his cigar—for timing."[18] This probably explains what he does with a cigarette case in *An Affair to Remember* and the many uses he has for a candlestick telephone in *His Girl Friday*. Notice also the joke he makes while emptying Tony Curtis's champagne bottle in *Operation Petticoat*.

We can now turn to the examination of specific films, bearing in mind that Grant had the benefit of working repeatedly with major Hollywood directors, among them McCarey, Hawks, Hitchcock, and Cukor, each of whom had a distinctive style and a preferred method of filmmaking. He adjusted to these very different directors while also bringing his own technical brilliance and imagination to their films. When he received his honorary Oscar, he mentioned them along with several of his screenwriters. "I trust," he said, "that they and all the other directors, writers, and producers, and leading women, have forgiven me for what I didn't know . . . I realize it's conventional and usual to praise one's fellow workers on these occasions. But why not? Ours is a collaborative medium; we all need each other."[19] They certainly needed Grant, as we shall see.

---

[19] Quoted in Marc Eliot, *Cary Grant: A Biography* (New York: Harmony Books, 2004), 18.

2

Farceur Cary

Comedy is hard, the saying goes, but it's especially hard in films because the actors don't have the response of an audience. There are stories of Leo McCarey doubling up with silent laughter during the shooting of *The Awful Truth*, but his players had no assurance that their jokes and timing were working. "Your timing had to be modified for the screen," Grant once said. "Since a laugh rolling up the aisles of a big-city movie theater took longer than one bouncing off the walls of a tiny rural vaudeville house, you had to time what you thought would please all audiences . . . The film crews don't laugh. They are too busy doing their own jobs."[1]

Grant was good at imagining an audience and could sense how quickly a small joke could be delivered—as in *The Philadelphia Story*, when the drunken James Stewart hiccups and Grant immediately says, "Excuse me." Grant improvised the line, and the surprised Stewart controlled his laughter with an "Umm?" Throughout the scene, the contrast between Grant's quick, vaguely British speech and Stewart's Midwestern drawl is amusing; Stewart takes time to react, and Grant's instinct for humor allows him to keep making swift comic returns.

In Grant's more farcical, rapidly paced screwball comedies, especially the ones directed by Howard Hawks, the dialogue depends less on jokes than on speed, and Grant controls his timing with nonsensical mumbles. "Cary was quite a mumbler," Irene Dunne recalled. "He'd go mmm-mmm-mmm—he'd throw in little yeses and nos and mumbles all the way through . . . He was a lot of fun to work with. He was a lot of fun *between* scenes as well."[2] Many actors who knew Grant made similar remarks about his sense of humor. The exception to the rule was the possibly jealous Robert Mitchum, who once co-starred with Grant and thought his jokes were old fashioned. Although Grant was intensely serious and even anxious about his job, he liked to amuse

---

[1] Quoted in Nelson, 96.
[2] Dunne quoted in Harvey, 687.

Some Versions of Cary Grant. James Naremore, Oxford University Press. © Oxford University Press 2022. DOI: 10.1093/oso/9780197566374.003.0002

people on the set with Cockney imitations and off-color stories from English music halls. This usually relaxed the players, putting them in the right mood and facilitating performance.

Grant's love of the lowbrow music hall and the physical talents he had perfected in his youth also gave him a strength apart from handling dialogue. He could do the acrobatic comedy of a Chaplin or Keaton, adjusting it to the world of talking movies while somehow never forsaking his essential attractiveness and urbanity. In *Bringing Up Baby*, Katharine Hepburn seems to fall in love with him the moment his feet slip beneath him and he lands on his hat. Irene Dunne has a similar reaction in *The Awful Truth* when a chair slides from under him and he becomes entangled in a broken piece of furniture. These physical gifts also contribute to his comic reactions. His swift double-takes in *His Girl Friday*, for example, are executed with such precision that he has time to express an aftereffect of contemplation or amusement.

Grant has long been appreciated as an expert at the skills I've just described. What has often been overlooked, however, is that the skills were adjusted to different characterizations. For those who might think he always played the same thing or that all screwball comedies are fundamentally alike, I submit the following films as evidence to the contrary. Grant gives us three very different personalities and three different ways of being funny.

The Awful Truth (1937)

Grant almost didn't make his twenty-ninth picture, which was one of the best of the screwballs and an Oscar-winning hit that secured his star image. He was upset because director Leo McCarey began principal photography without a final script, and in the first four days did little other than sitting around the set, chatting with the cast, and playing the piano. The habitually anxious Grant became almost ill, writing a letter of complaint to Harry Cohn, production chief of Columbia Pictures, asking to be released from the assignment and offering to pay Cohn five thousand dollars. When that didn't work, he proposed switching roles with supporting actor Ralph Bellamy (a terrible idea). Cohn again refused. For a while, Grant stopped speaking to McCarey, who held a grudge against him for years. But eventually Grant and the entire cast realized McCarey was a comic wizard and became willing collaborators.

In his memoirs of Hollywood, Garson Kanin gives an amusing account of how McCarey took an off-the-cuff approach to his work. Kanin was Samuel Goldwyn's assistant in the late 1930s and was called into the producer's office with the rest of the Goldwyn staff. "Gentlemen," said Goldwyn, "Mr. McCarey here has a great idea for a great picture and he is going to do us the honor this afternoon of telling us."[3] Whereupon the handsome, dapper McCarey surprised everyone by lying down on Goldwyn's expensive office sofa, crossing his well-shod feet, putting his hands behind his head, and, according to Kanin, telling this story:

Well, the guy in my story is a cowboy. I'll introduce him with four hundred feet of spectacular cowboy stuff . . . the manliest, sexiest, bravest, ballsiest son of a bitch you could ever imagine . . . *Wham*! Cut to Saturday night. In town. A little town. Arizona . . . it's kind of a dance hall . . . modern, you understand . . . and the orchestra's playing. [McCarey sang a few bars.] There's hardly any women there . . . Cowboys dancing with cowboys . . . there's nothing fairy about this, mind you. It's just that there aren't enough dames to go around . . . In the part of the *main* cowboy, . . . the image I get in my mind is . . . somebody like say—well, say, *Gary Cooper* . . . *Wham*! We cut to *another* dance hall. There's a string trio playing some kind of waltz. [McCarey hummed a few bars.] We're in the ballroom of the fanciest damn girls' finishing school on the East coast . . . And one of them, the one who's leading, is *really* class . . . I'll tell you who could do it. *Merle Oberon*! . . . Oh, by the way, did I tell you the title? Oh, get this . . . *The Cowboy and the Lady*!

McCarey knew Cooper and Oberon were under contract with Goldwyn. Kanin thought he was a spellbinding salesman, but the middle of his story was fuzzy; he had told his audience "virtually nothing, but it was a *funny* nothing." Finally he rose and said, "Well . . . let me know. By Friday, huh?" Two days later, Goldwyn paid McCarey $50,000 for the story. He then learned that McCarey wasn't interested in writing or directing the film, and that his proposed title, *The Cowboy and the Lady*, was owned by another studio. Goldwyn bought the rights for the title anyway and produced the picture in 1938, to lukewarm reception.

---

[3] Garson Kanin, *Hollywood* (New York: The Viking Press, 1974), 68–72.

McCarey had won an Academy Award a year earlier as director-producer of *The Awful Truth*, which he probably sold to Harry Cohn in similar fashion. (While describing the film he played the piano and sang to Cohn; McCarey fancied himself a songwriter, and Cohn had begun life as a pitchman of Tin Pan Alley songs.) The completed screenplay, credited to Viña Delmar but worked on by others, including Dorothy Parker, was loosely based on a 1923 play that had been filmed in 1925 and 1929. McCarey wrote some of the picture as it was being photographed, using his own experiences. When an idea came to him, he would describe a scene to the actors, have them improvise blocking and business, write down dialogue for them, and run through the scene again. As Irene Dunne explained to critic James Harvey, "Leo wrote an awful lot of it while we sat on the set and waited . . . He'd give you the scene and see what happened. And of course he was a great man for routines . . . But that was Leo's early training—that was his background."[4]

McCarey's background included directing two-reel silent films starring Charley Chase and Laurel and Hardy, plus the Marx Brothers' most surreal feature, *Duck Soup* (1933). At the height of his fame he made few all-out comedies and was better known for poignant, sentimental pictures; nevertheless, he was skilled at improvising "routines," jokes involving slapstick and public embarrassment. *The Awful Truth* is a string of these routines supported by a thin plot, and it depends crucially on actors who can be both funny and charming. Grant's early training suited him perfectly for the job; once the film was underway, he enjoyed improvising and used it often in later pictures.

Grant and Dunne play Jerry and Lucy Warriner, a wealthy couple with no family relations apart from a sophisticated Aunt Patsy (Cecil Cunningham) and a surrogate child named Mr. Smith (Skippy, a talented wire terrier who had become famous as Asta in the *Thin Man* films and later appeared in *Bringing Up Baby*). Exactly how the Warriners make their money isn't clear— something to do with investments and a coal mine. Like many screwball couples, they inhabit a metropolitan world, wear fine clothes, and frequent nightclubs. They're similar to the supernatural duo played by Grant and Constance Bennett in *Topper*, but they aren't ghosts, and their marriage is in trouble because Jerry seems to be having extra-marital affairs. I say "seems"

---

[4] Harvey, 682–83.

because the film tiptoes to the edge of Production Code rules for the treatment of adultery; we never see the woman Jerry is involved with when the
film begins, and Dunne isn't much interested in the two men around her, a
foreign music teacher and a rich bumpkin.

The Warriners have a mansion with a black maid (regrettably typical of
movies in the period, but at least McCarey doesn't make jokes with her).
When the film begins, Jerry has been living for weeks in the Gotham Athletic
Club and acquiring a deep sun-lamp tan while pretending to be on a trip to
Florida. He invites a couple of rich pals, one with a wife and the other with a
lady friend, to join him when he returns home. Standing in the doorway with
one hand in his pocket and the other holding a fruit basket ostensibly from
Florida, he calls, "Hey, Lucy! That man is here!" Mr. Smith joyfully barks and
leaps into his arms, but Lucy isn't home. Trying to hide his disappointment,
Jerry tells the maid to make a bowl of eggnog for the guests.

The scene is a paradigmatic McCarey "routine" (calmer than most) and
a definitive moment for Grant because it requires an actor who can be debonair and execute relaxed, skillfully timed comic reactions. It also involves
performance-within-performance—moments when we sense that the
leading characters are acting for the people around them. Throughout
the film, the Warriners perform for each other or for their social set,
playing the piano, singing, engaging in deceptions, and attempting to
hide their true feelings. The film's comedy is largely a matter of Jerry and
Lucy giving comically transparent or failed performances, acting that's
obvious to us but not to their audience, or acting that causes their masks
to slip.

In this case, Jerry (from now on I'll call him Grant) puts on a kind of
show by assuring his invited audience of his happy marriage. He strolls
around in stagy fashion, dispensing eggnog and using a shaker to sprinkle
the drinks with nutmeg. Then he casually puts a hand in his pocket and
makes a public speech filled with Grant's characteristic stressed syllables,
explaining that civilized marriages are ruined by mistrust: "The *road* to
Reno is *paved* with sus*picion*—first thing you know they all end up in
di*vorce* court." Sitting atop the back of a couch, he crosses a leg and says
that Lucy is probably with Aunt Patsy in her charming mountain cabin.
He reaches out a hand in a theatrical gesture. At that moment Aunt Patsy
enters from behind him. Grant is disconcerted and waves the hand at her
almost dismissively.

He tries to cover by claiming unconcern about Lucy's whereabouts. The guests look a little dubious, and just then Lucy enters (from now on I'll call her Dunne) swathed in a cloud of ermine and an evening dress. "Darling!" she cries with theatrical flair, and Grant embraces her, giving her his biggest grin. Cut to a close-up as he peeps over her shoulder through a billow of ermine and reacts wide-eyed to a foreign playboy type, mustachioed and tuxedoed, standing in the doorway.

Dunne explains that he's Armand Duvalle (Alexander D'Arcy), her music teacher. His car broke down while they were out, she says, airily waving her hand. They had to spend the evening at "the nastiest little inn you ever saw." The guests are relatively deadpan but realize it's time to leave. Armand congratulates Grant on having a "continental mind." "Yes," the un-smiling Grant says, "I have a *continental* mind." He pauses a beat and asks in an unfriendly voice, "Will you have an *egg-nog*?" Armand says yes, and Grant swiftly crosses to the punch bowl, looking over his shoulder with a quick comic reaction as Armand follows right behind him. The guests are departing. "You don't *all* have to *leave*, do you?" Grant asks. Armand replies, "Go? No." Grant pauses another beat and sits atop the back of the sofa again, this time with both feet on the armrest, head cocked toward Armand.

Once the guests and Aunt Patsy are gone, Grant turns to Dunne and Armand and congratulates them: "That wasn't a bad *performance* consid-ering there were no *rehearsals* or anything." The line serves as a reflexive comment on the film's improvisation and performance-within-performance. Even more important, as Andrew Sarris has observed, Grant's position atop the luxurious sofa (not so different from McCarey's treatment of Goldwyn's sofa) differs from what audiences had seen in Noël Coward-like comedies of manners: "His posture is that of infantile irresponsibility. The talkies had found at last a well-tailored romantic gentleman with the physical gifts of a baggy-pants comedian."[5] During the scene, Grant occasionally conveys an Oliver-Hardy exasperation or Stan-Laurel confusion in ways that enhance his attractiveness as a romantic leading man, and his accent adds to the effect because it blends a hint of upper-class British enunciation with comic Americanness.

Dunne, who was mostly associated with women's melodramas and had a contract stipulating she would sing in her pictures, turned out to be one of Grant's best partners. They clicked, she told James Harvey, because "comedy is timing mostly . . . Cary Grant always said I had the best timing of anybody he ever worked with."[6] She, too, later perches on the arms of furniture. In this scene, as she pets Mr. Smith and explains how her car broke down, she pouts and repeats Grant's own argument: "Can't have a happy life if we're always suspicious." He hesitates and says, "Of course not," but it's obvious that they're both lying. Armand says that he's simply Lucy's teacher, who occasionally "pats her on the back" and oversees her "development." He insists on his pedagogical role: "I am a great teacher, not a great lover!" Dunne agrees, "Yes, no one could say you're a great lover," then catches herself for an instant and trails off. "That is, what I mean to say . . ."

As Armand leaves, Dunne almost giggles with pleasure, but Grant becomes huffy. "I have no *faith* left in anyone," he announces. Dunne takes an orange from the "Florida" gift basket and finds that it's stamped "California." She tosses it to him. Grant catches it neatly, never taking his eyes from her, then looks down at the orange. A quarrel ensues, observed by Mr. Smith, with both characters feeling suspicious and trying to preserve their dignity by agreeing to a divorce.

Stanley Cavell has called *The Awful Truth* a "comedy of remarriage," but technically it isn't quite one; the law requires a long waiting period before the Warriner divorce decree becomes valid, and the remainder of the film takes place while the couple's relationship is in a liminal state. Grant is awarded "visitation rights" for Mr. Smith, which provide a reason for the couple to keep meeting one another. From this point on, the plot is composed of loosely connected, increasingly screwball routines in which the two are nominally split, keep encountering one another, and

---

[5] Andrew Sarris, "Cary Grant's Lasting Legacy: Screwballs and Beyond," *Observer*, June 6, 2004, observer.com/2004/06/cary-grants-lasting-legacy-screwballs-and-beyond.

[6] Harvey, 688.

ultimately reunite. Their relationship is never seriously threatened because they're so much alike, and despite what they pretend, they're still in love. They share a mixture of sophistication and polite ordinariness that Grant embodied more than any other male star, and it's only a matter of time before "infantile irresponsibility" makes them acknowledge they're made for each other.

Dunne moves into an apartment with Aunt Patsy, who unsuccessfully tries to convince her to go on the town and meet men. It turns out that living across the hall with his mother is Dan Leeson (Ralph Bellamy), a handsome, oil-rich lug from Oklahoma. When Aunt Patsy invites him over, he sits close to Dunne with a goofy, adoring smile and almost salivates. Mr. Smith growls. Just then Grant arrives—chipper, brisk, insisting on his visitation rights and showing his legal papers. "This is my husband," Dunne says, waving her hand as if to dismiss him from consideration. Grant goes to the piano, grins extravagantly, and just to annoy everyone begins cheerfully playing; he had learned to play piano during his youth in Bristol and plays in several of his films, but in this case he's almost certainly thinking of Leo McCarey's habit of playing piano on the movie set. After a couple of bars, he turns to Mr. Smith and says, "Take it!" Mr. Smith goes, "Arf. Arf."

We next see Grant and Dunne in one of those high-end nightclubs dear to Hollywood in the 1930s and 1940s, filled with evening dress and bubbling champagne. Grant has a date with a pretty young singer at the nightclub (Joyce Compton) who has changed her name to Dixie Bell Lee and adopted a parodic southern accent. He's mopey until Dixie Bell spots Dunne and Bellamy entering; they're now engaged, though Dunne doesn't seem happy about it. Grant puts on his best grin and dances with Dixie Bell toward the couple's table, acting surprised. He fairly prances from the dance floor, asks to join them, and arranges the seating—himself and Dunne on one side, Bellamy and Dixie Bell on the other.

A moment of comic silence descends as the four people look at one another. The humor derives from the tempo of the cutting, but especially from the facial expressions and exact timing of Grant's and Dunne's small movements. In a two-shot, they're seated side by side. Grant folds his arms in mischievous satisfaction, smiles like a Cheshire cat, and stares at Dunne, who looks down and adjusts her glove. After a pause, she uncomfortably looks back at Grant. Then they simultaneously, almost mechanically, turn their heads, looking in the direction of Dixie Bell. Grant maintains a fixed smile and Dunne tries to make the best of it. Cut to Dixie Bell and then back to Grant and Dunne, who, like puppets on the same string, simultaneously turn to look at one another. Grant is still smiling—he moves nothing but his head during the sequence—and Dunne is still trying to maintain poise. After another pause, they simultaneously turn to look back toward the camera, this time in the direction of Bellamy.

The ensuing conversation is equally funny. Sarah Kozloff, author of an excellent study of dialogue in Hollywood genres, points out that the classic screwballs often use a kind of speech derived from Noël Coward but with an Americanized spin. Like Coward, they don't employ wit or repartee. Kozloff explains the style in italics: "*Perfectly ordinary phrases, which are funny because of their context and because of the way in which they are delivered.*"[7] One of the typical speech acts, she points out, is teasing. This scene is an ideal example, dependent on Grant's stressed enunciation, Dunne's relative silence, and Bellamy's languid drawl:

Grant: So you're going to live in *Oklahoma*, eh Lucy? How I *envy* you. Ever since I was a *small boy* that name has been filled with *magic* for me. *Ok-la-homa!*

Bellamy: We're gonna live right in Oklahoma City.

Grant: Not *Oklahoma City* itself? Lucy, you *lucky* girl. No more running around the *night spots*, no more *prowl*ing around in *New York shops*. I shall think of you every time a *new show* opens and say to myself, she's *well out* of it!

Bellamy: New York's all right for a visit but I

Grant (FINISHING THE SENTENCE WITH HIM): wouldn't want to live here.

Dunne (QUIETLY BUT FIRMLY): I know I'll enjoy Oklahoma City.

---

[7] Sarah Kozloff, *Overhearing Film Dialog* (Berkeley: University of California Press, 2000), 176.

Grant: But of course! And if it should get *dull*, you can always go over to *Tul*sa for the weekend!

As good as the writing is, Kozloff observes that what makes the scene is the acting: "Irene Dunne's pained expression, and the way she uncomfortably shifts her gaze, and Grant's mischievous glee, and the way he delivers the lines, from his stringing out 'Ok-la-homa' to his mocking 'she's well out of it,' to the way he hits the word 'Tulsa.' Of course, all dialogue needs to be performed skillfully, but the impeccable delivery that Noël Coward expects is particularly crucial in screwball comedy."[8]

Soon after Grant's moment of triumph, he suffers embarrassment. Like nearly all the comic routines, this one involves characters who avoid acknowledging public discomfort. As James Harvey puts it: "Controlled dismay in the face of some unspeakable noise or sight, some vulgarity or gaucherie, is the basic McCarey joke."[9] McCarey once explained to an interviewer that such jokes depend less on the person who commits the faux pas than on the witnesses who don't react to it. The hypothetical example he gave, cited by nearly everyone who has written about him, is a scene at a polite dinner party where somebody farts and the people around the table remain deadpan.

Dixie Bell Lee is called to perform her singing number and appears on stage as the band plays a softly romantic introduction. In a sweet Southern voice, she sings "My Dreams are Gone with the Wind" (no relation to the 1939 movie or the jazz standard). Each time she comes to the title phrase, there's a special effect—a whoosh of wind from below that blows her gauzy, floor-length gown over her head and reveals her panties. The spectacle is funny, but what gives it punch is the restrained reaction of the three people watching from the nightclub table. Dunne lifts her head slightly, arches her eyebrows, and worries her necklace, behaving with aplomb. Bellamy looks slightly askance, his brow raised a bit, as if he might be interested but doesn't want to show it. Grant, who sits between them, exhibits "controlled dismay." Elbow on the table, he puts a hand to his brow, partly shielding his face and looking sidelong for Dunne's reaction. After a moment, he gestures toward Dixie Bell and matter-of-factly says, "I just met her."

Next, Dunne has to endure dancing with Bellamy. The music suddenly changes to a fast number and Bellamy lunges into a wild, clod-hopping

---

[8] Kozloff, 177.
[9] Harvey, 261.

jitterbug embellished with moves left over from the 1920s. The other dancers give him and Dunne room while McCarey's camera observes them without much cutting. (There were retakes, and Bellamy's hilarious imitation of gracelessness required a great deal of energy and skilled movement.) From his front-row seat at the table, Grant grins with good cheer and sends money to the band with a request that they repeat the number, forcing Dunne to do it again.

The next day, Dunne and Bellamy are at the piano in his apartment, attempting to harmonize on "Home on the Range." If Bellamy lacked something as a dancer, as a singer he's plain awful. It's the first of three songs Dunne performs, and it came about when McCarey saw her and Bellamy at a piano and asked them to sing. Bellamy explained that he couldn't sing, but McCarey insisted. He filmed them, and by all accounts almost fell down laughing. Part of the scene's comic charm has to do with Dunne's mix of enjoyment and dismay when she plays for Bellamy. When he urges her to join him, she not only sings but also whistles à la Crosby. She can't hide her laughter as she tries to keep the enthusiastic Bellamy in key and winces discreetly when he gives her a hearty cowboy punch on the arm.

Grant arrives with a briefcase, ostensibly dealing with financial business but using every opportunity to tease Dunne by insinuating naughty details of their previous love life. He sits on a couch alongside Bellamy to show him papers, and Dunne sits across from them on the arm of a chair, crossing her legs. Grant looks at them as Bellamy reads. She pulls her skirt down over her knee and Grant does a subtle double-take. Then Bellamy's "Ma" (Esther Dale) arrives. She's just heard rumors of an affair between Dunne and her teacher Armand, which supposedly caused the divorce from Grant. Bellamy grows increasingly uneasy, and Grant quickly stands and comes to Dunne's defense, giving an ostentatious, theatrical speech worthy of old-fashioned melodrama. It fools Bellamy and Ma and at one point almost fools Dunne. Their divorce, Grant says, putting a hand over his heart and breaking into blank verse rhythm, was the story of "a *trust*ing woman and a *worth*less man." He was "*never* good enough for Lucy," who is "as *pure* as the *driven snow*, as *pure* as she is *fair*." "*Would* that I had been *worthy* to *kiss* the *hem* of her *garment!*" Dunne can see him crossing his fingers behind his back. He sits beside Ma, who has moved to the couch, and says to her, "Excuse me, you're sitting on my prospectus." As he gathers his papers and makes a proud exit, he proclaims, "I'm sure the *three* of you will have a *happy* life out where the *West* begins." Dunne holds out a foot and trips him momentarily off balance.

The comedy becomes increasingly slapstick, each routine requiring a quickened pace. Grant goes across the hall to Dunne's apartment and mixes a drink. When she arrives, he leans a hand elegantly on the piano and the lid falls on it. As he's preparing to leave, Bellamy knocks. Dunne opens the door and Grant hides behind it, listening as Dunne tries to keep the randy, excited Bellamy from entering. Bellamy has written a doggerel poem ("To you, my little prairie flower") that he takes from his pocket and reads. Grant uses a pencil to reach around the door and tickle Dunne, who giggles and tries to act as if she enjoys the verse. The telephone next to Grant rings and he picks it up, hearing Armand's voice. Bellamy begs for a kiss, and Dunne gives him a small one, which causes him such delirious joy that he hugs her tight, lifting her from the floor and swinging her back and forth like a rag doll. When Bellamy rushes off to tell Ma, Grant hands the phone to Dunne and listens as she makes an appointment to see Armand at 3:15 the next day.

The appointment with Armand causes Grant to behave like a jealous husband and leads to a routine that makes full use of his acrobatic skill. Arriving at the appointed place at precisely 3:15, he's greeted at the door by Armand's diminutive Asian servant (Miki Morita), who refuses to admit him. When he forces his way into the foyer, the servant executes a jujitsu move that flips Grant, landing him flat on his face.

Their battle foreshadows the elaborate melee between Inspector Clouseau
and his servant Cato in Blake Edwards's *Return of the Pink Panther* (1975),
but it doesn't use doubles or special effects. Grant gets up, hat still on, and
retaliates with a trick that lands Morita on the floor. He turns and angrily
bursts into Armand's large room, only to find Dunne performing an aria from
Ruperto Chapi's opera *La Serenata*, with Armand at the piano and an audience gathered around. Surprised and struck by the beauty of Dunne's singing,
he takes a chair against the wall and listens. What follows is like a gag from a
Laurel and Hardy movie. Relaxing, he tips the back of the chair against the wall
and it slips beneath him, sending him crashing to the floor. When he gets up,
he steps on an upended side table, which breaks apart and becomes entangled
on his foot. Hair disarrayed, he struggles to extricate himself, looking apolo-
getically at an elderly fellow sitting nearby, who remains stone-faced.

Dunne keeps singing, reaching the end of the aria, which concludes, "ha,
ha!" But on the next day, she confesses to Patsy that she still loves Grant; she
recalls the laughs they had and intends to break it off with Bellamy. During
the conversation, she plays a hide-and-seek game involving Mr. Smith and
his favorite toy. As the scene develops, however, it becomes a Georges-
Feydeau-style farce with a dog as one of the stars.

Here we should recall Stanley Cavell's influential commentary on "remarriage comedy," in which he argues that such films are different from Feydeau because of their attitude toward sexuality and marriage. In the context of analyzing *Bringing Up Baby* (in which there's no marriage), Cavell says that "Feydeau and Hawks are as distant conceptually as the Catholic and the Protestant interpretations of the institution of marriage, hence of the function of adultery."[10] *Bringing Up Baby* is indeed different from Feydeau's nineteenth-century theater, though no less a farce, and it's true that Hollywood's screwball films always respect marriage; nevertheless, the scene in *The Awful Truth* clearly derives from Feydeau. It may or may not have a different attitude about adulterous sex, but that has less to do with Protestantism vs. Catholicism than with the strictures of the Production Code. (It seems odd to associate the screwball cycle with Protestantism, given that the 1930s Production Code was created because of pressure from the Catholic Church and was administered by Joseph Breen, who, like Leo McCarey, was an Irish Catholic.)

Feydeau's hugely popular sex comedies were designed for the limited space of proscenium theater and were about people trying to avoid one another who were brought together as soon and as often as possible. In a general sense, the whole of *The Awful Truth* resembles Feydeau because almost every scene involves comically awkward meetings between the Warriners. The farcical action in Feydeau, however, usually takes place in a single room with more than one door and involves rapid entrances and exits. That's how the scene in question works, with the exception of two brief moments when McCarey cuts away to show something outside the main room.

Immediately after Dunne's talk with Patsy, there's a knock at the door and Armand arrives, wearing a bowler hat. Patsy exits, and Dunne asks Armand in a fluttery, apologetic way if he will try to convince Grant she's been faithful. Armand agrees but wants to be sure Grant doesn't have a gun. Cut to the hallway outside to show Grant arriving, also wearing a bowler hat. Mr. Smith barks happily at the sound of his master, and Dunne hides Armand in the bedroom, forgetting to hide his hat. Grant enters on his hands and

---

[10] Stanley Cavell, *Pursuits of Happiness: The Hollywood Comedy of Remarriage* (Cambridge: Harvard University Press, 1981), 129. For an important critique of Cavell's argument about screwball comedies, see David Shumway, *Modern Love: Romance, Intimacy, and the Marriage Crisis* (New York: NYU Press, 2003).

knees, laughing and greeting Mr. Smith. He apologizes to Dunne about his behavior at her recital and laments, "At the mere mention of Armand's name, I feel positively murderous." Meanwhile, Mr. Smith has retrieved Armand's hat, which he thinks is part of the hide-and-seek game. Dunne surreptitiously hides it behind the couch where she's sitting with Grant and then behind a wall mirror, but Mr. Smith finds it, bringing the mirror down with a crash.

Armand's bowler hat not only determines the plot of the scene but also serves as an expressive object. Grant uses it to create one of his simplest but funniest moments. Hoping to reconcile with Dunne, he proposes they go for a ride together. She agrees, nervously telling him to get his car and wait for her on the street. He puts on the hat, mistaking it for his own, and prepares to go. Then he notices something wrong. McCarey shoots over Grant's shoulder as he goes to a mirror and looks at himself. The hat falls over his head like a helmet, bending his ears, making him unrecognizable and weirdly ridiculous. There's a long, silent pause, during which he reacts almost inexpressively. Like a man in a haberdashery, he stands stiffly, turning his head this way and that, staring suspiciously at himself, assessing the strange phenomenon.

There's another knock at the door. Bellamy and Ma arrive, and in the confusion Grant hides in the bedroom, taking the hat with him. McCarey cuts inside the room to show him listening at the closed door. Turning around, he sees Armand next to him, smiles slightly, nods, and politely returns Armand's hat; then he pauses a beat and slaps the hat out of Armand's hand. Cut to the main room. Dunne is talking to Bellamy and Ma as crashing sounds come from the bedroom, a cacophony intensified by Mr. Smith's barking. Dunne keeps talking, trying to ignore the racket, until the bedroom door bursts open and Armand runs through it, pursued by Grant, who chases him out of the apartment. The astonished, disillusioned Bellamy says, "I guess that shows a man's best friend is his mother."

Grant later apologizes to Dunne about "that two men in a bedroom farce" but drifts unenthusiastically into an engagement to the beautiful Barbara Vance (Molly Lamont), known in the press as "the madcap heiress." When he and Barbara become items in the gossip columns, Dunne intervenes, going to visit Grant. There's a quiet scene in which he opens champagne to celebrate their forthcoming divorce and she reads an old poem she once wrote. Everything is centered on Dunne, but Grant skillfully registers repressed sadness when the champagne tastes flat and he recalls the poem. Suddenly the phone rings and Dunne answers it. It's Barbara calling. Grant takes the phone and explains that the female voice she heard is his sister, just arrived from Europe, who would of course enjoy coming to a dinner that evening at the Vance's but probably can't make it. Dunne is amused. She's a character who often performs, aiming to deceive, tease, or entertain, and performance is a weapon she can use against the snobbish Barbara.

The occasion is the Vance dinner, a formal affair celebrating the impending divorce, which becomes official at midnight. It eventuates in Dunne's third singing number, filled with McCarey-esque jokes involving gaucherie and "controlled dismay." Grant arrives at the Vance mansion in top hat and tails, and in a wide shot walks across the vast entrance hall in his graceful Cary Grant stride. He greets the family and takes a seat beside Barbara, explaining that his sister, who was educated in Switzerland, can't attend because of fatigue from her trip. No reason for Barbara to be suspicious, he says, echoing the speech about marriage and suspicion he gave at the start of the film. As he begins reminiscing about his father's school loyalty to Princeton, Dunne suddenly arrives, echoing her surprise arrival back in the opening scene. This time she's dressed in rhinestones and a fringed skirt, and introduces herself as Lola, Grant's sister. The Vance family is quietly appalled. She asks for a drink, signaling the butler to bring a highball rather than sherry. "I had a few before and they're beginning to wear off," she loudly says, "You know how that is." As she sits on the arm of Grant's couch, she recalls that he used to be known as "Jerry the nipper," and their father was the groundskeeper at Princeton.

There are two jokes about posteriors, one involving a scarf and the other a purse. Dunne squeezes between Grant and Barbara on the couch, and Grant, who plays straight man, looks perturbed and tries to manage his pocket handkerchief. "Don't anybody leave this room!" Dunne says, "I've lost my purse!" It turns out she's sitting on it.

The biggest joke comes when she reveals that she's a singer-dancer and offers to demonstrate. Grant tries to dissuade her, and she almost yells, "I'm not going to do it like at the *club*!" Improbably, the Vances have a recording of "My Dreams are Gone with the Wind." Dunne explains that she usually does this song with a wind effect, but she compensates with an awkward bump and grind, all the more funny because it feels improvised. When Dunne rehearsed the number, McCarey wanted her to swivel her hips, but when she tried, she laughed and said, "I never could do that." McCarey had her repeat the remark for the film, even though it breaks character.

Grant is at first subtly disconcerted, unable to reveal Dunne's identity but aware that she's out to shock everyone. Now and then he frowns or registers surprise. As Dunne's performance proceeds, however, he becomes amused and seems to realize she's his ideal partner. "Not for the first time," James Morrison has observed, "Jerry sees Lucy anew, perceives—and is moved by—something of the desperation just beneath her act, and even gets into the spirit if it, playing along, however passively-aggressively."[11] When her song ends, Grant rises, takes her by the hand and moves with her to the archway leading out of the room. They turn, smile at their audience, and slightly bow. They exit like two stars leaving the stage.

[11] James Morrison, *Auteur Theory and* My Son John (New York: Bloomsbury Academic, 2018), 101.

Dunne keeps up the drunken act when she and Grant drive from the mansion. En route there's silly business, a reprise of the "laughs" Dunn remembers from their past; she mischievously breaks the car radio, plays tricks with a couple of motorcycle cops, and while nobody is looking deliberately wrecks the car. The cops obligingly give her and Grant a ride on their handlebars, with Dunne whooping joyfully, and deliver them to Aunt Patsy's cabin in the country, which was mentioned near the beginning of the film. This becomes the site of the couple's reconciliation. We might expect the film to end with a Hollywood kiss, but McCarey has something more touching and suggestive in mind.

One of the puritanical Hollywood conventions of the time was that a married couple always slept in twin beds. As this film nears its end, Dunne runs upstairs, Grant follows, and they take separate bedrooms with single beds, the arrangement joined by a creaky door that has a bad lock. It's obvious they want to reunite, but given their history neither wants to say so. Above the door on Dunne's side is a cuckoo clock that chimes on the quarter hour, at which point two small doors open and figures of a male and female in alpine costume dance out, turn, and reenter, the doors closing behind them. (The figurines are played by real dancers who behave mechanically.) At the stroke of midnight, the Warriner divorce will become final. Dunne turns out the lamps in her room, and in the moonlight dons silken lingerie. She gets in her narrow bed and shoos a black cat away from it. The door to Grant's room opens and he stands just inside, wearing socks and a striped nightshirt. He smiles, does a comic, hopping dance, and describes his costume as "air conditioned."

Photographer Joseph Walker provides a glamourous, soft-focus closeup of Dunne, who looks lovingly at Grant. They have an awkward conversation in which Grant says in a boyish, indirect way that perhaps if they behaved differently, everything could be the same. An acknowledgment that he hasn't been faithful, it's effective because Grant delivers it with a mingling of tentativeness, reticence, and desire. He goes back in his room and closes the door, which rattles in the wind. Then he behaves decisively, opening a window to admit more wind. The rattling door is blocked by the cat, which Dunne shoos away. When the door blows open, the cuckoo clock strikes twelve. The two alpine figures emerge and dance, but the male, wearing lederhosen rather than a nightshirt, does a little Cary Grant hop and follows the female into her doorway.

Bringing Up Baby (1938)

The wildest of the screwball comedies, Howard Hawks's *Bringing Up Baby* was based on a *Colliers* magazine story by the woman writer Hagar Wilde and adapted for the screen by Wilde and Dudley Nichols. The plot, analyzed by such distinguished critics as Robin Wood, Stanley Cavell, and Gerald Mast, needs no detailed discussion here. Suffice it to say the film involves a romance between David Huxley (Grant), an absentminded professor who is reconstructing a brontosaurus skeleton, and Susan Vance (Katharine Hepburn), a dizzy heiress who involves him in a series of absurdly chaotic misadventures. She appropriates his golf ball and damages his car; she causes him to slip on an olive and do a pratfall on his top hat; she inadvertently rips his tailcoat; she flusters him so much that he accidentally rips the back of her dress; she conks his potential benefactor on the head with a rock; and on the eve of his forthcoming marriage, just when he receives the "intercostal clavicle" that completes the brontosaurus skeleton, she calls him for help with a tame leopard named Baby that her brother has sent her. When he comes to her aid, she drives him into a collision with a truck full of live chickens and a swan, has him purchase a giant lump of raw sirloin for Baby, and takes him to her Connecticut farm, where he meets a troublesome wire terrier named George (Skippy, from *The Awful Truth*) and a gallery of comic stereotypes. Many ridiculous events ensue. "How can all these things happen to just one person?" David asks himself. "It isn't that I don't *like* you, Susan," he says, "because, after all, in moments of quiet, I'm strangely *drawn* toward you. But, well, there haven't *been* any quiet moments."

According to Hawks biographer Todd McCarthy, RKO originally offered the role of David to Ronald Colman, Robert Montgomery, Fredric March, and Ray Milland, all of whom turned it down.[12] We should be grateful to them because it's difficult to believe anyone but Grant could have made such important contributions to the film. *Bringing Up Baby* isn't free of problems, but one of its strongest pleasures is Grant's performance.

David Huxley is a radically different character from Jerry Warriner in *The Awful Truth*—in fact, all of Grant's roles in the comedies are more or less distinct from one another, requiring different behavior. He was at first insecure about playing a scientist or intellectual, but Hawks suggested he should think of what was known as the "Glasses" character in Harold Lloyd's silent pictures. This was probably all the direction Grant needed. In the early 1930s, he had developed a close friendship with Lloyd, and had long admired silent-era comics. He found a pair of glasses identical to Lloyd's, creating a character who isn't quite like the shy, all-American go-getter Lloyd embodied, but whose mannerisms and physical talent are worthy of him.

Like McCarey, Hawks was a director who encouraged improvisation. He worked with the best screenwriters but enjoyed what he called "kicking around" scenes, allowing actors to ad-lib or invent business. It was Grant who proposed the scene in which David accidentally rips the back of Susan's dress and has to cover her panties as they walk in tandem through a crowded restaurant. (The scene was loosely based on something that once happened to Grant, and Hawks liked it so much he repeated it in *Man's Favorite Sport*.) Hawks praised Grant for "doing little things now, little gestures, facial expressions, that he wouldn't have dared to do when he first came to Hollywood."[13] When Katharine Hepburn broke a heel and had to hobble as she walked, Grant gave her the line, "I was born on the side of a hill." She later told an interviewer that Grant "taught me that the more depressed I looked when I went into a pratfall, the more the audience

---

[12] Todd McCarthy, *Howard Hawks: The Grey Fox of Hollywood* (New York: Grove Press, 1997), 247.
[13] Quoted in Glancy, 171.

would laugh."[14] Grant also taught her an old circus trick for the closing scene: when he stands atop a scaffold and saves her as she falls from a ladder, he holds her by the wrist rather than the hand, giving him a strong grip so he can lift her for a kiss.

Much of Grant's performance involves costuming, posture, movement, and habits of speech that don't belong to what had become his star image. His eyeglasses connote the intellectually preoccupied, socially timid scholar who, in popular American eyes, is unmasculine and therefore comic. Hawks has described David Huxley as, at least initially, a "caricature," and Grant's behavior is appropriately stylized. When we first see him, he's wearing a white lab coat and sitting atop the scaffolding for the brontosaurus in the pose of Rodin's *The Thinker* (a pose he used less ostentatiously in *Sylvia Scarlett*). He frowns in exaggerated puzzlement—like all his expressions, it's telegraphed in the manner of silent comedy. He holds up a bone, wondering aloud if it belongs "in the tail." The film is sprinkled with sexual innuendo that Hollywood censors seem not to have noticed, and Grant's style here would be appropriate for a burlesque skit.

David is under the control of his attractive fiancée, Alice Swallow (Virginia Walker), whom he plans to marry the next day. She wears masculine clothing, keeps her hair in a tight bun, and at the beginning of the first scene has a pince-nez. He stands stiffly beside her and gives her an eager, birdlike kiss on the cheek, which she resists because, she says, a museum is no place for such displays. When he anticipates their honeymoon, she tells him it will be cancelled; as soon as the marriage is over, "we're coming directly back here and you're going on with your work... marriage must entail no domestic entanglements of any kind." He registers submissive disappointment: "Oh, Alice, gee whiz." His nervous, milquetoast "Oh," or "Oh, oh," becomes a signature mannerism and can be heard at least twenty times during the scene, sometimes because he's excited ("Oh, oh, the expedition!"), sometimes because he's meekly frustrated ("Oh, well, Alice, I was sort of hoping,"), and sometimes because he's forgetful ("Oh, have I [an appointment]? Uh, what for? Oh, *that* Mr. Peabody!"). As he exits, he opens the door, bumps into it, and says, "Oh, dear, excuse me."

---

[14] Quoted in McCarthy, 251.

Grant retains vestiges of his glamourous image but is acting the humiliated male of Hawksian comedy. The Grant smile is seldom evident, nor the graceful Grant walk, and this film involves him in much more physical comedy than *The Awful Truth*. At his golf game with Mr. Peabody, who might help him fund the Stuyvesant Museum of Natural History's dinosaur exhibit, he looks sporty, but when he hooks his ball into another fairway, he runs after it with rapid, short steps, hopping in concern. ("I'll be with you in a moment, Mr. Peabody!") Then he meets Hepburn, who is almost everything Miss Swallow isn't. Hawks was an excellent director for her because, although by no means a feminist, he liked confident female characters—his only difficulty, he explained, was that Hepburn tried too hard to be funny and had to learn how to deliver lines fairly straight. He emphasizes Hepburn's aureole of loose hair softly blowing in the wind and athletic, I-know-where-I'm-going stride, which is so different from Grant's hopping attempt to retrieve his golf ball. She sinks a thirty-foot putt in a wide shot as the hapless Grant goes running up to the cup.

When they meet, she immediately dominates Grant, but in a way different from Miss Swallow. An upper-crust type, she isn't snobbish but ignores his frantic concern, blithely assuming that he's mistaken— it couldn't possibly be his golf ball. When he proves it is, she walks off saying, "What does it matter? It's only a game, anyway." It also couldn't possibly be his car, which she damages and drives from the parking lot. What's most infuriating is her casual self-assurance and complete self-centeredness; she isn't dumb or innocent, and it's hard to tell how much of her dizzy behavior is inherent and how much calculated manipulation. (She will soon become infatuated with Grant, at which point her dizziness is more like a clever act.) When we last see Grant, he's whizzing past as she drives off with him standing on the running board of his car, clinging to the door and crying out, "I'll be with you in a moment, Mr. Peabody!"

At the dining room of the Ritz Plaza Hotel, dressed in top hat and tails, Grant hopes to reunite with Mr. Peabody. He enters stiffly and hesitantly, holding his hat in both hands as if he doesn't know what to do with it. Grant uses the hat cleverly throughout this episode. Out of place in the ritzy setting, he walks toward the dining room with an almost Chaplinesque gait and has an awkward, apologetic conversation with the headwaiter. Unsure what to do with the hat, he becomes confused, drops it, and almost bumps heads with a woman offering to check it. Then he again encounters Hepburn. She's at the bar, where the bartender is teaching her a trick with olives and martini glasses. As she drops an olive on the floor, Grant walks past and executes a perfect pratfall, feet high in the air, landing on the hat. She apologizes, and he says, "Well, I might have known. I had a feeling just as I hit the floor."

It's the first sign that Hepburn is attracted to Grant; she becomes flirtatious, and he tries to escape. She follows at a distance, stopping to chat with the first of the film's many caricatured bit players—a psychiatrist (Fritz Field) with a monocle, a German accent, and a nervous twitch. He gives her the happy news that Grant may have a "figzation," a "love impulse" manifesting itself as conflict.

Thanks largely to Grant, a great deal of what happens next would be funny as a silent movie. Hepburn mistakenly takes a purse from the psychiatrist's table and crosses to Grant, then realizes something and asks him to hold the purse while she goes away for a moment. He stands uncomfortably, ridiculously holding his crushed hat in one hand and the purse in the other. The psychiatrist's wife, returning to their table, finds her purse gone. Grant crosses toward Hepburn and is stopped by the wife, who wants her purse. Grant struggles with her husband and won't surrender it. Then Hepburn returns with her own purse, which is identical.

After lots of overlapping chatter, the problem is resolved; the jokes, however, derive not from what's said but from Grant's behavior. When the wife tries to retrieve her purse, Grant is bewildered and alarmed, stiffly holding the valuable item to his chest, turning away and guarding it with his elbow. At one point he's unable to speak because of the argument of the other three characters, and he does a kind of proto-Lou Costello routine: he taps the psychiatrist on the shoulder, he opens his mouth a couple of times in a futile attempt to get a word in edgewise, and he's almost frantic when everybody ignores him.

The dialogue isn't unimportant, though it's even more ordinary than in *The Awful Truth*. Hawks has a distinctive way of handling dialogue, which is delivered at high speed in matter-of-fact style with a good deal of overlapping at the beginning and end of speeches. Sometimes the actors talk completely over one another, but Hawks reserves important information for the middle of sentences and wants the actors to overlap by rattling off something insignificant at the start—as when Hepburn says, "No, wait a minute," or Grant says, "Now, just a minute." The dialogue is funny not because of wit (Hawks, whose memory was faulty, once said, "I can't remember ever using a funny line in a picture"[15]) but because of speed, timing, and the quality of

[15] Joseph McBride, *Hawks on Hawks* (Berkeley: University of California Press, 1982), 260.

voices. Notice the moment when Hepburn realizes she has the wrong purse; as usual, she and Grant talk at cross-purposes, creating a fast-paced duet of New England and mid-Atlantic accents:

Hepburn: Now, you see, the trouble with you is you have a kind of fix . . .
Grant: Now, look, look. All I'm trying to do is find the gentleman, whom, thanks to you, I abandoned on the golf course today. That's all I'm trying to do here. Now, please, go . . .
Hepburn: But I . . . Say, this isn't . . . Where do you suppose I . . . Here, hold this a minute, will you please? I'll be right back.
Grant: Yes.

A high point of the film's physical comedy begins not long after, when Hepburn, trying to restrain the fleeing Grant, grabs one of his coat tails and rips the back of his coat. "Oh, you've ripped your coat!" she says. He closes his eyes and tells her to be gone by the time he can count ten. She takes offense and marches up a stairway, but he's inadvertently standing on the train of her long dress, which rips up the back and reveals her underwear. He runs after her, trying to explain what happened, and uses a distinctive move typical of his crazy comedies: the Cary Grant crouch, often accompanied by

open-mouthed astonishment or alarm. Bending low at the knees, he almost embraces Hepburn and looks frantically up in her eyes. Then he slaps his crushed top hat against her bottom with a loud pop (probably augmented by a foley effect). "What's the matter with you?" she asks, turning away in shock and exposing herself to everyone in the room. Still crouching, the wide-eyed Grant starts moving around her, shifts the hat to his left hand, and whaps it over her bottom again.

The gag is enhanced by Grant's timing, by the public humiliation of two "classy" movie stars, and by sexual innuendo. Once Hepburn realizes her backside is exposed, Grant puts the crushed hat straight atop his head, gets directly behind her (which might suggest the bone-in-the-tail joke at the beginning of the picture), and does another of his silly walks. Almost glued together, the two march swiftly across the crowded dining room, Grant taking precise, mechanical steps. As they exit through the door of the Ritz, Grant looks sideways and spots Mr. Peabody at the hat check. "Oh, I'll be with you in a minute, Mr . . ." he cries. "Be with you in a minute, sir. I'll see you in a minute. Uh, I'll see you in a minute."

Absurd situations and slapstick jokes accumulate, but Grant is also funny in relatively ordinary situations, as when he's safely at home talking on the telephone with Miss Swallow and hears the doorbell ring. The result is a confused flurry of improvised phrases combined with an attempt to open the door without tripping over the phone cord: "Wu . . . no . . . I . . . I don't know . . . Well . . . How do I know, well, because, because . . . Well, there's someone at the door." He opens the door and finds a delivery man chewing gum and holding a box. The delivery man leans calmly against the door jamb and waits while Grant tries to be assertive with his fiancée: "Yes, Ali . . . Oh . . . Now, Alice, be . . . before we're married . . . there's one thing we must have clear. I don't want any woman interfering with my affairs." The delivery man casually says, "That's the stuff, buddy." Phone at his ear, Grant turns and sternly asks, "What do you want?" To Alice, he says, "Oh, just a minute, Alice. Have to sign something . . . Oh, Oh, Alice, it's arrived! The intercoastal clavicle!" Most of the humor has to do with his precise articulation, difficulty forming sentences, and quick shifting from bumbling subservience to failed assertiveness to childlike joy. The delivery man (Jack Gardner, uncredited) is also important. A perfect Hawks character, he has a relaxed professionalism and dry wit that counterpoint Grant's frantic confusion.

When Hepburn learns that Grant's fiancée is waiting to meet him, she says, "I mean, if I were engaged to you, I wouldn't mind waiting at all. I'd wait forever." The arrival of the pet leopard provides a stratagem to delay the marriage and begin the single-minded pursuit of Grant. She calls him and feigns being attacked by the leopard. "Susan! Susan!" he cries, "Be brave! Be brave! I'll be right there, Susan!" Running to the door with the telephone, he trips on the cord and does another pratfall. During their drive to Connecticut with Baby, she collides with a poultry truck and Grant, who has to pay for the chickens Baby consumes, is covered with feathers. He reacts with a slow burn, like Oliver Hardy hit with a custard pie. For Hepburn, it's a fortuitous accident. While he is taking a shower at the farm, she delays things further by sending his clothes to the laundry.

Grant's costuming always contributes to his performance. Arriving at the Ritz Plaza in fancy dress, he's insecure about his top hat and his movements are tentative. He normally wears either a lab coat or the sort of baggy tweed suit Jerry Warriner in *The Awful Truth* would disdain. (See the wide shot when he stands on a Park Avenue sidewalk and finds that Baby has followed him.) Now, emerging from his shower in desperation (Miss Swallow, the bone), he looks for his clothes and finds them gone. Susan is in her own shower, so he dons the only thing available, appearing sans glasses in an elaborate white negligee with marabou trim. In one of the most famous scenes in the film, the front doorbell rings, and the angry Grant, hopping barefoot across the floor, throws open the door, confronted by Aunt Elizabeth (May Robson, garbed in mannish style) and George the dog. There's a repeated exchange of "Who are you?" and "Who are *you*?," with Grant becoming more furious by the moment. Aunt Elizabeth asks, "But, why are you wearing those clothes?" Grant explodes, jumping up and down, waving his hands and yelling, "Because I just went *gay* all of a sudden!"

Grant improvised that line, causing many later commentators to wonder if he was a closet homosexual and if audiences at the time understood the sexual implication of "gay." In answer to the first question, biographers haven't described Grant as homosexual and disagree about whether he was bisexual. In answer to the second, the general audience in 1938 wouldn't have known "gay" as homosexual code; like "camp," it had sexual meaning chiefly in the backstage world of theater and movies, which Grant would surely have known. Whether or not the audience got his joke, it was typical of the sexual innuendo of the film as a whole.

A more interesting aspect of the scene is Grant's behavior in drag. Ironically, this is the point at which he's most "masculine." He may be wearing a woman's outfit (and doesn't seem uncomfortable in it), but his glasses and timid reserve are gone and he's on the edge of violence. He sits on the stairway—hairy legs spread, elbow on his knee, chin in his hand—and glares at George, who keeps barking at him. When Hepburn enters and tells her aunt that Grant has had a nervous breakdown and should be "allowed to wear a negligee if he wants to wear a negligee," he again goes into his proto-Lou Costello behavior, trying to speak. Then he rises and silences the two women, yelling "QUIET!" and stomping Susan on the toe. With controlled ferocity, as if he might knock somebody's block off, he says to Aunt Elizabeth, "Perhaps you can help me find some *clothes*."

Classic Hollywood always treated male cross-dressing this way. Dietrich and Hepburn could wear pants and be sexy, but a man in a skirt had to look masculine and ridiculous—see, for example, Mickey Rooney's imitation of Carmen Miranda or the male chorus line in *South Pacific* (1958). In *Hawks on Hawks*, the director tells Joseph McBride that he thinks men in drag are funny, and that when Grant cross-dressed in *I Was a Male War Bride*, Hawks instructed him to "just act like a man in woman's clothes."[16] To show what he meant, Hawks attended a military party in a wig and a dress, put a cigar in his mouth, and asked an army general for a light. As Peter Wollen has

[16] McBride, 260.

pointed out, this type of comedy breaks certain taboos, but it "serves primarily to allay anxieties about . . . male homosexuality, evoking laughter rather than panic."[17]

Hepburn counts her toes ("He loves me, he loves me not.") and follows Grant as he finds an old riding outfit, a pair of socks, and sandals. "Ooo, ooo," she says, "You're so good-looking without your glasses!" (Harold Lloyd wore glasses in his films because Max Roach told him that without them he was too handsome to be funny.) From this point on, her infuriating screwball behavior masks her anxiety that he might leave. Soon the dog George comes to her aid by finding the dinosaur bone and burying it. Grant and Hepburn crawl around on their hands and knees as George digs holes around the twenty-six-acre garden, searching for the priceless bone. "Oh, look at that nasty little *cur!*" says Grant.

Comic stereotypes accumulate: the dotty aunt, the Germanic psychiatrist, the dim-witted country sheriff (Walter Catlett), the drunken Irish gardener (Barry Fitzgerald), and the effeminate "Major Applegate" (Charlie Ruggles), who claims to be a big-game hunter. But the comedy flags somewhat. As Hawks told Peter Bogdanovich, "I think the picture had a great fault and I learned an awful lot from it. There were no normal people in it. Everyone you met was a screwball . . . If the gardener had been normal, if the sheriff had just been a perplexed man from the country—but as it was they were all way off center."[18]

There are nevertheless delightful moments, as when deadpan Grant sits with a group at dinner and keeps turning his head away to stare at George, or when he and Hepburn attempt to get Baby off the psychiatrist's roof by harmonizing "I Can't Give You Anything but Love." Key episodes, however, lack vivacity. The midsummer night search for Baby and George—Grant armed with a rope and a croquet mallet, Hepburn with a butterfly net—doesn't have the inspired slapstick of earlier scenes; some critics believe it's intentionally dark, but to me its best attribute is the subtle, childlike expression of affection between Grant and Hepburn, especially when he gets his head caught in her butterfly net. The business about Baby's doppelganger escaping from the circus isn't as comically suspenseful as it wants to be, and the climactic scenes when everybody winds up at the local jail are more bedlam than genuine fun. When the upper-class Hepburn tries to imitate a gun moll, she's so unconvincing that it's difficult to believe

[17] Jim Hillier and Peter Wollen, eds., *Howard Hawks: American Artist* (London: British Film Institute, 1996), 7.

[18] Peter Bogdanovich, *The Cinema of Howard Hawks* (New York: Museum of Modern Art, 1962), 26.

that even the goofy sheriff could fall for her act. Grant, in the next cell, is more amusing; when he tries to explain things to the sheriff, he turns into a proto–Lou Costello again, speechless and sputtering with desperation. One of the funniest bits is an in-joke about *The Awful Truth*: Hepburn tells the sheriff that Grant's alias is "Jerry the Nipper," and Grant says, "*Constable*, she's making all this *up* out of *motion pictures* she's seen!"

Another problem, perhaps unnoticeable until long after the film is over, has to do with the resolution of the plot. Unlike the Warriners in *The Awful Truth*, the characters played by Grant and Hepburn have almost nothing in common; they fit the Hollywood formula of an attractive, initially mismatched couple who fall in love, but they're so different it's hard to imagine them having a life together. The film can't fully solve the id vs. superego conflict at the root of its comedy; it may be a picture about what Robin Wood calls "the lure of irresponsibility" or about regression from the hyper-civilized to the natural (dinosaurs, leopards, dogs, childlike play), but it remains just on the edge of nightmare. Near the end, Grant tells Susan that his time with her was "the best day I ever had in my whole life," and yet the only suggestion of pleasure he's shown was during the nighttime search in the woods. Otherwise, Grant's performance as a bewildered, desperately frustrated scientist is the only thing that gives the film what balance it has between farce and gravitas.

In the last scene, the intercoastal clavicle is restored, Hepburn's ladder sways giddily, and four years of work on the skeleton come crashing down. "I trained Kate myself," Grant later said and recalled there was no mattress on the ground. The stunt of grabbing her before she fell was the "scariest thing I've ever done, but Kate said it was wonderful."[19] Just before the skeleton hits the floor, David says to Susan, "I love you, I think," which perfectly captures the way he's suspended between joy and reason. After he rescues her, she confesses responsibility for the first time: "Oh, David, look what I've done ... I'm so sorry." He can only say, "Oh, dear," wrapping his arms around her and adding, "Oh, my. Humm."

His Girl Friday (1940)

Usually classed as a screwball or "remarriage" comedy, this film might easily be discussed under the rubric of "dark Cary," because Grant plays the

---

[19] Quoted in Glancy, 167.

unscrupulous newspaper editor Walter Burns, a charismatic anti-hero created by Ben Hecht and Charles MacArthur for their 1928 play *The Front Page*. The wonder of his performance is that he gives the scoundrel such comic likeability.

A major success on Broadway, *The Front Page* was revived five times on the New York stage, became the source of four movies, and led to a decade of fast-talking, stop-the-presses pictures about journalism. Perhaps more importantly, it affected Howard Hawks's entire career. Hawks saw it when it first appeared and was impressed by its rapid overlapping dialogue, which he used in many subsequent films. He later collaborated with Hecht on *Scarface* (1932), and with Hecht and MacArthur on both *Twentieth Century* (1934) and *Gunga Din* (1939)—the last of which cannibalizes a plot element of *The Front Page*, but which Hawks lost the opportunity to direct. His admiration for the play reached full expression with *His Girl Friday*, the best of the film adaptations. He had a brilliant idea: the bromance between star reporter Hildy Johnson and editor Walter Burns could be turned into a variation of screwball comedy involving a female reporter and her male editor.

This wasn't a difficult transformation. *The Front Page* was already a farcical, repressed love story. You don't need to change the two leading characters' names, and when they become an ex-married couple, the comic potential and dramatic intensity of their relationship is heightened. Moreover, by 1940 the "girl reporter" had become a familiar Hollywood type. An independent, wise-cracking female inspired by the real-life reporter Adela Rogers St. Johns, she was epitomized by Glenda Farrell in a series of nine B pictures about Torchy Blane (1936–1939), who became the inspiration for Lois Lane in the Superman comics; she also appeared in Frank Capra's populist melodramas, played by Jean Arthur in *Mr. Deeds Goes to Town* (1936) and *Mr. Smith Goes to Washington* (1939), and by Barbara Stanwyck in *Meet John Doe* (1941). One of her incarnations was in an early Grant vehicle, *Big Brown Eyes* (1936), in which Grant is a detective and Joan Bennett a manicurist-turned-reporter. (At one point in that film, Grant imitates Mae West and Bennett responds, "Come up and see me sometime.") But Hawks's Hildy Johnson, played by Rosalind Russell after Jean Arthur turned down the role, is the best and toughest of the lot; she not only outsmarts a room full of rival newsmen and writes a better story than theirs but also breaks into a run in high heels, hikes up her skirt, and executes a flying tackle.

To develop a screenplay, Hawks hired Charles Lederer, a longtime friend of Hecht and MacArthur, who had also been the co-writer for Lewis Milestone's

1931 adaptation of *The Front Page*. His chief task was to "open out" the play and satisfy censors by polishing its rough edges, all the while remaining true to its half-cynical, half-romantic portrait of the world Hecht and MacArthur experienced as Chicago reporters in the 1920s. It was Lederer who contributed the important idea of making the editor and star reporter a divorced couple, and the uncredited Morrie Ryskind helped provide dialogue. Once the action moves to the press room of the criminal court building where Earl Williams is about to be executed, the film hews very close to the original play; and when Hawks, Lederer, and Ryskind make alterations, they're mostly improvements.

Walter Burns, the editor-in-chief played by Grant, was based on Walter Howie, the editor of Chicago's Hearst newspaper and a leading exponent of lurid yellow journalism; as reporter Arthur Pegler once wrote, the Hearst papers resembled "a screaming woman running down the street with her throat cut."[20] But even though Howie specialized in lowbrow, sensational material, he was something of a dandy; he was played by fancy-dressed Osgood Perkins in the original play, and by sophisticated Adolph Menjou in Lewis Milestone's adaptation. This may explain why Grant, in contrast to the newsmen around him, doesn't have a tough accent and looks more like a movie star, tanned and groomed as if he just emerged from a spa.

In Russell's first appearance, she's also done up, wearing the latest fashion in 1940s hats, which doesn't diminish her swagger. She enters the *Morning Post* (city unidentified) with her fiancé, Bruce Baldwin (Ralph Bellamy, less silly than in *The Awful Truth* but no less a mother's boy) and leaves him eagerly waiting outside the press-room gate while she confronts her ex-husband/ editor in his office. The camera tracks at a slightly low level as she marches across the bustling room like a returning hero, smiling modestly, acknowledging "Hi-ya" welcomes from other female reporters, and commiserating with the older woman who does a lovelorn column. She's long-legged, and as James Harvey has noticed, a little ungainly, which is part of her charm.[21]

The scene in Grant's office, shot on the first day of filming, is a masterpiece of blocking and performance in a tight space. Hawks boasted that *His Girl Friday* had twice the dialogue of an ordinary movie, and Grant and Russell make a bushel of it whiz by accompanied with nicely timed beat changes and short, pregnant moments of silence. Hawks claimed that he didn't care for jokes in dialogue, but this scene and the film as a whole has plenty. The pace

[20] Quoted in Ben Hecht, *A Child of the Century* (New York: Ballantine Books, 1970), 137.
[21] Harvey, 433.

is relentless, filled with quick movements, speeches that provide back story, and clever use of objects. The two actors seldom bite one another's lines, but there's a lightning ping-pong of exchanges between them, and they some-times overlap completely with indecipherable yada-yada-yada.

When Russell enters, Grant is seated with his back to us, shaving with an elec-tric razor and conversing with a gangster named Louie (Abner Biberman) and the city editor Duffy (Frank Orth, whose character was named after Ben Hecht's Chicago editor). In a flash, he checks the smoothness of his cheek, removes the napkins at his neck, gets rid of Louie, and shoves Duffy out, ordering him to find the lazy Republican governor and promise him the paper's endorsement if he gives accused killer Earl Williams a reprieve. A world-class double-crosser, he sits cockily in a swivel chair, boasting that he's now going to double-cross a governor. Turning to Russell, he asks, "And what can I do for *you*?" She makes a pointed request to sit down. He taps his knee and grins: "There's a light burning in the window for you, honey, right here." She sits atop a desk.

Business with cigarettes in a Hawks movie is often more significant than the dialogue. Grant lights up, and Russell asks if she can have one. No ro-mantic, he tosses it to her. "And a match?" she asks. He tosses the match-book. She lights up and a verbal duel begins. She wants him to stop sending messages (including by sky-writing airplane), and he wants her to return as reporter and sexual partner. "How long has it *been*?" he asks, his sly grin leaving no doubt what "it" means. Sitting beside her on the desk, he reminds her that he's "still got the dimple in the same place." When she recalls how their marriage was a failure from the start, he apologizes for spoiling their honeymoon: How could he know there would be a cave-in in a coal mine? When she spent two weeks in the mine getting a story, "We beat the *whole country*!" He begins pacing around, arguing that divorce is just a bunch of words uttered by some judge; he always meant to do something about it, but "you never miss the *water* till the *well* runs dry." At this, he makes a charac-teristic Grant double-take and quick grin of I-got-you-there amusement. He tells Russell that if she comes back, "we'll get married again." She tells him he's wonderful in a "loathsome sort of way."

The mood quickly changes and gestures become wild and caricatured. Grant begins pacing, shouting "I made a *reporter* of you!" According to him, when they met she was a baby-faced hick just out of school, but now she's a real journalist. It would have all worked out, he laments, "if you'd just been a *reporter*, but *not you*, you had to *marry* me and *spoil* everything!" He imitates her: "Oh, *Walter*!" he gushes, batting his eyes and striking an effeminate pose.

He turns away and crosses to a phone on his desk, saying she would never have accepted his proposal if she'd been a "gentleman." At this, she throws her purse at him and misses. He smiles and remarks that she "used to have a better arm." (Hawks encouraged Grant and Russell to improvise, and this was one of their spur-of-the-moment inspirations.) Then his face changes slightly, exhibiting what Stanley Cavell has called "Cary Grant's photogenetic quality of thoughtfulness."[22] One reason he excels as a movie actor is that he has the ability to show thinking without speech, sometimes without evident gesture or movement, using his eyes. Here he performs it ostentatiously, portraying Walter Burns as an inveterate schemer and plotter, quickly maneuvering to gain advantage. He uses his brief pause at the candlestick telephone (an object that figures prominently in both the play and the film) to indicate quick calculation: turned away from Russell, his eyes shift restlessly for a second, then he makes a sudden call to Duffy, pretending to talk about a reporter named Sweeny. He turns to Russell in despair over Sweeny's fate. "Dead?" Russell asks, unconcerned because she's never going to fall for anything Grant tries. No, Grant says, Sweeny has "picked *today* to have a *baby*!" Earl Williams is about to be executed, and Sweeny, the only good writer left at the *Post*, is probably "walking up and down in the *hos*pital!" In another imitation, he grasps his hands behind his back, bows his head in worry, and paces like an expectant father outside a delivery room.

Russell takes a compact from her purse, ignores him, and begins powdering her nose. Suddenly, Grant acts as if he's had an inspiration: "*Hildy!*" he says. She scoffs, snaps the compact shut, and casually drops it in the purse like a depth charge. He offers her a series of raises and withdraws them when he finds she doesn't have a job with another paper. When he tries to embrace her, she pushes him away, telling him to stop acting like her osteopath. "You can't quit the newspaper business," he moans as he continues pacing. "You're a *newspaperman*! You're a *journalist*!" She aloofly calls attention to her engagement ring.

There's another beat change as Grant realizes the seriousness of the situation. Russell talks about a normal life and an actual home with the man she's found on a Bermuda vacation, and Grant turns away, moving to the telephone again, fingers drumming on it, eyes thoughtfully restless.

[22] Stanley Cavell, *Pursuits of Happiness: The Hollywood Comedy of Remarriage* (Cambridge, MA: Harvard University Press, 1981), 164.

"Sounds like a guy *I* ought to marry," he says and uses another object to hide his thinking—a carnation, which he picks up from the desk and slides in his lapel.

Suddenly he becomes gentle, crossing and taking her by the arms. "I'm more or less particular about who my wife marries," he says. "Mind if I meet him?" She resists, but he's already headed for the door, which he closes in her face. "Oh, I *am* sorry, Hildy," he says.

Predictably, the meeting results in calculated humiliations of Bellamy, who, nice fellow that he is, doesn't seem to notice. Russell opens the press-room gate for Grant, who quickly introduces himself to an elderly stranger standing near Bellamy. After a good deal of overlapping dialogue, the so-called confusion is cleared up; Grant spins, smiles broadly, and shakes the umbrella handle sticking out from under Bellamy's arm. (Bellamy, an insurance man, also has a raincoat and galoshes because it might rain.) Grant apologizes, explaining that Russell gave him the impression she was engaged to "a much older man." Then he rushes the two out to a nearby restaurant for lunch. At the restaurant, Grant moves fast, gracefully slipping into Bellamy's chair as he's trying to sit down, positioning himself between the couple. There's more business with cigarettes—Russell lights one and Grant takes her hand, using her lit match to light his own.

Once again dialogue goes by speedily, but this time everyone talks while having lunch. Eating scenes in movies are tricky for actors, especially here because of the amount of dialogue. According to Todd McCarthy, the scene took four days to shoot.[23] Grant and Russell, who have most of the lines, play with their food or take small bites—Grant doing this while holding a knife, a fork, and a burning cigarette. Russell is archly silent when he says she's a great reporter, and he'd "*kill* her if she wanted to work for anyone else." He turns to face Bellamy almost nose to nose and expresses interest in insurance. It's important to have when you die, Bellamy explains. Grant nods sagely, does a quick double-take, and says, "I don't get it." When he learns that Bellamy lives in Albany with his mother, he gazes toward heaven, softly delivering a line reminiscent of *The Awful Truth*: "A home with *Mother*, in *Albany*, too!" He looks at Russell and chuckles, remembering a naughty moment in an Albany hotel room when they were covering a story; then he does another double-take, pretending to realize he shouldn't mention that.

The rhythm changes slightly when Grant discovers the couple are leaving for Albany in two hours and will be married the next day. There's another moment of quick calculation in his eyes. He pretends to have a spill on his coat and arranges for the waiter to announce that he's wanted on a telephone. While

[23] McCarthy, 285.

he's gone, the innocent Bellamy tells Russell he finds Grant charming. "His grandfather was a snake," Russell says. Grant returns, disconsolate because Sweeny now has twins. Russell immediately exposes this lie, but Grant has a better way of hooking her: he begins discussing the impending execution of Earl Williams, the importance of "the colored vote" (Williams allegedly shot a black policeman), and the need for the newspaper to do something. Bellamy is concerned about the poor man who's about to be hanged. As Russell listens, we see her become interested; she has an idea—Grant could hire an "alienist" to interview Williams and rebut the sherriff's claims.

Now Grant knows he's got her. "I can't write that," he says, "It needs a *woman's* touch, something with *heart!*" He frowns with concern, patting his chest to prove he has a heart, and pleads that it will "only be an hour or so." She agrees on the condition that Grant purchase a twenty-five-thousand-dollar insurance policy from Bellamy—and, she insists, the policy must be paid for with a certified check. As they depart, Grant tries to have Bellamy pay for the meal. Russell stops him, but he borrows the tip from Bellamy.

Cut to the press room of the criminal court, overlooking a plaza where a scaffold is being constructed for the Williams execution. We're now in the enclosed world of the original *Front Page*. A gaggle of bored, blasé reporters has assembled, playing poker, chatting, talking on the phone with their editors, commenting that the sheriff and mayor have just put a hundred more of their relatives on the payroll to protect the city against the Red army. This is also the world of the skilled, exclusive male group that figure in many of Hawks's adventure films, and he gives their fast-paced conversation a typically Hawksian, low-key quality. Also typically, he brings an independent woman into the group. In this case, the woman is superior to the men in every way. The middle section of *His Girl Friday* belongs to Russell, whose performance is one of the best in her impressive career, and it's impossible to talk about the film without paying tribute to her. (Hawks's only instruction for her scenes with Grant was "just keep pushin' him around the way you're doing.") She enters the press room with a casual, confident walk, wearing a different hat, sweeping its brim up from her brow like a cowgirl returning to the ranch. The other reporters clearly admire her. She's leaving the business for good, she explains with mixed pleasure and nostalgia, just as soon as she's done some work on the Williams case. But when a siren goes off outside, she pauses a second, reacting with the alertness of a war horse called to action. Realizing that it's only a practice drill for the hanging, she says, "I thought it might be a good fire."

We next see Grant at the newspaper, where he's being examined by a doctor while Bellamy sits at a desk, intent on making out the life insurance policy. The scene is a good example of how Grant makes the audience feel amused rather than appalled by his machinations. He and Bellamy play in a slightly exaggerated comic style that turns the characters into types: Bellamy isn't just a dull provincial, he's a clueless rube; and Grant isn't just a trickster, he's a theatrically obvious con man.

The cheerful Grant has his shirt open as the doctor checks his heart and pronounces him of sound health. He bends over Bellamy's shoulder with the polished, polite smile we associate with his drawing-room comedies, and asks, "How are you doing, Bruce?" Bellamy wants him to name a beneficiary. Puzzled by the term, Grant leans in further, tying his tie; when Bellamy explains what a beneficiary is, Grant names Hildy, at which Bellamy looks sadly apologetic: "That'd make me feel pretty funny." Grant reacts in comic concern, bending closer and assuring Bellamy that the "whatever it was," should be regarded as a "debt of honor." With stagy sincerity, drawing out a key syllable, he leans close to Bellamy's ear and says, "I was a *baad* husband!" Standing upright, he announces, "She wouldn't take alimony . . . too independent." He boasts that he has at least twenty-five years to live, bends down to Bellamy's shoulder again, and adopts a faraway look. "Think of Hildy!" he says, "I can see her now—white hair, lace. Can you see her, Bruce?" Bellamy looks off, and Grant drags out another syllable: "She's *oold*, isn't she?" He goes into another of his imitations, holding an aching back to signify old age, insisting that Hildy is entitled to "spend her *remaining* years" in security.

Unseen by Grant, the long-suffering Duffy enters, pauses at the door, and shakes his head at the corny act. Now fully dressed, Grant shifts into the stentorian tone he used for his unworthy-husband speech to Bellamy in *The Awful Truth*. "And the beauty of it is," he says, looking dreamily into space, "she'll never have to know until I've *passed on*! Maybe she'll think *kindly* of me after I'm gone." He removes the display handkerchief from his pocket and wipes a tear. To make sure Bellamy sees this, he taps him on the shoulder. "Gee," Bellamy says, and uses his own handkerchief to blow his nose in sadness.

Duffy tries to speak, and Grant snaps his head around as if a switch had been thrown: "*Whaddya want*?" Duffy has brought the certified check, which Grant happily gives to Bellamy, rubbing his hands together in a gesture of reserved, gentlemanly satisfaction. He suggests that Bellamy call Hildy with the news and steps outside. Through the half-obscured window of the office, we glimpse Grant speaking with the crook Louie, who is quite short. Grant quickly lifts him up like a doll so he can see Bellamy through the window.

Back at the criminal court building, Russell has two important scenes, the first when she bribes a jailer and gets an interview with Earl Williams (whiney-voiced, meek John Qualen, as effective here as he was soon after in Ford's *The Grapes of Wrath*). In the play, Williams is an anarchist, but Hawks and Lederer make him a timid bookkeeper who, after losing his job of fifteen years, desperately wandered the streets and accidentally shot a policeman. As Russell enters, a crane shot looks down on the isolated, bird-cage cell where Williams is in solitary—an unusual angle for Hawks, who usually keeps the camera at eye level. Throughout the interview, Russell's voice is soft; it's the only slow-paced dialogue in the film and provides important dramatic contrast. She offers Williams a cigarette, which he puffs once and gives back to her, explaining that he doesn't smoke; she uses it expressively, holding it downward and sadly dropping it on the floor. Williams seems to have no politics and has never used a gun until he shot the policeman. He doesn't know why it happened, but Russell reminds him of a slogan he's heard—"production for use"—and he thinks maybe that was the reason. "I'm not guilty," he says, "it's just the world."

The second scene involves the pathetic Mollie Malloy (Helen Mack), a prostitute with a heart of gold (the film isn't explicit about this cliché) who is in tearful rage over the way the reporters have treated her and "Mr. Williams." They've written that she and Earl are lovers and plan to marry on the gallows. They shrug, sneer, and brutally insult her until she wonders why "a bolt of lightnin' doesn't come down and strike you dead!" Russell hustles Mollie out the door, explaining that it's no wonder the men are monsters—"they're reporters." When she returns, she stands in the doorway for her finest moment. I've praised her lanky charm and ability to battle with Grant, but one of her distinctive attributes as an actor is a slightly regal quality, which probably explains why she was often cast as a career woman. One of her typical mannerisms is to tilt her head up slightly as if she were looking down her nose at the world. She emphasizes it here, gazing around the room with a hint of disdain, quietly delivering her best line: "Gentlemen of the press!"

A telephone rings and Russell learns that Bellamy is in jail. "I've never stolen a watch in my life," he tells her—an allusion to the famous closing line of the play ("The sonofabitch stole my watch!"). In addition to being arrested, his wallet has been stolen, along with four hundred and fifty dollars and "that picture of us in Bermuda." After rescuing him, Russell makes him wait in their taxi, goes to the press room, flops her hat on the table, and grabs a phone to call Grant. She rips her Williams story from the typewriter and takes it to the phone. "Get this you double-crossing baboon," she says, and makes Grant listen as she tears it to pieces. Struggling with her coat, she determines to leave, bidding farewell to the reporters: "So long, you wage slaves!"

At this point, the film, like the play, begins piling one *coup de théâtre* atop another. Machine-gun fire is heard outside. Earl Williams has escaped.

Russell grabs the phone, reports to Grant, and sprints out in high heels, dodging a hoard of police cars and motorcycles, running through tear gas, and, with a little help from a stunt double, tackling Williams's fleeing jailer. Back in the press room, she gleefully calls Grant and gives him the story— the psychiatrist sent to interview Williams asked him to reenact his crime, whereupon he shot his way out, wounding the shrink in the posterior.

Russell knows that Grant is responsible for Bellamy's arrest and robbery, and wants the money back. "Bruce's money?" Grant says on the phone in innocent surprise, eyes widening and laughing quietly to himself. He swears on his mother's grave that he'll send Louie right away with four hundred and fifty dollars. Russell reminds him his mother isn't dead. When Grant hangs up, he turns to Louie, who is standing behind him with a platinum-blond moll, and tells him to get four hundred and fifty dollars of counterfeit money—which, as it turns out, Louie has on him. Grant also tells Louie to find a certain guy in a taxi outside the criminal court building. Louie wants to know what the guy looks like. Grant improvised his response: "looks like that fellow in the movies, Ralph Bellamy."

In a film rich with gifted character actors, Billy Gilbert has an especially funny turn as Joe Pettibone, a chubby fellow with a bowler hat and umbrella, who shows up to deliver the Governor's pardon for Earl Williams. The city's Mayor (Clarence Kolb), a cigar-smoking political boss, does everything he can to delay the delivery and get rid of this sweet simpleton; an election is nearing, and if Williams is pardoned the Mayor could lose votes. "You never arrived," he says to the bewildered Pettibone, who gestures helplessly at the door he just entered. "What's your salary?" the Mayor asks. "Who, me?," says Pettibone. The Mayor keeps upping his offers as Pettibone politely sputters in confusion: Pettibone will get a good job, his family will be moved from the country to the city, and his son will skip a grade in school. "Well, I don't know, my wife . . .," Pettibone says. When the Mayor promises to take care of the wife, Pettibone does a double-take. Finally, after giving Pettibone cash and shoving him out the door, the Mayor tells the Sherriff to issue a shoot-to-kill order for Williams. We now have characters who can make us root for Cary Grant.

Surprise entrances and exits keep coming, resulting in a dark farce. Alone in the press room, Russell gets Bellamy's money and wallet from Louie, but just as she sends him away, Earl Williams enters through the open window; he's climbed down a drain-pipe outside, and has his gun. After calming him, Russell lowers the window shades, locks the door, and grabs a telephone: "Get me Walter Burns, quick! Tell him I need him!" At that moment, Bellamy calls on another phone, and she has to talk at speed into both receivers, head swiveling from one to another. She learns that Bellamy has been arrested again, this time as a "masher." The strange woman involved was blond, "very blond."

The action in the press room becomes increasingly frenetic. Mollie Malloy arrives and she and Russell hide Williams in a roll-top desk. Reporters begin filtering in, calling their editors, wandering around, raising the blinds, and wondering if Williams might be hiding in the building. Suddenly a dignified older lady enters—Bellamy's mother (Alma Kruger), insisting that she be given his stolen money. Russell has told Bellamy about the finding of Williams, and Mother knows this. The reporters grow suspicious and crowd around Russell. Sitting with her back to the roll-top desk, Mollie urgently needs to create a distraction. She leaps out of her chair and cries, "*Now* you want me to talk! . . . I'll give you a story!" Then she jumps straight through the open window to her death.

Hawks treats the defenestration differently from the 1931 adaptation of *The Front Page*, not milking it by having Mollie stand dramatically in the window before she jumps. She literally runs through it, and before the audience can catch its breath there's a virtual match cut to the opening door of the press room: Mollie flies out, and Grant enters, wearing a stylish fedora.

As the reporters rush out to investigate Mollie death, Grant moves straight across the room in lithe, athletic style and goes into a Cary-Grant crouch in front of the roll-top desk. "You're sitting pretty," he tells Williams. It's as if a baton had been passed from Russell to Grant, who now dominates the action. Mother tries to intervene, and Grant, as assertive and dangerous as he was in the cross-dressing scene in *Bringing Up Baby*, says, "Who are *you*?" He gives Russell a signal with his thumb, like an umpire signaling out. Louie tosses Mother over his shoulder and carries her through the door as Grant stuffs a gag her mouth and Russell straggles helplessly behind. "Don't worry, Mother," she cries, "it's only temporary!"

Grant closes the door and confronts Russell, moving in close and looking sternly down at her. He advances almost menacingly, so that she's walking backward and they look like dancers. As they keep circling a desk, Grant angrily delivers his longest speech—a racing, non-stop lecture about her achievement and the importance of *The Morning Post* discovery of Williams. "You've done something *big*, Hildy," he says, putting a hand Napoleon style inside his coat: "It's a *career*! . . . There'll be *statues* of you in the *park*!"

Russell is gradually swept up by the excitement. She puts her hat on the back of her head and goes straight to the typewriter, beginning to type a lead while Grant seizes a phone and calls Duffy. "Tear out the *front page*," he orders, "never mind the European war!" In the pre-digital era, the art of holding an imaginary conversation on a telephone was a common training exercise for actors; Luise Rainer and Barbara Stanwyck were nominated for Academy Awards for emotionally talking to unseen people on the telephone, and it's a wonder Grant and Russell weren't nominated for this picture. Grant's performance is striking for the sheer amount of time he spends talking to an unseen person while using the telephone as an expressive object. In this scene, the door opens and Bellamy tentatively enters while Grant is gripping the phone tightly and almost yelling at Duffy: "*No*, never mind the *Chi*nese *earth*quake!"

What follows is a virtuoso performance requiring careful timing from the three actors, who are tightly framed, with Grant and Russell seated and Bellamy standing. The dialogue, as fast as ever, never quite overlaps, but the trio of players produce an illusion of comic chaos while allowing us to hear everything they say. The slower talking Bellamy vents anger and frustration; his reputation in Albany has been affected by his arrests, and he plans to return home on the nine o'clock train with or without Russell. Exasperated, Russell tries to deal with him gently while writing her story, and at one point inadvertently types something he's said. Grant, always on the phone, intervenes: "leave her alone, *buddy!*" But Bellamy wants his stolen money returned. Preoccupied with her story, Russell gets out the cash she received from Louie, and Grant, still on the phone, takes it for a moment. "Just wanted to look at it," he says (making sure it's counterfeit). Bellamy becomes wounded and indignant, and Russell, still intent on what she's writing, says, "Can't you see this is the biggest thing in my life?"

All the funny lines in the scene, however, belong to Grant, who is like a jazz drummer performing occasional flourishes and licks while the melody is carried by the other two players. "Take all those Miss America pictures off page six," he tells Duffy on the phone, "Take Hitler and put him on the funny page!" "Keep the rooster story, that's human interest!" Russell pauses in her mad typing and asks him, "the Mayor's first wife, what was her name?" Grant pauses in the phone conversation and says, "The one with the wart on her . . . *Fanny!*"

Once Bellamy has gone, Grant hangs up the phone, looks out the window, and tries to figure out how to move the desk where Williams hides. "*Aw*, the *moon's* out," he complains. There's a knock at the door and he opens it for another arrival—the reporter Bensinger (Ernest Truex). He's a problematic aspect of the film, not because of his performance but because Hecht, MacArthur, Lederer, and Hawks seem to have delighted in gratuitously mocking a stereotyped homosexual. Earlier, Russell has affectionately told Bensinger that he can be a bridesmaid at her wedding. A tiny, effeminate man, he stands in the open doorway and gazes up in awe at Grant, who instantly figures out a way of getting rid of him. Using his most charming smile, Grant says, "I was just talking to our Mr. Duffy about you!" Bensinger is astonished that Grant knows him and has read his reporting. "On the *contrary*," Grant says, his hand gently brushing off the shoulder of Bensinger's suit like a tailor grooming a client. Bensinger asks what Grant thought of the poem he wrote for his story on Williams, and recites a few lines. Grant glances toward Russell at the typewriter and acts pleased, remarking, "All we've got is a lot of lowbrows, like Johnson here." He offers Bensinger a job with a raise and grabs the phone again, calling Duffy and telling him to expect the arrival of "Roy B. Bensinger, the poet." Then he practically shoves Bensinger out the door, ordering him to get to work on a story about Williams, giving readers the sense of "an animal at bay." Bensinger salutes and says, "*au revoir, mon capitaine!*" As soon as he's gone, Grant whirls and phones Duffy, telling him in a tough voice to inform Bensinger that his poetry stinks, and to "kick him downstairs."

Grant goes into his crouch again, measuring the desk with his arms and realizing it won't fit through the window. The next arrival at the door is a beaten and battered Louie, returning from an auto collision with police involving Bellamy's mother. "Was she killed?" Russell asks in alarm. A closeup shows Grant's eyes widening in pleasure: "Yeah, was she?" Russell goes to a phone to find out if Mother has survived, and Grant simultaneously gets a call from a fellow named Butch, who could help remove the desk.

Butch puts his wife on the phone, and Grant needs to persuade her that he's loyal to her husband. "I'd put my arm in the fire up to *here* for him," he shouts, using the telephone earpiece to indicate his elbow. The wife hangs up, and this provokes a frenzied reaction that Grant uses in his wildest comedies: the Cary-Grant whinny. (It's an expression that Hawks suggested to him.) He immediately calls Duffy for assistance, and whinnies again when he learns Duffy is suffering from diabetes. "I ought to know not to hire anybody with a *disease*," he moans as he slams down the receiver. He turns to Louie.

"You're the best friend I've got," he says, ordering him to recruit men with "hair on their chest" who can move the desk.

Grant's performance becomes progressively animated and makes an interesting contrast with Adolph Menjou's more realistic style in the Milestone version of *The Front Page*. He moves with exaggerated steps and reacts with comic ostentation, almost winking at the dialogue. When Sheriff Hartwell and a gaggle of reporters come rushing into the room, he stands proudly, puts a hand in the pocket of his double-breasted suit, and with his other hand calmly checks the knot of his tie, as if advertising his elegance and savoir faire. He glares at the sheriff and asks in a theatrical voice, "Whataya *mean* by *break*ing in here like this?" Gesturing like a melodramatic rhetorician, he orders Hartwell out, threatening legal action. When Hartwell discovers that Russell has Earl Williams's gun, Grant claims it's his gun; a hand still in his pocket, he fiddles again with the knot of his tie, gazes down at Hartwell, and reacts with mock outrage: "My dear man!" Then Bellamy's bruised mother appears, pointing a finger at Grant and announcing, "There's the man who did it!" Grant looks around for someone behind him, pauses, puts a hand on his chest, and says, "*Excuse* me, Madame, are you referring to *me*?"

As an argument develops, Grant presses his lips together, turns to the roll-top desk, and indignantly pounds it three times, calling the Sheriff a "*cock-eyed liar!*" He's forgotten that three knocks are an agreed signal to Williams, who knocks in response. Guns are drawn and pointed at the desk; a count-down for the shooting begins, with a montage of closeups as reporters call their editors. But before anybody can shoot, Williams emerges. The reporters roil with excitement, giving their newspapers wildly different tales of the capture, and follow the police out as the weary, despairing Williams is hauled off to his fate. Through the open press room door, we glimpse Bellamy and his mother reuniting. The Mayor arrives, congratulating the Sheriff, who glee-fully has an officer handcuff Grant and Russell together. "You're through!" the Mayor boasts. Grant improvised his response: "The last man who called me *that* was *Archie Leach*, just a week before he *cut* his *throat!*"

Grant boasts that "an unseen power" watches over *The Morning Post*, and sure enough a *Deus ex Machina* arrives in the person of Joe Pettibone, who returns with the Governor's pardon for Williams. Mildly indignant, Pettibone doesn't want the job the Mayor promised him as City Sealer. He explains that he tried to deliver the pardon earlier. When Grant asks him to recall this for a newspaper story, he begins thinking back: "Well, nineteen years ago I married Mrs. Pettibone." The Sheriff and Mayor try their best to weasel out of the situation, unlocking the cuffs on Grant and Russell, who smile at each other in triumph. Everyone exits, leaving the two in the empty press room.

The only issue to be settled is the relationship between the ex-married couple—a difficult problem in a film that melds the cynicism of *The Front Page* with the heterosexual romance of Hollywood's farcical remarriage comedies. We've known from the beginning that Bellamy isn't a satisfactory mate for Russell; she's talked herself into marrying him on the rebound from Grant, who clearly deserves her resentment. Compounding the difficulty, she's a professional female in a period of limited opportunities for women, when movies insisted that happiness was best fulfilled through marriage. Genre conventions dictate that Russell and Grant should be brought together, whatever the odds, but to its credit the film doesn't completely evade the problem. Its chief strategy is to give Grant a moment of tenderness and Russell a moment of tears (plus the only bit of non-diegetic music in the film), all the while maintaining a comic/satiric spirit.

Russell is thrilled by what she and Grant have accomplished and begins reminiscing about the newspaper fun they've had in the past. ("Fun" is the keyword in the screwball comedies.) She tells him, "Remember the time we had to hide out for a week?" Grant turns away in a businesslike posture and starts to make a phone call to Duffy; then he pauses, telling Russell that she's earned to right to go to Albany and have the kind of life he couldn't give her. He'll write the Williams story himself, he announces, and confesses to making fun of Bruce and Albany only because of jealousy. "Goodbye and good luck," he says in stagy sincerity, taking her by the shoulders and giving her a gentle kiss. She's bewildered: "What's that with you?" Putting her purse in her hands, he explains, "I'm trying to do something *noble* for once in my life." As she reluctantly heads for the door with her overcoat and suitcase, a phone rings. Grant says it's for her, and not wanting to leave she rushes back to sit at the desk. The call is from Bruce, who's been arrested again, this time for passing counterfeit money. Grant, standing behind Russell and about to call Duffy on another phone, raises his eyebrows and comically reacts to the situation. He starts to sneak out the door, but stops when Russell puts her head on the desk, fumbles the receiver, and breaks into tears. Concerned, he crosses and leans down, putting his hand on the desk beside her. "Aw, honey," he says, "don't cry, please . . . you never cried before." But she's beside herself. "I thought you were on the level for once and didn't love me," she sobs.

Grant smiles joyfully and gets on the phone to Duffy, announcing that Russell is going to write the Williams story and "We're going to get married!"

She stands beside him, holds her suitcase under her chin, and says she wants to go to Niagara Falls for the honeymoon. Grant cheerfully agrees, but frowns when he hears something on the phone. He learns from Duffy that a big strike is going on in Albany. It's on the way to Niagara Falls, and he and Russell can cover it. "I wonder if Bruce can put us up," he says as he exits with Russell trailing behind him, carrying her luggage. As in *The Awful Truth* and *Bringing Up Baby*, the relationship hasn't fundamentally changed and never will.

3

Dark Cary

David Harvey has made the important point that there's "something dangerous, menacing even" behind Cary Grant's charm, which is "quite different
from the equivalent qualities of Cagney or Gable . . . that note of deep-seated
anger that arms or energizes him, that separates him so markedly from the
other farceurs and sophisticates." Grant seldom expresses outright anger
(except in *None but the Lonely Heart* when he goes toe to toe with Ethel
Barrymore and becomes enraged over the poverty of East End London), but
in all his films he has what Harvey calls an "elusiveness," an "intelligent fierce-
ness," and an ability to seem "a sardonic bystander."[1]

Those darkly shaded qualities are most apparent in the films Grant
made with Alfred Hitchcock, who nevertheless knew that audiences liked
the comic/romantic Grant and didn't want him to be different. Hitchcock
once told Peter Bogdanovich, "One doesn't direct Cary Grant, one simply
puts him in front of a camera. He enables the audience to identify with the
character."[2] But the term "identify" in this context is vexed: Do any of us resemble Cary Grant? Hitchcock was doubtless thinking of identification as
the audience's tendency to root for certain characters; the great Hollywood
stars could play ordinary people, but at the same time they were extraordinary beings, their charisma reinforcing our concern about what happened
to them. In any given film, our attachment could be deepened by the camera
and the mechanics of narrative. Thus, in describing a famous scene in *North
by Northwest*, Hitchcock said, "you and Cary Grant are now—because you
are identified with him—left alone. Then suddenly the airplane comes down
and shoots him all over the place."[3]

But Hitchcock sometimes tested our ability to identify with Grant by
having him play characters with unattractive traits. This is true even in *North
by Northwest*, which is not only a suspenseful adventure but also a romantic

---

[1] Harvey, 303.
[2] Quoted in Nelson, 124.
[3] Quoted in Albert J. LaValley, ed., *Focus on Hitchcock* (Englewood Cliffs, NJ: Prentice-Hall,
1972), 23.

Some Versions of Cary Grant. James Naremore, Oxford University Press. © Oxford University Press 2022.
DOI: 10.1093/oso/9780197566374.003.0003

comedy with an undertow of amusing, subtly satiric comments on Grant's stardom. In a conversation with screenwriter Ernest Lehman during the making of the film, the perpetually anxious Grant complained, "This is ridiculous. You think you're writing a Cary Grant picture? This is a David Niven picture!"[4] Actually, it's a definitive Grant vehicle. Given that I've written extensively about it in other books, I've de-emphasized it here, but I can't avoid briefly repeating myself because it so beautifully displays Grant's wit, athleticism, and romantic appeal in a role that initially provokes disapproval.

Grant asserts his familiar star image in *North by Northwest* even before we know who he's playing. Exiting a crowded elevator, he tosses a joke over his shoulder and strides across a busy entranceway, hunching slightly to accommodate a secretary who is copying a memo he dictates. We recognize his springy step, clipped accent, polished handsomeness, beautifully tailored suit, and chipper behavior suitable for comedy. But we quickly learn that he's playing a character named Roger O. Thornhill (the "O" both a sly reference to David O. Selznick and an initial signifying nothing), a shallow, self-absorbed, Madison Avenue ad man. His memo ends with a suggestion that he and his client "colonize at the Colony one day next week," and he follows this with a message for one of his many women friends, to be accompanied by "something for your *sweet tooth*, baby." Then he prevents a man from entering a taxi and enters it, claiming that his secretary is a "*very* sick woman." He orders the taxi to take him to the Plaza Hotel, where he plans to consume two martinis.

Like Cary Grant, Roger keeps himself trim (he dictates a memo to himself: "Think thin") and has been married several times. In the midst of his martini lunch at the Plaza, he's kidnapped by a sinister duo who believe he's not Roger but an actor—according to them, he's really George Kaplan, a US government spy. He's then taken to a Glen Cove estate on the North Shore of Long Island, where he meets the villainous Vandamm (James Mason), who tells him, "With such expert playacting, you make this very room a theater." After he narrowly misses being killed with "bourbon and sports car," nobody—not even his sophisticated mother (Jessie Royce Landis)—believes him because he's always been irresponsible. He soon finds himself being photographed holding a knife that has just killed a man at the United Nations. Fleeing the police, he slips aboard the 20th-Century Limited, where he meets the beautiful Eve (Eva Marie Saint). Sitting across from her in the dining car, he removes a pair of Hollywoodish sunglasses and says, "I know,

---

[4] Quoted in John Brady, *The Craft of the Screenwriter* (New York: Touchstone Books, 1982), 226.

I look *vaguely* familiar." Before long he will be attacked by a crop-dusting airplane and barely survive a cliff-hanging rescue of Eve atop Mount Rushmore.

Grant's performance is filled with graceful athletic moments, including a sprint away from the crop duster and a Douglas Fairbanks–style search for Eve outside Vandamm's grand lair in North Dakota. To reach Eve, he escapes from a hospital room, edging along a ledge outside the building and entering an open window, where he finds a beautiful woman in a bed. "Stop!" she cries. He begs her pardon. She puts on glasses and ardently cries, "Stop!" as if she's looking at a movie star.

Alongside the adventurous moments are grace notes and important acting skills that are barely noticeable. Consider the dining car scene with Eve, which could easily have become vulgar or lascivious. Grant plays it with polite amenity, giving Roger Thornhill more polish and likability than we expect of a boozing womanizer, while bestowing wit on the simple dialogue. His chief job is to react to Saint's breathy voice and seductive stillness, and a great deal depends on his tone—the mildly knowing way he says "Well, here we are again"; his distinct enunciation when he writes out an order for "*Brook ... Trout*"; and his charm when he manipulates his sunglasses, napkin, fork, and matches. As the conversation becomes sexual, he achieves comic expressiveness by a slow, quiet, drawing out of syllables, almost as if this were a musical and he were about to break into song:

She: It's going to be a long night.
He: *True ...*
She: And I don't particularly like the book I'm reading.
He: *Ahh ...*
She: You know what I mean?
He: Now *let* me *think ...*

Equally important is Grant's performance with almost nothing in the slow buildup to the crop-duster attack. The scene gets its surreal charge from the mere fact that he's standing alone on an empty road somewhere in a flat Indiana countryside, wearing a well-tailored gray suit of the kind he's worn in many drawing rooms. He's waiting for a rendezvous. Hitchcock draws out the scene, omitting music, and Grant just keeps standing there, squinting uneasily in the sun and frowning slightly. He looks right, then left. He uses his arms and shoulders expressively, raising and lowering them in a slight coiling and uncoiling movement as he takes his hands out of his pockets to button and unbutton his coat. It's a perfect instance of Soviet-era theorist Lev Kuleshov's idea that film actors should be experts at small, ordinary, but precisely controlled movements suited to an editing scheme. Grant himself attributed this skill to his early training in pantomime for the Bob Pender troupe, where he learned "How to establish communication silently with an audience, using the minimum of movement and expression; how best immediately and precisely to effect an emotional response."[5] It was exactly what Hitchcock needed.

There are also dark moments, as in the love scene aboard the train. Saint asks, "How do I know you're not a murderer?" Unsmiling, he says, "You don't" and slowly raises his hands along the wall behind her head as if to grasp her neck. "Maybe you're about to murder me right here, tonight," she says. "Shall I?" he replies, putting his large hands behind her head and stroking her hair. Later, when he believes she arranged the attack by the crop duster, he meets her at the Ambassador East in Chicago and becomes fierce, taking her roughly by the wrist, pulling her close, and trying to dominate her. In a Chicago art auction, he and James Mason stand facing one another behind Saint's shoulders, as if she's an art object they're vying to possess. "You had this one here hustle me on the train last night," Grant says to Mason, gesturing toward Saint and then turning to her. "Good night, sweetheart," he says bitterly, "Don't think it hasn't been nice." In the fairytale ending, however, Roger and Eve are reunited and spend their wedding night on the train. Maybe it will be a happy marriage, but when the film closes he's still an ad

[5] Quoted in Nelson, 44.

man. The dark notes in Grant's work with Hitchcock were more thoroughly elaborated in two other thrillers, discussed here.

Suspicion (1941)

Alfred Hitchcock's fourth American film and his first with Cary Grant, *Suspicion* was among the most profitable pictures of the year, despite going considerably over budget. Hitchcock, however, was disappointed. He thought the photography too glossy and the sets too posh, he hated the title RKO had imposed on him, and he resented the Production Code Administration and RKO executives because they forced him to make compromises and abandon what might have been an impressive ending. Among the redeeming pleasures was that he and Grant got along swimmingly; they respected one another's talent, had a mutual dislike of co-star Joan Fontaine (who won an Academy Award), and were both unhappy with the released film's ending. In the same year, Hitchcock tried unsuccessfully to cast Grant in *Mr. and Mrs. Smith*, a relatively bland screwball comedy Grant may have rejected because he was weary of the genre. *Suspicion*, on the other hand, had great appeal to the actor, not only because of the chance to work with a director he admired and with whom he shared a similar background but also because Hitchcock offered him a chance to play a charming murderer.

The film was based on the excellent 1932 novel *Before the Fact* by Francis Iles, a pen name of British author Anthony Berkeley Cox. Hitchcock had hoped to adapt this novel when he was in Britain, and when he came to America he found it was the property of RKO. He believed he could overcome the potential objections of censors while maintaining its title and basic situation, which Iles stated in the opening two sentences: "Some women give birth to murderers, some go to bed with them, and some marry them. Lina Aysgarth had lived with her husband for nearly eight years before she realized that she was married to a murderer."[6] The shock of the novel is that Lina allows her husband, Johnnie, to kill her. As she lies in bed with a case of flu, he brings her a poisoned glass of milk and soda, which she knows is lethal. She drinks it down and asks Johnnie to leave the room because she doesn't want him to see her die. In the sardonic last sentence, Iles writes, "It did seem a pity that she had to die, when she would have liked so much to live."[7]

---

[6] Francis Iles, *Before the Fact* (London: Arcturus, 2011), 5.
[7] Iles, 254.

The novel is both a dark satire of British manners and a disturbing psychological portrait of a woman's masochistic enslavement to an attractive rotter. Narrated in the third person but from Lina's point of view, it leaves no doubt as to Johnnie Aysgarth's character. Before he succeeds in murdering Lina, he lies, forges, swindles, murders a close friend, and openly commits serial adultery, even impregnating his and Lina's pretty household servant. He's the black sheep of an aristocratic family that has lost its estates and money, and his chief interest in Lina McLaidlaw—an interest that at first Lina doesn't allow herself to see—is her potential wealth. The well-educated, proto-feminist daughter of a conservative, landed family in Dorset, she thinks herself unattractive and feels suffocated by the horsey, doggy young males of well-to-do provincial society. Johnnie is an extremely attractive visitor from London who is adored by the local females and immediately fascinating to Lina: "She thought: he looks as if he knows me down to the most secret detail . . . She felt stripped." Once he begins seducing her, "she would have gone to meet him along a mile of public road on her knees."[8]

The novel couldn't have been adapted straightforwardly by Hollywood in 1941. There were successful films in the period about *hommes fatales*— among them Hitchcock's own *Shadow of a Doubt* (1943) and Cukor's *Gaslight* (1944)—but they made sure the killer didn't get away with it. Hitchcock wanted to follow that pattern, making the sex less explicit, tilting the atmosphere more toward gothic romance á la *Rebecca* (1940), and adding a twist to the ending. In his version, which he described to François Truffaut, Johnnie would bring Lina poisoned milk, but before dying she would ask him to post a letter to her mother. Johnnie wouldn't realize that the letter describes his plan to kill her. After she drinks the milk, he would go whistling out to a postbox, and as the film ended he would drop the letter in the slot.[9]

Hitchcock never got a chance to film this ending, which foreshadows the dark humor of his later television series and which he prepared for by a motif of postage stamps and letter writing. (One of Lina's nicknames in the novel is "Letterbox," and Hitchcock makes his cameo appearance in the film as a man dropping a letter into a postbox.) Unfortunately, the screenplay, written by Hitchcock's assistant Joan Harrison, his wife Alma Reville, and long-time Ernst Lubitsch collaborator Samson Raphaelson, was plagued from the start by fears of Breen Office censorship and pressure from RKO to avoid making Grant a villain. Several endings were tried (in one, Grant becomes a heroic air force flier

[8] Iles, 20.
[9] François Truffaut, *Hitchcock/Truffaut*, rev. ed. (New York: Simon & Schuster, 1985), 142–43.

going off to attack Berlin) and at least three were filmed. Audiences at a preview showing were put off by the inconsistent tone, and the problem was exacerbated when RKO underwent a change of management, installing Joseph Breen, the censorship czar, as temporary production chief. Probably under the influence of Breen, producer Sol Lesser cut all scenes that made Grant look sinister, resulting in a 55-minute picture. Hitchcock objected, and the scenes were restored.[10]

The ending we have was arrived at by Hitchcock and Joan Harrison: Lina doesn't drink the milk and decides to leave Johnnie, who angrily drives her to her mother. En route, the door of the speeding car pops open; for a moment it looks as if he might push her out over a cliff, but he saves her instead. Lina realizes the milk wasn't poison, and Johnnie confesses that he's been plagued with guilt about his behavior. He turns the car around (driving a bit close to the edge of the cliff, a threat suggested by a brief surge of Franz Waxman's music), and they drive toward home. In the last shot, we see the backs of their two heads as he puts his arm around her. Hitchcock was fond of showing the back of Cary Grant's head in sinister moments and may have intended a concluding irony. But if you look closely at this shot, you can see that neither Grant nor Fontaine were present—they were played by doubles.

[10] Production history of *Suspicion* is discussed in Christina Lane, *Phantom Lady: Hollywood Producer Joan Harrison* (Chicago: Chicago Review Press, 2020), 118–23. See also Dan Aulier, *Hitchcock's Notebooks* (New York: Avon Books, 1999), 62–95.

The film is centered on Joan Fontaine's point of view, and most of Hitchcock's characteristic subjective (POV) shots belong to her. Partly for that reason, critics Donald Spoto and Mark Crispin Miller have described *Suspicion* as the portrait of an insecure, neurotic woman who, after the death of her father, fantasizes that her husband is a murderer.[11] But as Tania Modleski has pointed out, there are good reasons why Fontaine should be suspicious—among them Grant's irresponsibility, his freewheeling spending of her allowance from her father, his deceptive pawning of a wedding gift from her father for gambling money, his secret attempt to borrow from her life insurance policy, and his embezzlement from a relative who employs him. There are also scenes, clearly not imagined by Fontaine, when Grant seems potentially violent. Modleski argues that "the clash of moods and styles along with the notorious impossibility of ending the film plausibly are evidence of a stalemate, a standoff between the sexes . . . We are each of us caught up in our own genres, our own fantasies or compulsions: Gothic fantasies in Lina's case, gambling in Johnnie's."[12]

Whatever the case, the key to Grant's performance is a sustained ambiguity—repeated shifts between warmth and chill abetted by the lighting and framing of shots. Physically, he's quite different from the Johnnie Aysgarth of the novel, who is short, muscular, and curly haired; but his tall/dark/handsome attributes, combined with his typical air of refinement and reserve, give him a greater opportunity to suggest charm mixed with restrained menace. Despite his apparently genuine expressions of love for Fontaine, which are often a little detached, and his occasional admissions of guilt, which are always played with understated sincerity but never end in reform, the ending can't expunge suspicion of him.

In the film's sexually suggestive opening scene, he's slightly comic—a hungover playboy who behaves with a mixture of politeness, manipulation, and childlike rudeness. Hitchcock begins in darkness, with the sound of a train going through a tunnel and Grant's distinctive voice saying, "Oh, I *beg* your pardon. Was that your *leg*?" Light breaks out, and we see two

[11] See Donald Spoto, *The Dark Side of Genius: The Life of Alfred Hitchcock* (Boston: Little, Brown, 1963), 246; and Mark Crispin Miller, *Boxed In: The Culture of TV* (Evanston: Northwestern University Press, 1988), 268–69.

[12] Tania Modleski, "Suspicion: Collusion and Resistance in the Work of Hitchcock's Female Collaborators," in *A Companion to Alfred Hitchcock*, ed. Thomas Leitch and Leland Pogue (Chichester: Wiley-Blackwell, 2011), 175. For an account that takes in additional literature on the film, see also Michael Walker, "Suspicion Revisited," *Hitchcock Annual*, no. 24 (2020): 1–38.

strangers on a train at either side of a first-class compartment. Grant has entered to escape "*vile* cigar smoke" in the next car, which, "after last night," he can't stand. Hitchcock, who began as a silent filmmaker, makes him and Fontaine clearly readable even without Raphaelson's dialogue. While Grant chatters away, she says almost nothing except "no." From her POV, he looks fashionably dressed and well groomed, if a bit flashy. Rubbing his hungover brow, he peers from beneath his hand, and we see his POV of Fontaine, beginning with her sensible shoes and traveling up her attractive legs to her plain tweed dress and her eyeglasses (which the film will make much of). She's an emblem of repression, reading a dull-looking book on child psychology.

The conductor enters, and Grant complains that the railroad has given him a third-class ticket; he asks if he can change a five-pound note, then admits he doesn't have one. He asks to borrow change from Fontaine ("I hate to presume on our short acquaintance"), and when she puts a purse in her lap and opens it (more sexual suggestiveness), his eyes light up and he eagerly leans across to look inside, taking out her postage stamps.

"Legal tender!" he declares to the dubious conductor, waving him away and telling him to "write to your mother"—a line that would have been ironic if Hitchcock had filmed the ending he planned. Grant leans back and rubs his forehead as Fontaine opens *The Illustrated London News*, where, to her surprise, she sees a picture of him on the society page.

We next see Grant and Fontaine at a Wickstead fox hunt; as Oscar Wilde put it, the "unspeakable" are chasing after the "inedible." Grant is surrounded by female admirers, and a society photographer wants to take his picture. He notices Fontaine atop one of the horses, and Hitchcock cuts to a Sternberg-like closeup of her beautiful, rapturous smile as her horse rears. (Hitchcock would have known that a woman's pleasure in horseback riding was a favorite trope of British Victorian novelists who wanted to suggest repressed sexuality—as with Gwendolen Harleth, the heroine of George Eliot's *Daniel Deronda*.) Cut to a big close-up of Grant, his eyes lighting with a cocksure glint. "I can hardly believe it," he says, "It can't be the same girl."

On Sunday, accompanied by a group of young females, Grant appears at Fontaine's wealthy home, entering just behind the women through her windowed garden door. Fontaine, who has been reading, quickly removes her glasses and tries to look less dowdy. Grant has clearly engineered the meeting, but he stands aside, looking eager, as the women invite Fontaine along on a walk to church services. It's as if he's read Iles's novel or been told about it by Hitchcock, because his manner is similar to what Iles describes: "Johnnie's eyes twinkled at her, just like those of a schoolboy." When she goes off to put on a Sunday frock, he glances down at what she's been reading and sees a picture of him that she's clipped from *The Illustrated London News*.

On the way to the church, Grant walks ahead, whistling confidently— probably the same whistle Hitchcock planned for the film's ending. Outside the church, he takes Fontaine's arm, smoothy detaches her from the group, and says, "You don't really want to go to church, do you?" When she demurs, he tosses a coin for a walk with her in the countryside. Hitchcock cuts to a wide shot of the couple standing atop a windblown hill, where, accompanied by Waxman's emotional music, Grant holds Fontaine roughly and she struggles against him. It looks as if he's assaulting her. When Hitchcock cuts to a closer view, Grant smiles and says, "What did you think I was going to do, kill you?" But he still seems threatening, holding her wrists and calmly twisting her arms across one another, his large hands in complete control, contradicting his pleasant smile.

"I'm just beginning to understand you—thought I was going to kiss you, didn't you?" he says. Of course she did, so did we. When he releases her, he says he was merely trying to fix her hair, though there seems nothing wrong with it. This is the first sign of the ambiguity in Grant's performance, which repeatedly makes us unsure of how dangerous he might be. Fontaine, who thinks herself unattractive, says, "I don't understand men like you. I always feel they're laughing at me." Grant apologizes, explaining that for a moment he became "a passionate hairdresser." She relents, allowing him to toy with the back of her hair, which he arranges in a comic, stand-up pigtail. "What does your family call you," he asks, "Monkeyface?" This tease becomes his way of expressing endearment, and to make sure she doesn't resent it, he makes a sexy, flattering joke: "Your occipital mapilary is quite beautiful." No such term exists; he's referring to the "sternal notch," or small cavity between the collar bones at the base of the neck. He points at it and touches it.

Every step in the seduction and eventual marriage has a push-pull dynamic that that keeps Fontaine oscillating between deep unease and passionate happiness. Her father, General McLaidlaw (Cedric Hardwicke), declares Grant a wastrel who shouldn't be allowed in their home, but this tends to drive Fontaine toward him; even if McLaidlaw is right, he's a stuffy patriarch who thinks his daughter too unattractive to have a handsome lover. Fontaine secretly begins mooning over a glossy photo of Grant, but he cancels a date with her. When the annual Beauchamp Hunt Ball approaches with no word of him, she falls into extravagant, wilting depression. Has he forgotten her, or is he torturing her? At the last minute, she gets a telegram, using her glasses to read the thrilling news: he'll be at the ball, and she should bring her occipital mapilary.

At the ball, Grant arrives late, attired in glamourous tails, and claims falsely that he's one of the McLaidlaw party. Fontaine rescues him, breaking away from a dance with a bald fellow named Reggie. In an instant, he sweeps her out to the dance floor and twirls her around to a waltz that will become their theme song. Smiling, eyes twinkling, biting his lip mischievously, he says, "Hello, Monkeyface," and waltzes her to an exit door. Is he a Prince Charming? Despite his devious maneuvering and bad reputation, he seems genuinely delighted. When he takes her outside to sit in an automobile, he asks without looking at her if she's ever been kissed in a car, and his behavior hasn't a trace of the lothario. Part of the effect has to do with Grant's looks, unique accent, and rare ability to be both polite and sexually forward at the same time. (He makes a different impression from what an actor like Zachary Scott, for example, would have made.) Fontaine says she'd like a kiss, and he gives her their first, Hitchcock's shot favoring her occipital mapilary.

They drive to Fontaine's family home, where Grant becomes forthright, almost somber. "I'm honest with you," he tells her, because "I think it's the best way to get results." With a resigned look, he explains that he stayed away from her for a week because "I was afraid of you." Given what we've seen, this is implausible, but Fontaine seems to believe it. Grant's face is more serious than at any previous point, as if resisting her but unable to help himself. He sits on the arm of a chair, and Fontaine pours him a drink. "I think it's because for the first time in my life I know what I want," he says. If you believe him, dear reader, I have a romance novel to sell you, and yet he's quite convincing. They kiss again, and Hitchcock employs his signature method of depicting erotic passion: a 180-degree track around the couple, circling the back of her head and stopping on his profile, foreshadowing the more elaborate, 360-degree track in Vertigo . After they kiss, Grant asks if she likes the room. "Very much," she says, and he turns to look at a large portrait of McLaidlaw père in his general's uniform covered with medals. His very name signifies the Law of the Father. Grant stands, hands in his pockets, and walks over to the portrait to look up and address it: "I say old boy, isn't that going a bit too *far*?" He turns to Fontaine, smiles broadly, and says, "He doesn't *like* me." His reading of the simple line is complex; mainly with his eyes, he gives it a wry, slightly triste inflection—an acknowledgment of what they both already know, an implicit recognition that he can't do anything about it, and a sort of challenge to Fontaine. It won't be long before she agrees to elope with him, sneaking out of her home and dropping a letter to her family in a nearby postbox.

Grant's performance after the wedding is remarkably like his screwball comedies, emphasizing his well-to-do attractiveness and infantile irresponsibility but putting them in a repressive, Hitchcockian context. After a honeymoon in Europe, he and Fontaine return to Wickstead, where Grant has purchased a home without paying for it. It's completely different from Fontaine's family home—bright, modern, with a wide circular staircase and a cobweb pattern on the entranceway created by shadows cast from windows across the room. He's also hired a pretty young maid named Ethel (Heather Angel). "Oh, I've forgotten your name," he says when he introduces her to Fontaine. A telegram arrives announcing that he owes a thousand pounds, and he sweetly tells Fontaine he borrowed it for their honeymoon. He has no money, "not a shilling," but she shouldn't worry her monkeyface, not at this wonderful moment; charming, chipper, almost zippy, he talks at speed and showers her with endearments. He lights a cigarette, smiles, and says, "I've been broke all my life!" Then he mentions her father as a source of income. She's not as wealthy as he thinks, she explains, and he had many opportunities to marry better. Adopting a maternal attitude, she tells him she's just realized he's a child.

Ethel brings them tea and wedding cake, and as he and Fontaine sit together on a couch Fontaine says he will have to find work. Hitchcock cuts to a close-up of Grant, who does a comic double-take; his eyes widen, his eyebrows go up, and his head jerks to the side to look toward Fontaine. "Work?" he says. He'll make a list of possible jobs, he says, and crawls over Fontaine to get paper and pencil. Just then father calls to announce he's sending a gift. Grant scoots behind Fontaine, goes into his Cary Grant crouch, and listens to the conversation. Comically animated, he encourages her to invite father for dinner or perhaps a game of golf. When she frowns with maternal disapproval and returns to the telephone, he looks boyish and chews his pencil.

Ethel announces that the gift has just arrived. A close-up shows Grant breaking into delighted anticipation, saying, "Bring it in!" It's a pair of antique chairs from Fontaine's old home; she loves them, but they're in grotesque contrast with the room. While Fontaine talks with father on the phone, the disappointed Grant sprawls in one of the stiff chairs and puts his shoes on the other. It's the same behavior that made him amusing in *The Awful Truth*, but Fontaine signals him to take his feet off the furniture.

Not long after, Grant invites his London friend Beaky as a house-guest (Nigel Bruce, playing the sweetly dimwitted type he made famous as Dr. Watson in the Sherlock Holmes films). Fontaine is fond of Beaky, who simply chuckles at Grant's irresponsibility: "That Johnnie, he'll be the death of me." Then she sees the chairs in a local shopwindow, and at the same time Grant comes home loaded with gifts. Again Grant's comic traits are evident. Fontaine sits in depression, but he's ebullient, going into the Grant crouch, lovingly gazing at her face and smiling. Talking nonstop, he presents her with jewels, a fur coat, two boxes of hats ("Do you remember that funny little hat you wore on the train?"), and a pet terrier reminiscent of *The Awful Truth* and *Bringing Up Baby*. He also has a cane for Beaky and a fox fur for Ethel. Most of his interactions with Nigel Bruce are redolent of the English music hall, and he often accompanies his joking with a characteristic Grant expression: he smiles and his eyes gleam mischievously as he bites his lower lip, rather like an adult teasing a child.

He explains that he's sold the chairs and hit the jackpot from a horserace, but this does nothing to change Fontaine's mood. He crouches and tickles her under the chin, saying, "Give us a smile," while Beaky tries to amuse her by making the sound of a duck. What finally redeems him in Fontaine's eyes is a surprise he's saved for last: a receipt showing that he's used his winnings to purchase the chairs.

In the film's next phase, Grant's performance becomes tightly controlled, much less comic, allowing Hitchcock to emphasize his potentially sinister qualities and giving Fontaine more opportunity to become suspicious. She learns that he's been discharged for embezzling two thousand pounds and writes a letter to say she's leaving him. She tears the letter up before posting it, and at that moment he arrives, standing darkly behind her with a telegram saying her father has died. When General McLaidlaw's will leaves nothing but her allowance, Grant pours himself a drink, and Hitchcock shows the back of his head as he toasts the father's portrait: "You win, old boy." Driving home after the reading of the will, he quietly tells Fontaine, "Monkeyface, marrying you is the one thing I've never changed my mind about. I want nothing but to spend my life with you, and if you were to die first . . ."

When Grant devises a real-estate scheme using the wealthy Beaky as partner, Fontaine becomes concerned and tries to warn Beaky. As they talk, Grant opens the door and stands there, his eyes for the first time a bit dangerous, as if a mask were removed. Dismissing Beaky, he confronts Fontaine in quiet fury: "What the devil do you have to do with my business?" Stiff with anger, a hand in his pocket, he leads her to the stairway and marches ahead of her, saying, "I don't want any interference from you or anybody else!" It's the first of three times we see him mount the stairs, each time with a different attitude.

Hitchcock designed the next scene as a sequence shot. Fontaine is trimming a hedge in the garden and Grant appears from behind the camera, the back of his head looming in the foreground. His dark coat, broad shoulders, and height make him look threatening, but he says, "Hello, Monkeyface." Smoking a cigarette, he walks around to her side of the hedge and is revealed as no longer angry. He quietly tells her that he's decided to abandon the real-estate scheme, "maybe because I'm too lazy." A hand in his pocket, he smiles slightly with an undertone of ironic resentment, and walks off.

From this point on, nothing alleviates Fontaine's mounting suspicion, yet she's unable to leave Grant. A major problem with the film is that because of Production Code censorship and the studio's desire to make Grant innocent, Hitchcock and the actors have little opportunity to convey the sexual dynamic at the core of Iles's novel. There are two romanticized kissing scenes near the beginning, but Grant has no chance to generate a sadistic eroticism so remote from any of his movie roles, which would help explain his hold over Fontaine. Hitchcock can only toy with Fontaine's fears, using impressive cinematic technique.

First there's an evening game of anagrams, with Grant, Fontaine, and Nigel Bruce dressed as if they were attending a glamourous soirée. It's a good example of a trick Hitchcock uses often, cutting away from a conversation between two characters so that we hear it while watching the silent reaction of a third. During the game, Grant says that because he doesn't want to be responsible for backing out of a deal, he wants Beaky to come with him for an early morning look at the proposed site of the real-estate development—a high cliff overlooking the ocean. In close-up, Fontaine listens to the off-screen conversation, suspects that Grant wants to kill Beaky for his money, and moves pieces of the game to spell "murder." Hitchcock shows her mental image, in which Grant pushes Beaky over the cliff. She faints and falls to the floor, the long, dark skirt of her dress spilling out from her like a pool of blood. (It's an idea Hitchcock employed again in the color film *Topaz* [1969], shooting from a high angle and using a red dress.)

Grant doesn't push Beaky over the cliff; in fact, he saves him from a fall. This gives Fontaine only temporary relief because Beaky then travels to Paris on a financial errand, apparently accompanied by Grant, and dies after drinking a large beaker of brandy. (In an earlier scene, we see him almost die from brandy.) Fontaine is visited by the Wickstead constabulary investigating the death, and Hitchcock makes a sly joke, juxtaposing the big portrait of General McLaidlaw with a modernist painting, probably belonging to Grant—the latter an object of fascination for one of the policemen. Grant returns, carrying a murder novel under his arm, and looks grimly unhappy about Beaky's death. "Next to you," he tells Fontaine, "I loved him more than anyone in the world." But his expressive eyes register subtle tension when he asks Fontaine what she told the police. He seems to be lying when he tells an officer on the telephone that he wasn't in Paris.

Because Grant is a fan of murder mysteries, he and Fontaine are invited to dinner by Isobel Sedbusk (Auriol Lee), a local author specializing in Christie-style detective novels. The other guests are Isobel's brother, Dr. Sedbusk, who is a coroner, and Phyllis Swinghurst (Nondas Metcalf), whose mannish attire suggests that she's Isobel's lesbian lover. Phyllis isn't a character in the Isles novel and she troubled Joseph Breen, who insisted that all hints of a lavender relationship be excised. Somehow they survived, and Joan Harrison's biographer Christina Lane has suggested that "perhaps Joan wanted to make a point about the unspoken perversity of heterosexual relations and institutional marriage."[13] But the entire group at dinner

---

[13] Lane, 124.

is perverse, and Hitchcock's taste for black humor is evident throughout. Phyllis is not only mannish but also vaguely sadistic, like Mrs. Danvers in *Rebecca* (1940); and Dr. Sedbusk, wearing thick, creepy-looking eyeglasses, seems to enjoy reminiscing about exhuming a body as he slices into a glistening roast bird. (Hitchcock, a known gourmand, enjoyed sick jokes about food—see the moment in *To Catch a Thief* when a dowager puts a cigarette out in a fried egg.) As for Isobel, she's obviously speaking for Hitchcock when she says her villains are her favorite characters and there's no reason why they shouldn't be happy.

Of all the guests, Grant most relishes conversation about murder. Because of the amount of dialogue, he artfully plays with his utensils, creating the illusion of eating. He says to the doctor, "If you're going to kill somebody, do it *simp*ly! Am I right?" To Isobel, he says, "Seems to me that by now someone would have discovered a poison that couldn't be traced." When she tries to avoid giving him an answer, he smiles and his eyes light. Is he playful or slightly crazed? He insists that Isobel answer: "No, no, please! After all, do I look like a murderer?" Then his face changes. "Look at the expression on his face," Isobel says, "Trying to look serious, aren't you? You couldn't [murder] in a hundred years." Grant looks at Fontaine and smiles. "No," he says, "I don't believe I could." His smile fades.

That evening Fontaine feels ill. "Do you suppose you're catching cold?" Grant says as he locks the front door and explains that Ethel and the cook are away. Holding out a hand, he leads her up the dark stairway. She asks, "Would you mind sleeping alone?" Late the next day she awakes from a sleeping pill and finds Grant and Isobel hovering over her bed, caring for her. Isobel jokes that Grant has been "worming all my secrets out of me," especially the one about an "undetectable substance available anywhere" that leads to a "most pleasant death."

The most dramatic scene comes the next night. A crane shot looks down from the top of the stairs as a doorway opens, sending a shaft of light across the dark floor. Grant emerges, carrying a glass of milk on a tray. Hitchcock told Truffaut there was a lightbulb in the glass, and he may also have fastened the glass to the tray. Waxman's music plays a spooky waltz, but Grant also contributes to the shot. His graceful walk is always a pleasure to watch; he ascends almost as if gliding, the camera pulling back as he approaches. It's appropriate for an ending that might have been.

Notorious (1946)

The first Hollywood film on which Hitchcock was his own producer, *Notorious* became one of the director's highest achievements and resulted in an enormous payday for Grant, who earned the then astronomical sum of $300,000. Amazingly, Grant almost didn't get to play the leading role of Devlin, the US agent who recruits Alicia Huberman (Ingrid Bergman) to spy on Nazi conspirators in Brazil. The film was initially under the control of David Selznick, who thought Grant would be too expensive and wanted Joseph Cotten. (Cotten later played Devlin in a radio adaptation.) Its distant origins were in a property Selznick owned, a 1921 *Saturday Evening Post* serial about a Mata-Hari type who seduces a German spy during World War I.[14] Selznick intended Hitchcock to direct it but gave up the project because of his preoccupation with *Duel in the Sun* (1947). The screenplay went through a

[14] See Matthew Bernstein, "Unrecognizable Origins: 'The Song of the Dragon' and *Notorious*," in *Hitchcock at the Source*, ed. R. Barton Palmer and David Boyd (Albany: State University of New York Press, 2011), 139–58.

variety of iterations, including an unsatisfactory version by Clifford Odets, who had recently worked with Grant on *None But the Lonely Heart* (1944). The bulk of the writing was done by Ben Hecht, but according to Bill Krohn, Hitchcock independently and without credit created many scenes, especially at the film's conclusion, with Hecht filling in dialogue.[15]

In certain respects *Notorious* echoes or reverses *Suspicion*, perhaps intentionally. In *Suspicion*, the back of Grant's head has a minatory quality, and in *Notorious* Hitchcock introduces Grant with the back of his head. Early in the film, Bergman awakes from a hangover and finds that the darkly dressed Grant has brought her a milky white glass of medicine. Near the end, when Grant leans over the bed of a desperately ill Bergman, the shot is quite similar to one in *Suspicion* when he leans over the bed of Joan Fontaine. Even the plots have affinities: *Suspicion* was a film about a man who may or may not be a poisoner, and *Notorious* is about a man who, after putting a woman in danger, saves her from a poisoning. *Suspicion* has a motif involving the postal service, which Hitchcock planned to end with an ironic twist, and *Notorious* has a motif of drinking: Bergman is a near alcoholic who tries to drown her revulsion over her Nazi father with drunken benders, and in a twist she almost dies from poisoned coffee. Hitchcock's cameo in *Suspicion* shows him dropping a letter in the mail, and in *Notorious* he appears drinking champagne.

One of the important differences between the two films is a matter of tone or mood. Most of Grant's performances, including *Suspicion*, have light comic moments, but *Notorious* has none. With the exception of a few scenes at a party in Brazil where he's pretending to be one of Bergman's ex-lovers, even Grant's dazzling smile is either subdued or in abeyance. In at least three respects, however, he's ideal for the film. First, he contributes to its air of luxury, beauty, and perverse romanticism; second, despite his typical elegance, he's able to play a hard-boiled, tightly coiled character who has neurotic intensity; and third, he's gifted at what early Soviet theorists and directors called "bio-mechanical" acting, which involves control over precise movement and enables him to serve Hitchcock's editing techniques.

In an often-quoted 1937 encyclopedia essay on direction, Hitchcock wrote, "I would almost say that the best screen actor is the man who can do nothing extremely well."[16] Grant exemplifies that skill. Billy Wilder, who kept trying

---

[15] Bill Krohn, *Hitchcock at Work* (London: Phaidon Press, 2000), 80–103.
[16] Alfred Hitchcock, "Direction," in *Focus on Hitchcock*, ed. LaValley, 35.

without success to star Grant in his films, said of him, "He makes the hard things [opening a door, taking a seat] look simple . . . You don't value the skill until you see a less skilled actor try the same thing. It's pure gold."[17] Soviet-era theorist Lev Kuleshov made a similar point, noting that theatrically trained players "cannot content themselves with such an elementary task as how to enter a room, take a chair . . . If you ask an actor to perform this task several times, you will see it is performed variously."[18] Kuleshov wanted actors who were more like Chaplin, able to execute and repeat simple movements with precision. Grant mastered that skill in his earliest theatrical training, and it made him exactly the kind of actor Hitchcock needed.

Grant's first scene in *Notorious* is a case in point. At a drunken party in Bergman's Miami apartment after her father has been sent to prison, he barely moves and rarely speaks. In a long take (a technique Hitchcock began to favor in the 1940s), he's sitting in the shadowed foreground with his back to us, almost like a member of the audience at a movie, but because he's in the center of the shot, he looks mysterious and attracts our attention and curiosity.

[17] Cameron Crowe, *Conversations with Wilder* (New York: Alfred A. Knopf, 2001), 6.
[18] Lev Kuleshov, *Kuleshov on Film*, trans. and ed. Ronald Levaco (Berkeley: University of California Press, 1974), 101.

Bergman wanders around dispensing liquor for several guests and a wealthy older gentleman (perhaps her suitor), assuring everyone that "important drinking hasn't even started yet." When she approaches Grant, the camera moves toward his head. She pours a generous amount in his glass and says, "Hello, handsome, haven't we met before?" He's silent. The tipsy Bergman says, "You know something? I like you." The camera tracks in farther on the back of his head until it fills the screen. Fade out, and fade in to mark passage of time; the camera is in almost the same position, but it circles to the right, revealing Grant's face. He's smiling slightly, and Bergman, clearly intoxicated, drinks from his glass. The wealthy older man departs along with others, reminding Bergman that a trip to Havana has been arranged for tomorrow. Bergman sits facing Grant, and Hitchcock gives us shot/reverse close-ups of two of the most beautiful stars in movie history. On the verge of passing out, Bergman needs air and decides to give her good-looking, unidentified guest a ride in her convertible. Grant, completely sober, again offers an understated smile, and as they step outside makes his first significant movement, tying a scarf in gentlemanly fashion around her bare midriff to protect against the night air. It's pure gold.

Hitchcock often created suspenseful automobile rides not by showing the car racing down the road, but by staying inside it and cutting to POV shots of the road ahead. In this case, Bergman's POV is obscured when her hair blows in her eyes. Grant's face wavers between calm and subtle tension; he glances at Bergman with a slight grin and lights a cigarette, but his close-ups show him eying the speedometer and the gearshift, ready to intervene. This is the first of many instances when his chief job as a performer is simply to look off-screen and react, giving Hitchcock just enough expressiveness to collaborate with the editing. His silent reserve irritates Bergman, who says, "I want to make it eighty and wipe that grin off your face. I don't like gentlemen who grin at me!" Soon a motorcycle policeman pulls her over, and when Grant shows his credentials the policeman salutes and rides off. "Why you double-crossing buzzard," the drunk Bergman yells, "you're a cop!" She begins wildly slapping and hitting Grant, who wants to take over the driving. He gives her a discreet karate chop to remove her hand from the wheel and says in a soft, stern voice, "Are you going to get calm?" Flying into a rage, she tries to hit him again. He pulls her to his side, swiveling his back to us and shielding her from the camera's view. Then he bends over her, and we hear the sound of a short, quick, knockout punch, delivered with precision. As Scott Eyman has observed, throughout the film Grant gives "a completely contained performance, and the clear implication is that if Devlin ever cuts loose, objects—or people—will be broken."[19]

I've long been surprised by Raymond Chandler's mention of Grant in a 1951 letter to D. J. Ibberson, in which he describes Philip Marlowe: "The expression 'passably good looking' would not satisfy him in the least. I don't think he looks tough. He can be tough. If I had ever had an opportunity of selecting the actor who could best represent him to my mind, I think it would have been Cary Grant."[20] Nobody can object to Humphrey Bogart as Marlowe in *The Big Sleep* (1946), and I suspect Grant wouldn't have accepted that role had it been offered; some may think the very idea of casting him as Marlowe is risible, but if you watch *Notorious* you can see what Chandler meant. It's the closest Grant ever came to a film noir (unless you count *Crisis* [1950]) and has several Marlowe-like moments.

Consider the scene in which Bergman awakes on the morning after the wild ride and sees Grant standing in her bedroom doorway—a

---

[19] Scott Eyman, *Cary Grant: A Brilliant Disguise* (New York: Simon & Schuster, 2020), 223.
[20] Raymond Chandler, *Selected Letters of Raymond Chandler*, ed. Frank MacShane (New York: Delta, 1987), 270.

shadowy figure, darkly clothed, one shoulder leaning casually against the doorjamb, arms crossed. When he walks toward her, photographer Ted Tetzlaff executes a complicated moving shot from Bergman's POV, the camera tilting dizzily until Grant looks upside down. "Feel better?" Grant asks. He's unsmiling, laconic, and the dialogue has a tough-guy flavor. "Got a job for you," he says grimly. He mentions a group of I. G. Farben executives planted in Brazil as "German gentry," and tells her, "You could make up for your daddy's peculiarities." When she resists, he says, "Relax, hard-boiled, and listen." He goes to a record player and lets her hear a phone conversation he's tapped in which she denounces her father and the Nazis. Standing beside her, he says nothing, but his eyes, especially important to this film, suggest a mix of stoicism, cynicism, and sympathy. "Well, what about it?" he says, "Train leaves tomorrow morning early." He lights a cigarette.

Grant, who is all business as an US agent, suspects Bergman is a hard-drinking, promiscuous femme fatale—a "Mata Hari," as she derisively remarks. Any attraction he might feel for her threatens his professional ego and gives him a hardened edge. On the plane flight to Rio, she softens but he remains guarded. He goes to the rear of the aircraft to speak with his spy chief, Paul Prescott (Louis Calhern), and when he returns Bergman asks him who was the "very nice-looking man." This heightens Grant's suspicions, and from the look in his eyes we can see that she's also a threat to his sexual ego. "I won't be seeing any men in Rio," she says. In response, he tells her that her father died that morning after taking a poison capsule in his prison cell. In an inexpressive tone, he adds, "Sorry." "We're coming into Rio," she says, leaning slightly across him to look out the window. He looks at her profile, and a small expression in his eyes suggests he's beginning to fall for her.

Later, at a sidewalk café in Rio where they order drinks, Grant radiates resentfulness and contempt, much like a jealous lover. The contrast between his sourness and Bergman's vulnerability undermines any idea that he's a conventional leading man. She tells him, "I'm practically on the wagon," but he isn't impressed: "You've been sober for eight days and as far as I know you've made no new conquest." She wants him to give his "copper's brain a rest" and challenges him to hold her hand. "Scared?" she asks. Hands crossed and elbows on the table, Grant barely moves. Like the love-scarred flier he played in *Only Angels Have Wings*, he answers toughly: "I've always been scared of women, but I get over it." She asks, "Afraid you'll fall in love with me?" An actor who makes the difficult seem easy, he says, "That wouldn't be hard," tossing off the line but suggesting a cross between a confession and an insult. Bergman decides to order another drink. "I thought you'd get around to it," he says. She orders a double.

Afterward, they go for a walk on a wooded hillside overlooking Rio's Guanabana Bay, with Sugarloaf visible in the distance (no sign of a favela in this completely glamourous film). When she taunts him with the idea that the "invincible Devlin" has fallen in love with "a no-good woman," his resistance breaks, leading to their first kiss. Grasping her arms, he presses his lips roughly to hers in an almost angry passion, the shot favoring his right profile but emphasizing her long, yielding neck. It's a rare instance of Grant behaving aggressively in a love scene. The film then moves to a government office in the city, where Calhern, in conference with local police officials, explains Bergman's mission. In a long take, the camera almost imperceptibly travels backward down a long table until the group of men sitting at the far end look conspiratorial. Calhern says that Bergman is "good at making friends with respectable gentlemen."

Next is one of the most famous scenes in the film, a sequence shot in which Grant and Bergman kiss one another for two and a half minutes. The Hollywood Production Code frowned on lengthy, eroticized kissing during the period—in the same year as *Notorious*, studio publicity for M.G.M's *The Postman Always Rings Twice* attempted to titillate audiences with news that John Garfield's steamy kiss of Lana Turner had been timed with a stopwatch. Hitchcock solved the problem by having the couple embrace for the whole time, giving one another short kisses with barely a break between them. The sequence required almost balletic collaboration of the actors and Tetzlaff's moving camera and demanded that the two beautiful lovers strike graceful poses as they move, never bumping noses. Ben Hecht wrote suggestive dialogue for Grant and Bergman, but Hitchcock told them to forget it and simply improvise a banal conversation to counterpoint their variety of sexy kisses.

The sequence begins when Grant walks out on the balcony of Bergman's apartment, which overlooks a process-screen view of Copacabana beach. She joins him and they kiss, the shot again favoring the right side of his face. Her arms are around his neck, and when they release from the kiss she keeps holding him, her head and hair thrown back, her eyes closed in ecstasy. The camera moves in for a larger close-up, and as they look in one another's eyes, she touches the cleft in his chin. "Let's not go out for dinner," she says softly, and he quietly responds, "We have to eat." They kiss again. "I'll cook," she says. "What about the washing afterward?" he asks. They pause and briefly kiss again.

A good deal of the effectiveness of the scene has to do with the contrast between the way Grant and Bergman deliver these lines. As usual with Grant, his speech is clipped and fairly rapid, in this case spoken with a quiet matter-of-factness; hers is slower, a Swedish drawl that's both teasing and passionate. He's relatively unemotional, almost impassive, but she tickles his earlobe, laughs, and gives him more soft kisses.

Still embracing, they kiss again and start to move in a kind of dance, the camera following toward a room and keeping them tightly framed. Bergman, who is responsible for most of the eroticism of the scene, is so enraptured she can't let go. "Where are you going," she asks as they move into the room. "I have to telephone," he says. They turn slightly, the back of his head to the camera. Still holding him, she kisses him and hands him the telephone receiver. He dials his hotel and they kiss again, her face to the camera.

"C. R. Devlin," he says, "Any messages for me?" She kisses him. "Read it to me," he says quietly. When he puts down the receiver they kiss. In a deadpan voice he says he's wanted "right away." Still kissing and tightly framed, they move toward a door. He opens it and slides out, saying he'll return at seven.

Grant's subsequent meeting with Calhern produces an emotional crisis. He's brought along a bottle of champagne for his evening with Bergman, but he learns of a plan to have her cultivate the wealthy Nazi operative Alexander Sebastian (Claude Rains). "Sebastian knows her," Calhern says, "He was once in love with her." Grant, who is standing, looks grim and paces a bit; when he turns to face Calhern, there's a mounting anger and fear in his eyes. "I didn't know that," he says. He's trying to keep his emotions under control, but his eyes disclose his disquiet. He grips the back of a chair to convey emotion. "I, uh . . . Nothing, sir," he says, and asks, "How is the *meeting* to be arranged?" He tightens his grip on the chair. As Calhern explains, Grant drums his fingers on the chair. "All right," he says. He taps the chair with his hands, turns, and exits, forgetting his bottle of champagne.

When he arrives at Bergman's apartment, she's in the kitchen wrestling with a roast chicken. He walks across the front room, clenches his hands, and rubs his forehead. With his back to us, he goes out to the balcony, where he puts his hands in his pockets, bows his head, and raises his shoulders in discomfort. When she appears and kisses him, he keeps his hands in his pockets. She asks what's the matter and jokes, "The time has come when you must tell me you have a wife and two adorable children." Grant looks her in the eyes and quietly says, "I bet you've heard that line often enough." His sexual vanity is threatened, and his cruel remark signals a turn in their relationship. "Do you remember a man named Sebastian?" he asks, keeping his hands in his pockets as if holding in his emotions. He explains the plan the US has in mind, saying, "I figured that was up to you, if you care to back out." He takes out a cigarette, using it to convey unease, followed by a hint of anger. "I'm waiting for your answer," he says, tapping the cigarette and lowering his head. She goes inside and pours herself a stiff drink. He joins her, frowning. "I had a bottle of champagne," he says, "must have left it somewhere."

The casting of Claude Rains as Alexander Sebastian was an inspired touch, not only because Rains was one of Hollywood's greatest character actors but also because his performance enhances the ironic qualities of the film's treatment of sex and politics. Short, unhandsome, and slightly effeminate, he contrasts with the tall, glamorous, heteronormative Bergman and Grant, and he becomes oddly sympathetic. Although he's a Nazi, he never makes ideological statements or shows inclinations toward the sadism or violence of some of his compatriots. Hitchcock often preferred charming but monstrous villains, but Sebastian is both charming and vulnerable, a victim of Bergman's deception and the jealous domination of his mother, Madame Sebastian (Leopoldine Konstantin). He may be planning an atomic bomb, but it's mom who has the killer instinct. Among the best of the film's dark jokes is the mother's wicked-witch entrance seen from Bergman's POV, and the later moment when the distraught Rains goes to her bedside and tells her of Bergman's betrayal; the mother rises triumphantly from her pillow and lights a cigarette with the flair of a Nazi dominatrix.

The relationship between Sebastian and his mother suggests incest and the pop-Freudian idea that a male's excessive closeness to his mother is a sign of homosexuality. Within the limits set by the Production Code, Hitchcock often explored such themes, hinting at murderous queers attached to their mothers, as in *Strangers on a Train* (1951) and *Psycho* (1960). In other ways, however, Rains serves as the ironic double of Grant—equally in love with Bergman, equally threatened by her possible involvement with another man, and equally responsible for her emotional and physical suffering. The film never gives its chief characters a completely normative sexuality, and its sexual triangle is clearly neurotic: Bergman turns to drink and casual relations with men because of her father, then becomes caught between two men, one trying to escape his mother's hold, the other threatened by sexual disloyalty.

When Grant devises a way for Bergman to meet Rains and have cocktails with him, Rains's insecurities are immediately apparent. She nods and smiles at Grant, who is sitting across the room, and Rains says, "He's rather handsome, isn't he? There's someone else again?" From this point on, the film gives us a series of performances within performances, scenes in which the actors lie and put on emotional masks, often letting the audience see the deception—as when Rains invites Bergman for dinner and she says, "Yes, how nice," with a nervous inflection. Later, when she and Rains go to the racetrack, she has a prearranged, supposedly accidental encounter with Grant, informing him of the Nazi group around Sebastian and odd behavior concerning a wine bottle. "You can add Sebastian's name to my list of playmates," she adds. Rains, sitting in a distant box with his mother, watches the meeting through his binoculars, and Grant and Bergman, knowing they're observed, put on an act. They smile as if having a polite conversation, but at the same time have an argument that contradicts their expressions. A large close-up of Grant, unseen by Rains, shows him reacting with jealous anger. In another large close-up Bergman loses control and breaks into tears, but when Grant sees Rains approaching he smiles, telling her, "Dry your eyes, baby, it's out of character. Here comes dreamboat." They revert to casual laughter and act like old acquaintances. When Grant leaves, Rains says, "I watched you. I thought maybe you were in love with him. He's very good looking."

Grant's resentment over Bergman's involvement with Rains doesn't turn him completely against her. During a meeting with the US and Brazilian officials, an American diplomat remarks that he dislikes working with "a woman of that sort," and Grant turns from a window with a challenging half-smile. "What sort is that?" he says, "She may be risking her life, but when it comes to *your lady*, she doesn't hold a candle, sir!" This helps recuperate Grant in the eyes of the audience and serves a larger purpose. *Notorious* was under pressure from censors not only to avoid offending the US and Brazil but also to keep the woman played by Bergman from seeming too loose. In Bergman's case, the problem was tricky because the film evolved from a story about a promiscuous woman; it retains a vestige of that origin, making Bergman seem notorious in the eyes of certain men, but it needs to assure us that she's actually virtuous. The solution is to give her an unsubstantiated bad reputation and an early drunken scene at a party, then have her fall in love with Grant. The film makes sure that it's obvious to us, if not to Grant, that Rains is of no sexual interest to Bergman, who isn't "a woman of that sort."

Grant's commitment to his job puts him in a psychological bind. He needs the woman he loves to behave like "that sort," yet his ego and repressed love for her is threatened when she does. The situation is exacerbated when Bergman arrives at the meeting of Brazilian and American officials with news that Rains has proposed marriage. Calhern is concerned, and asks, "What do you think, Devlin?" Grant steps forward in close-up, looking toward Bergman, and says with an undertone of bitterness, "Oh, I think it's a *useful idea*. May I ask what *inspired* it? He thinks you're in *love* with him?" His voice and eyes suggest a repressed, seething anger.

Here and elsewhere, Grant collaborates with Hitchcock's "subjective" style, which is dependent on cuts from a character looking off-screen to a reverse field of what the character sees. Hitchcock was well aware of the "Kuleshov effect," a legendary silent-era "experiment" by Kuleshov, supposedly proving that cinematic performance is determined less by the actor's facial expression than by the cut to an off-screen space. (*Rear Window* [1954] is devoted entirely to that principle, even though it depends on James Stewart's expressiveness.) But while it's true that facial expressions and gestures are polysemic, dependent on context for their meaning, Kuleshov oversimplified the task of film acting, and Grant shows how much an actor can contribute when he seems to do relatively little. Often an emotionally reserved actor, his work was engineered to fit the precise needs of a given sequence. He effected small actions with clarity, never complicating them with unnecessary movement, while at the same time he had control over *degrees* of expression, so that he could produce pieces of behavior for Hitchcock to manipulate. As this shot indicates, he was gifted with a strong off-screen "look," perfectly suited to editing.

Notorious is increasingly devoted to a drama of looking, a triangulation of gazes that requires actors to use subtle expressions. This strategy completely underlies a suspenseful party celebrating the nuptials of Bergman and Rains. Grant is invited on the pretext of being Bergman's former suitor, and he and Bergman use the occasion to investigate the mansion's wine cellar, where they discover the film's McGuffin: a bottle filled with what the film suggests is uranium ore. The evening begins with an omniscient, bird's-eye view typical of Hitchcock, in this case using an elevator and a zoom lens to descend from a very high angle down to a key hidden in the palm of Bergman's hand. (When the film was completed, Bergman gave the key to Grant as a souvenir.) Grant arrives late and looks across the grand entranceway toward Bergman and Rains.

From this point on, the three principal actors repeatedly look toward one another or toward a supply of iced champagne that grows progressively smaller, establishing a suspenseful timeline. The actors also engage in performance within performance. Grant crosses to Bergman and Rains, acting the role of Bergman's old friend, and Rains subtly conveys tension beneath his mask of civility. Bergman surreptitiously passes Grant the key to the wine cellar. Ostensibly renewing their old acquaintance, they sit for a while at a distance from Rains, who gazes toward them. As in their earlier scene at the racetrack, they know they're being observed and seem to be having a light conversation, but when Hitchcock cuts to a closer view, their dialogue contradicts their facial expressions.

As the two notice the supply of champagne dwindling, they find an opportunity to visit the wine cellar, where Grant accidentally dislodges a bottle, causing it to crash to the floor. Hitchcock cuts to an intense close-up (what he called a "big" shot) of Grant looking downward.

In the reverse angle, we see that the bottle contains dark granules rather than wine. By the time Grant collects a sample and cleans the floor, he and Bergman realize that Rains is looking for more champagne. Grant quickly takes Bergman out to the garden and tries to distract Rains by staging a scene in which the faithful wife suffers the attentions of an overly aggressive former lover. We see their kiss from Rains' POV, but when Hitchcock cuts to a closer view there's no counterpointed dialogue; a big shot of Bergman shows her almost swooning with love and desire.

Rains eventually discovers the double betrayal: Bergman is not only an unfaithful wife but also a spy, and if Rains's Nazi companions find out, he'll be exterminated. Madame Sebastian takes charge of killing Bergman by slow poisoning, while Rains continues to act the solicitous husband. During Grant and Bergman's next clandestine meeting in a Rio park, he says he's being sent on a mission to Spain. She's feeling ill. He assumes she has a hangover and tells her, "You look all mashed up." She gives him the scarf he tied around her bare midriff at the beginning of the film.

They plan to meet again, but Bergman doesn't show up because she's near death and has collapsed. Concerned by her absence, Grant visits Calhern; the brief scene is cleverly staged by Hitchcock, who gives it interest by having Grant lean against the wall while the almost fully dressed Calhern relaxes on a bed, spreading pâté on crackers. In quasi-Chandleresque fashion, Grant says, "She looked like the ragged end of nowhere." He doesn't believe Bergman had a hangover and wants to pay a "social call" to the Sebastian mansion.

Several versions of the concluding scenes were written, some by Hecht and one by Clifford Odets, but Hitchcock was the chief author of the version we have, which eliminates gunfire and violent action. Grant drives to the mansion and has a conversation with the butler, who tells him Bergman is ill. The camera moves in on Grant's face as his eyes move anxiously from side to side and he says, "Oh, I'm sorry to hear that. Has she had a doctor?" The butler goes away to announce him, and from Grant's POV we see Madame Sebastian leaving a room at the top of the stairway. Grant quietly ascends the stairs, taking several steps at a time, and enters the room where Bergman lies in bed, near death.

One of the brilliant features of the scene is the way it ironically rhymes with earlier moments in the film. From Bergman's POV, a shadowed Grant moves from the doorway toward the bed, just as he did when she had a hangover in Miami. But this time he's Prince Charming come to rescue Sleeping Beauty. The camera moves close as he leans down, kisses her, and begins a whispered conversation. He lifts the weakened but enraptured Bergman to a sitting position, puts on her robe, and they continue to whisper, brushing each other with light kisses, the light favoring Bergman's face. Hitchcock's camera makes a 180-degree circle around their heads as Grant tells her he was leaving for Spain only because he loves her and was a "fat-headed guy." They continue to hold each other as he lifts her to a standing position and says "keep moving." The camera keeps its tight framing of their faces as they cross—an echo of their extended kissing scene earlier in the film, but this time it's a powerful mixture of romance and suspense.

In the hallway outside the room, they meet Rains and his mother. The four are observed by the Nazi conspirators at the bottom of the stairs, and Grant quietly tells Rains and his mother they must help him get Bergman to a hospital or "I'll raise quite a rumpus." He puts a hand close to his pocket as if he's carrying a gun. The group look off-screen at the Germans below—a collective off-screen look with everyone except Bergman registering emotion. Rains and his mother know they have no choice.

Rains descends the stairway, ineffectively pretending he's trying to help Grant and Bergman, and when he follows them out to Grant's car, he tries to leave with them. Hitchcock gives the film a final irony: Grant locks the car door and drives off, leaving Rains to his fate. On one level, this provides the audience with a happy ending: Grant is a hero, Bergman is saved, and love is restored. But Grant's psychology has been such that an audience can also feel he's taking pleasure in locking out a rival. The last shot is of the lonely Rains, a pathetic figure, walking to his doorway and his certain death.

4

Romantic Cary

The usual formula for heterosexual romance in Grant's day was that the film's plot, which could be comic or melodramatic, was nearly always presented in linear fashion and began with an ostensibly mismatched couple who meet by chance. At first there's a tension between them, but as they come to know one another, they fall in love. Then an impediment or complication of some kind arises—a psychological problem, a marriage, a rival lover, or an unexpected catastrophe—that keeps them apart until they reunite happily at the end. This familiar narrative survives today: a recent example is *The Last Letter from Your Lover* (2021), an enjoyable melodrama featuring two couples who represent different generations, with one couple's story told through flashbacks.

In classic Hollywood, the trans-generic formula was tailored for particular stars. In the underrated romantic comedy *Teacher's Pet* (1958), for example, tough newspaper editor Clark Gable meets university journalism teacher Doris Day. He's a man of action who is contemptuous of college types, and she's an idealist who dislikes anti-intellectuals. They clash, but when he grabs and kisses her she goes weak in the knees. One impediment is her boyfriend, Gig Young, a sort of junior Cary Grant who is not only polished and attractively modest but also an author, a mean player of bongos, and a skilled dancer of the cha-cha. This and other problems, however, are eventually overcome. Gable, for all his mistakes and comic humiliations, gets Doris Day. The couple realize what they have in common, and Gig Young becomes a lightly comic help to their relationship.

The plots in Cary Grant's romantic films followed a somewhat similar pattern but were different in important respects. Grant was a romantic ideal, not an aggressive lover; furthermore, as we can see in the following two films, the impediments to happy endings in his pictures, whether melodramatic or comic, had nothing to do with the potential incompatibility of the couple.

Some Versions of Cary Grant. James Naremore, Oxford University Press. © Oxford University Press 2022.
DOI: 10.1093/oso/9780197566374.003.0004

An Affair to Remember (1957)

Grant hadn't appeared in a Leo McCarey film since *Once Upon a Honeymoon* (1942), and his reunion with the director almost didn't happen. For over a year, Twentieth-Century-Fox producer Jerry Wald had been working a color and Cinemascope remake of one of McCarey's best pictures, *Love Affair* (1939), which starred Charles Boyer and Irene Dunne. Wald imagined he could turn it into a musical but soon abandoned the idea, opting instead for a screenplay that very closely followed the original version by McCarey, Delmer Daves, and uncredited Donald Ogden Stewart. Yul Brynner was offered the leading role but wavered, perhaps because McCarey, at a low point in his career, hadn't had a major commercial success since *The Bells of St. Mary's* (1945). The project was saved when Grant expressed interest.

An Affair to Remember got middling reviews and good box-office returns in the US but had a significant afterlife. *Cahiers du cinéma* listed it among the 100 best films of all time, Jonathan Rosenbaum included it among his list of 100 films overlooked by the AFI's top 100, Molly Haskell called it one of the last important flowerings of what were once termed "women's pictures," and the AFI eventually named it the fourth-best Hollywood romance. Sweetly alluded to in Charles Shyer's *Irreconcilable Differences* (1984), it provided the inspiration for Nora Ephron's *Sleepless in Seattle* (1993) and was badly remade as Warren Beatty's *Love Affair* (1994). Loosely adapted for a couple of Bollywood romances, it was also affectionately joked about in several later TV series, including *The Simpsons*.

Admirers of the film nevertheless have to overlook several problems, which invited condescension even in its own day. Grant's character is supposed to be a talented amateur painter who becomes a successful artist, but the few examples of his work we see are pure kitsch. (Wisely, McCarey gives us only a glimpse of Grant's *chef d'oeuvre*.) Although the film wasn't turned into a musical, it has six musical numbers, among them a bad example of midcentury pop sung by a male quartet and two syrupy tunes rendered by a chorus of Hollywoodish kids. (In the chorus are a pair of black children who do a dance that wasn't intended as racist but seems that way.) The singing voice of Grant's co-star, Deborah Kerr, was provided by the uncredited Marni Nixon, who had dubbed Kerr's songs in *The King and I* (1956), but Nixon should have been given the opportunity to do the title song behind the opening credits, which was performed by popular but unremarkable crooner Vic Damone. (McCarey was one of the writers of the song; the theme music in *Love Affair*—Jean-Paul-Égide Martini's eighteenth-century *Plaisir d'amour*—is far superior.) Besides all this, some viewers will find the film too heavily laden with McCarey's sentimental Irish Catholicism.

The working atmosphere on the production appears to have been a bit like what Grant had experienced with McCarey on *The Awful Truth*. Cinematographer Milton Krasner remembered that McCarey was fun: "It was a different way of making pictures . . . He'd come in in the morning and he didn't have an idea. He and Grant would get into a little talk and he'd sit down at the piano, then he'd call in the songwriter and say he had an idea for a tune."[1] In later years, however, McCarey told Peter Bogdanovich that he preferred *Love Affair* and had hesitated to do the remake because of Grant. "If you put the two pictures in a laboratory," he said, "Boyer came out much better than Cary. But Cary Grant meant more at the box office . . . Grant could never mask his sense of humor—which is extraordinary—and that's why the second version is funnier. But I still prefer the first."[2]

Love Affair is indeed more serious in tone. Photographed in radiant black and white, it's paced more crisply, perhaps because McCarey wasn't working in widescreen, and its dated elements are less obtrusive than in *An Affair to Remember*. Grant no doubt contributed to making the 1957 film more humorous, not only through his performance but probably also through his suggestions for individual scenes. (Boyer made important suggestions for scenes in *Love Affair*, which was a more McCarey-like in the sense that it was an original, make-it-up-as-we-go production.) Even so, Grant's acting in the remake is in some ways more delicate and various than Boyer's; it not only has quiet humor and touches of self-reflective commentary on his stardom but also an understated depth.

Grant plays Nickie Ferrante, an internationally famous playboy about to be married to Neva Patterson (Lois Clark), one of the richest women in the world. (Older viewers of the film may have been reminded of the "Cash and Cary" marriage of Grant and Barbara Hutton in 1942.) The film begins with parodic TV newscasts from New York, Venice, and London announcing the forthcoming marriage of the "big dame hunter," but we soon discover that Ferrante has left his fiancée for a few weeks and is aboard a luxury liner bound for Europe. One evening a purser on the ship walks along the deck

---

[1] Krasner quoted in Eyman, 294.
[2] McCarey quoted in Eyman, 295.

announcing a telephone call for "Signor Ferrante," and passengers react with excitement, almost as if the call were for Cary Grant. Like an actor stepping off a movie set, Grant appears on the deck garbed in a tux, one hand in his pocket, and waves off autograph hunters with a polite smile. He goes inside to sit beside a telephone, hand still in his pocket, and receives a call from one of his lovers, a fiery Italian beauty named Gabriella who has just learned about the wedding ("You beast!"). He pretends the connection is bad, hangs up with an amused look, and can't find a cigarette case Gabriella gave him. (In real life Grant was a collector of cigarette cases.) As he walks along the corridor in search of it, he sees a beautiful redhead walking on the deck outside with the case in her hand.

She's Terry McKay (Kerr), a nightclub singer engaged to a rich Texan (Richard Denning) who has sent her on a vacation while he closes a business deal. She wears a reddish orange coat that almost matches her hair—as Joseph McBride points out in a DVD commentary on the film, McCarey repeatedly uses a red and orange motif that becomes associated with Kerr. Grant is immediately attracted. He steps to a window between them and says, "I believe you have my cigarette case."

This is the first of several instances when the couple talk across a slight barrier of some kind that suggests an impediment. Flirtatious banter ensues, although Kerr isn't as effectively witty as Dunne in *Love Affair*. Wide-eyed in amusement, she reads the inscription in the case and says, "Oh, don't tell me you're Nicolo, I've read all about you in *Life, Look* . . ." Grant quickly adds, "and possibly *Good Housekeeping*." She gives him the case, and they walk along together toward their respective compartments.

The cigarette case provides a meet cute and becomes an object Grant deploys for roughly eight minutes as an expressive device. His handling of the small object is a good instance of what Joe McElhaney has termed "medium shot gesture" in Cinemascope films, which usually avoid the tight framing and shot/reverse shots of earlier Hollywood pictures, arranging the conversations between characters on a horizontal line rather than in depth.[3] As Grant and Kerr walk along, Grant shifts the case from hand to hand and flirtatiously says, "I'm in trouble, serious trouble." He turns the case over and over and uses it to point toward his compartment, where he hopes Kerr will join him. She invites him to hers instead: "My mother told me never to enter a man's room

[3] Joe McElhaney, "Medium-Shot Gestures: Vincente Minnelli and *Some Came Running*," in *Vincente Minnelli: The Art of Entertainment*, ed. Joe McElhaney (Detroit: Wayne State University Press, 2009), 322–35.

in months with an R." Inside the room, he looks around, smiling and thought-fully tapping the case with his fingers, holding it as he helps her remove her coat. For a moment he puts it in his pocket, but he takes it out again and turns it around in his hands. "I was *bored* to death," he says, leaning back and tap-ping the case on his palm, as if shuffling cards. "I hadn't seen *one* attractive woman . . . Then I saw *you*." He gestures toward her with the case.

Kerr is holding a small purse, but she covers it with her hands, ceding the gestures to Grant. She sits on a chair and Grant sits on a couch, twirling the case over and over in his hands, exercising charm. He crosses, sits on the arm of her chair, makes his shuffling move with the case, and proposes that they seize the day. They could enjoy champagne, he says, and she tells him she prefers it to be pink. He takes a cigarette from the case but doesn't have a light. She suggests he could use the hot inscription inside the case. She then explains that she's en-gaged to the man in a photo beneath a lamp in her room. Disappointed, Grant, still holding the case, starts to leave, but she allows him to take her to dinner.

Throughout this action, the cigarette case attracts our eyes and signals the emotional eddies in Grant's attempts at seduction—his uncertainties or frustrations, his compliments, his moments of amusement or confidence, his combination of sophistication and boyishness. After dinner, as he and Kerr enjoy coffee and brandy, he has the case on the table, touching it now and then. Because of the Cinemascope framing, there's relatively little cutting in the sequence, which means the actors have control over timing and tempo. Grant and Kerr take a leisurely approach to the pacing and dialogue, and the charm of their interaction has to do with small things, as when Kerr poses thoughtfully with her chin in her hand. She teases him about his many women. He says there haven't been that many—and besides, he tends to idealize them: "Every woman I meet I tend to put up there," he says, slowly raising a hand as if lifting an object on a pedestal, then lowering it to illustrate his eventual disillusionment. Kerr says that some of the women must have loved him. "I doubt it," Grant says briskly, looking away with a seriousness he hasn't shown.

The dinner leads to other encounters, but Grant's celebrity attracts unwanted attention. A boorish American (Charles Watts) keeps intruding, and a pesky photographer snaps pictures of Grant and Kerr. During one of their conversations on deck, a purser calls out their names because they've each received a telegram from the person to whom they're engaged. Grant disposes of the photographs, and they each toss their telegrams overboard after reading them; Kerr, however, says the continuing publicity could cause trouble for their relationships in New York. They try to eat dinner separately but end up back-to-back in adjacent booths, amusingly framed in Cinemascope with the wall at their backs creating a split-screen effect and causing other diners to stare and giggle. They dine at separate hours but accidentally meet at the bar, where they've both ordered pink champagne and are observed by gossipy witnesses. As they near the end of the journey, Grant dives into the ship's swimming pool, which, improbably, has no one else around, and accidentally bumps into Kerr's head. He says that at their Mediterranean port of call he plans to visit his grandmother in Villefranche-sur-Mer; she doesn't believe him, so he invites her along.

The grandmother (Cathleen Nesbitt) lives in an attractive old home with a flower garden overlooking the Cote d'Azur. It's a studio set designed to create an atmosphere of beauty, peace, and spirituality. "There's something about it that makes you want to whisper," Kerr says. Grant has brought along a wrapped painting as a gift for the grandmother but finds that she's at prayer in a small chapel adjacent to the house. He strides athletically across the garden and up a few steps, greeting a faithful collie dog. Returning to Kerr, he stands with one foot on a low stone wall, resting his elbow on a knee, and explains that his grandfather is buried behind the chapel and his grandmother expects to be buried there also. (Grant once advised a young actor who was playing a scene on the front steps of a house to stand with one foot on a higher step because it looks better that way.) When the aged, weakened grandmother emerges from the chapel with her shoulders covered in a white lace shawl, she and Grant embrace lovingly, speaking in French. Enchanted, Kerr asks to see the chapel. She goes inside and the grandmother smiles, telling Grant he should join her because he probably hasn't been in church "since you were an altar boy." Grant laughs softly and goes to meet Kerr.

In writing about *Notorious*, I've pointed out how Grant exemplifies Hitchcock's idea that the best screen actors are those who can do almost nothing extremely well. His performance in *An Affair to Remember* depends on that skill because much of the time he does little more than sit, cross a room, open a door, lean on a ship's deck, or hold a quiet conversation. The scene in the grandmother's tiny chapel is a good illustration of his poised treatment of small expressions and gestures. He finds Kerr praying to a small statue of the Virgin, kneels beside her, and there's a long silence. Her hands are together in prayer, but his are folded in an insincere attitude, half prayerful. He looks up at the Virgin and then at Kerr, whose head is bowed, her face hidden by her broad white hat. He thinks while she prays. Struck by her seriousness, perhaps feeling an awkward humility, he moves his eyes only slightly, as if something important is happening. She finishes her prayer, crosses herself, and rises to go. Still on his knees, his head bowed, Grant crosses himself half-heartedly and adjusts the knot of his tie.

Inside the house, Grant shows the painting he's brought—a portrait of his grandfather that he's done from memory—and goes to get drinks. While he's away, the grandmother tells Kerr, "Everything comes too easily for him." Grant returns with bottle and glasses, and once again does very little. As they raise their glasses, the grandmother looks at Kerr and proposes a toast: "I don't know how to put it. Would it have to do with his happy marriage?" Grant does a subtle exchange of glances with Kerr. The grandmother then goes to the piano and plays the film's theme music while Kerr looks at a music sheet and sings the lyrics in French. Grant stands quietly, one hand in his pocket and the other atop the piano, looking on in near reverence. (*Love Affair* puts stronger emotional emphasis on this scene, largely due to Boyer's suggestions for elaborating it and Irene Dunne's singing of *Plaisir d'amour*.) After the song there's the sound of a distant boat whistle, signaling the return trip to America and creating a moment of sadness. The grandmother says that one day she will send Kerr the white lace shawl as a gift. On the steps leading away from the house, Kerr pauses, turns, and rushes back to give the grandmother a tender embrace.

The spiritual aura of these scenes, their evocation of love, death, marriage, and memory, leads to a change in the relationship between Grant and Kerr. When they return to the liner, they no longer joke or engage in mild shipboard flirtation. The tearful Kerr says it's been "the loveliest and most memorable day I've known," and Grant moves to give her a chaste kiss. She says no, preferring to walk on the moonlit deck, but when Grant holds her hand and leads her down a stairway to the lower deck, she pauses midway. Holding her hand, Grant turns, looks up at her with an arm at his side and ascends like a theatrically romantic lover moving toward a lofty ideal.

When Grant reaches Kerr's level, McCarey keeps the camera in the same position, so that their lengthy kiss is out of our view, with only their legs visible. The off-screen kiss of approximately twenty seconds is the only moment of passionate sexual love in an affair that's strikingly free of sex, and is characteristic of Grant's image as what Pauline Kael called a "dream date." His films tend to avoid or slightly conceal passionate kisses; in part this has to do with the strictures of the Production Code (which were being liberalized in 1957), but even in his more sexy work with Hitchcock, Grant usually lets the woman lead, and as Kael has noted, avoids the sweep-her-off-her-feet techniques of Gable or Flynn. (When he's being aggressive with Suzy Parker in *Kiss Them for Me* [1957], the kisses are artfully obscured by a passing extra or by Parker's hat.) McCarey's films add to this effect in a different way. As James Morrison has pointed out, McCarey's pictures are "essentially *about* divided couples, joined by temperament but divided by circumstance . . . we see the members of the couple apart more than we see them together."[4]

When Grant and Kerr descend the steps, he holds her hand and says in a deeply serious tone, "We changed our course today." But they continue to hide their relationship. She returns to her room, and Grant knocks, speaking to her through the half-open door—another barrier between them. "We've got fast thinking to do," he says, and they agree to keep their love concealed for the time being. "One kiss!" he says, and she allows him to kiss her fingers. On the next day they walk separately around the stair where they previously kissed, trying not to encounter one another but comically failing. In the evening, they dance to the corny tune of the quartet, and to escape scrutiny of the crowd, they go on deck and joyfully twirl to the music. Grant reaches under her coat and embraces her.

As the ship nears New York, Kerr finds Grant alone on deck, lost in thought. "I've never done a day's work in my life," he tells her and wants to reform himself. In the film's most improbable but successful strategy to keep the couple apart and postpone consummation, Grant proposes that they break off their respective engagements and not see each other for exactly six months, during which time he'll find out if he can support himself as a painter. He kisses her hand again. A process screen behind them shows the skyline of New York moving past, and as they discuss where they can meet on that wonderful day, the Empire State Building comes into view: "The nearest thing to Heaven in New York," it's the best site for their rendezvous.

---

[4] Morrison, 81.

On arrival, they stand apart near the gangway, and in a more elaborate pantomime sequence than its equivalent in *Love Affair*, they smile, blow kisses at their respective American lovers, and steal glances at one another. When Kerr gets a hug from her fiancé Kenneth, Grant walks past and mischievously touches her hand. He then travels to Neva Patterson's mansion outside the city to break off their relationship but finds himself in an awkward situation. A television crew is set up for a live broadcast of an interview conducted by Robert Q. Lewis, a 1950s TV personality who plays himself. The broadcast is comically similar to Edward R. Murrow's *Person to Person* show of the period, which was devoted to live visits to the homes of celebrities and had a significant national audience. Grant gets humor out of the scene by doing little more than being elegantly uncomfortable. He sits tightly on the couch next to Patterson; he endures a makeup man who pats his tanned face with a powder puff; he frowns when he's asked if he happens to have a blue shirt; and as Lewis explains to him how TV works, he quietly points out that the camera light is on and the broadcast has already begun. Meanwhile, Kerr is tensely watching the show in her ritzy New York apartment. Kenneth arrives—he's a nice fellow, but she tells him their engagement is off.

Then Grant and Kerr begin managing their six-month separation. In a comfortable looking garret where he's been "painting my breakfast," Grant tells his art dealer (Fortunio Bonanova) that he needs to make money but won't trade on his fame by painting women. "You'd think it was the one thing I could remember," he says. Kerr returns to work as a nightclub singer and sings a couple of songs, one of them the film's theme. Grant gets a job painting a billboard (which looks better than his serious work), and his dealer arrives, shouting up to him that he's sold a picture. "I'm a painter!" Grant joyfully yells, and his co-worker on the scaffold says, "I've always been a painter."

When the day of Grant and Kerr's reunion arrives, Kerr shops for lingerie and takes a cab to the Empire State Building, where she shakes her cab driver's hand, tells him she's going to be married, and rushes off-screen toward the skyscraper. We hear the squeal of brakes, and pedestrians on the street begin running in her direction. At this late moment, *An Affair to Remember* swerves from its lightly comic, spiritual romanticism and becomes one of the last important Hollywood melodramas devoted to a woman's suffering—a popular genre the industry once called "women's weepies." Kerr has been struck by a car and her legs are paralyzed. She can't be at the rendezvous with Grant and will refuse to give him the news of what happened.

Grant walks briskly to the Empire State Building elevator, smiles, and travels to the top. A series of shots show him spending the entire afternoon and evening standing and waiting, moving toward the elevator each time it opens, showing eager then anxious anticipation whenever he glimpses a passenger wearing red. An ambulance siren is heard in the distance, but he ignores it. As darkness falls, he's leaning against a parapet, dejected. There's a melodramatic thunderstorm, but he waits in the rain until the building closes. Meanwhile, Kerr is on a hospital bed, writhing in agony.

Kerr has certain affinities with Jane Wyman, who is accidentally blinded by playboy Rock Hudson in Douglas Sirk's widescreen version of *Magnificent Obsession* (1954). Sarah Kozloff has pointed out that such films usually contain elaborate discussions of romantic relationships, as when Grant and Kerr talk about their plan for a six-month separation; paradoxically, however, they depend crucially on "the *not* said, the words that cannot be spoken . . . the driving tension of the plot stems from one character keeping some secret, a secret that the viewer knows." Rock Hudson doesn't reveal his guilty secret to Wyman because he wants to love and heal her; Kerr doesn't tell Grant of her accident because she wants to give him his freedom. But as Kozloff says, "We always know who really loves whom."[5] The films usually also have an emotionally powerful recognition scene, when a character learns the secret we knew all along.

Grant returns to Villefranch-sur-Mer, where his grandmother has died, and takes a brief tour of remembrance. He sighs. During the making of the film Grant told Robert Walker, "I finally figured out how to breathe in a scene!"[6] He may have been talking about this sort of expressive breathing, but he was also referring to the technique of getting enough air in the diaphragm in dialogue scenes with longer speeches. Here he says nothing. Walking around the room he and Kerr once visited, he uses minimal gestures to indicate its emotional resonance. Almost longingly, he touches the upholstery of the chairs where Kerr and the grandmother sat, as if he could still feel the warmth of their bodies. At the piano, he places his hand on its top, just has he had done when Kerr sang for his grandmother. He stands there for a long time, his head bowed, his expression changing from a fond smile to sadness and a troubled frown.

[5] Kozloff, 242.
[6] Eyman, 294.

From a servant, Grant collects the lace shawl the grandmother wanted to give to Kerr and returns to his solitary life in New York. Six months later, at the Christmas season, we discover that he's not reverted to womanizing and has become a prolific and successful artist. Kerr has taken a job leading a children's choir, which she conducts from a chair and her bed. But the plot makes a decisive change when Grant's former fiancée invites him to a ballet. There's a joke when they arrive: a beautiful young woman behind Grant stares at him and tells her date, "I love our seats." Grant turns to the woman, looks at Neva Patterson, and shrugs in an attitude of amused but helpless innocence. At the end of the performance, he and Patterson are among the last to exit, and as they walk up the isle they pass Kerr and Kenneth, who are still seated. Grant halts for a moment, staring at Kerr, and bends to retrieve a handbag she's dropped. Stone-faced, he says "Hello," and walks out.

This encounter leads to the film's last, most emotional scene, in which Grant pays a visit to Kerr's apartment (humbler than when she was engaged to the rich Texan). Kerr reclines on a couch wearing a red dress, her legs covered with a red blanket, a book in her hand and a fire burning in her hearth. The maid is leaving to join her family for Christmas, and as she opens the door, we see Grant standing there, his coat and hat in his hands.

The ensuing scene has virtually the same dialogue as in the 1939 *Love Affair*, and viewers who've seen both films will probably disagree about which version provokes more tears. But it's instructive to see how two different actors perform the same material. Boyer is lively, behaving as if he's cheerful, exuding Gallic charm, showing genuine affection but never revealing his purpose. He's pleased to see Irene Dunne and behaves a bit like a bon vivant; he lights his cigarette with flair, smokes as he explains how he managed to find Dunne, and smiles as he reminisces about their past. He often takes a seated position, casually moving from a chair to a piano bench while Dunn remains seated. He betrays almost no sign of resentment, and when he steps closer to Dunne he's vaguely seductive, perhaps a bit sad, as if remembering their past. Saying goodbye, he pauses at the door and recalls the painting he did of Dunne in the grandmother's shawl. Suddenly he realizes something and crosses, opening a door to another room and looking off-screen at his painting of her, which we see reflected in a mirror behind him. The close-up of his recognition is eloquent, in part due to Boyer's large, liquid eyes. The camera lingers on his face as it subtly changes, registering shock, grief, sympathy, admiration, determination, and love.

Grant plays the scene differently, more like a jilted lover concealing anger and making subtle accusations. (It's tempting to relate this approach to Grant's personal experience; his biographers agree that he was usually anxious and had moments of jealousy and depression, perhaps because for many years he thought his mother had abandoned him.) He drops his hat and coat on a chair, turns with a hand in his pocket, and takes a deep breath. Kerr says, "It's been a long time." Grant folds his arms across his chest in a judgmental pose and says lightly, "Yes, *hasn't it?*" Unsmiling, he takes a chair and explains he "accidentally" came across her name in a phone book. "I asked myself," he says, giving insinuating emphasis to certain words, "could that be Terry McKay, *my old friend?* . . . Then I said, after all, I haven't been very *nice* to Miss McKay. After all, I had an *appointment* with her and *I didn't make it.*" He gets up, a hand in his pocket, and walks around to the back of the couch. "So I said to myself—I talk to myself quite a lot these days—I should *apologize* to Miss McKay because don't you agree when someone doesn't keep an *appointment* they should *apologize?*" Surprised and touched, Kerr says, "That's very sweet," and Grant replies in a joking but slightly cutting tone: "*I* thought so."

"I've often wondered about you," Kerr says. Grant gives an almost bitter chuckle and says nervously, "*Really?*" He rubs his hands together and paces, asking her a series of questions: "How long did you wait? I mean, did you wait long? Until midnight? In a *thunderstorm?* Then what did you do?" Kerr says that she went home and got tight. Grant says, "*No!* You didn't do *that.* Maybe just a *little* one, every hour for about a *month.*" Rubbing his hands nervously and pacing again, he takes a cigarette from a tray but doesn't use it (he never smokes in the film). He goes to the back of the couch and bends toward her. In the last of their conversations across a barrier, he says, "We used to read each other's thoughts. Not the same is it?"

He crosses, paces, and tells her that he's become a restless world traveler seeing the sights alone. When he mentions Paris and the Eiffel Tower, he raises his hand as he did in their first dinner table conversation, as if lifting an ideal on a pedestal. Then he goes into the Grant crouch and performs a "say for," imitating what people say about him: "They say, 'There he goes, the *mad painter*, he doesn't *like women*!' " He tells her he's brought her a Christmas present—the lace shawl his deceased grandmother promised her. Kerr says she now understands why the grandmother didn't answer her letters and puts the shawl around her shoulders. Grant kisses her hand, says goodbye, and goes to the door. About to leave, he turns for one last look and remembers that he once did a painting of her in the shawl, and it was one of his best. He gave it away, he says, when his dealer told him of a young woman so admired it; she didn't have money, and besides . . . He stops, suddenly realizing who the woman was and that she couldn't walk. Crossing the room fast, he smiles and rubs his hands in excitement, turning around and explaining that he has "holly in my heart." (One of Grant's favorite personal expressions, and a line that wasn't in *Love Affair*.)

Now comes the recognition scene so important to Hollywood melodramas, and equally important to actors because it involves intense emotional expressiveness. Grant opens the door, steps in with a smile, sees the painting (which we see in the mirror behind him), and steps back as if hit with a blow. He freezes for a moment, his shoulders stiffening, his eyes closing in shame, guilt, and empathy with Kerr's suffering. He returns to the couch, takes a seat beside her, and for the first time we see the couple in a close-up kiss. Grant wipes Kerr's tears with the lace shawl and asks why, if this had to happen to one of them, it couldn't have been him. Kerr says it happened because it was her fault—she was looking upward at "the nearest thing to Heaven." They both smile as she promises him, "If you can paint, I can walk."

Indiscreet (1958)

The second of four Grant films made with director Stanley Donen and the first film on which he was his own producer, *Indiscreet* could be regarded as a bookend to *An Affair to Remember*. Both of the wide-screen, color pictures end with Grant smiling, kissing, and promising to marry a tearful woman who is seated on a couch. But *Indiscreet* is a sophisticated romantic comedy, more sexy and more keyed to middle-aged love. It was based on *Kind Sir*, a failed Broadway play of 1953 by Norman Krasna and Joshua Logan, which starred Charles Boyer and Mary Martin. Donen believed the play could be "opened out" into a film and its setting changed to London, where it could be shot on location and at Elstree studios. When Grant read Krasna's outline for a screenplay, he agreed immediately, his only condition being that Ingrid Bergman should be his co-star. Bergman had been ostracized by Hollywood during the puritanical uproar over her out-of-wedlock child with Roberto Rossellini and had turned down the female lead in *An Affair to Remember* because she didn't want to return to America. She was living in Italy, and her affection for Grant motivated her to join the cast of *Indiscreet* and work in London—this without even seeing an outline of the screenplay. When the film ended production, Grant returned the key she had given him from *Notorious*, saying it was her turn to keep it for a decade.

Grant plays Philip Adams, a diplomat and international banking expert, and Bergman plays Anna Kalman, a celebrated actor in the English theater. They're introduced by Anna's sister and brother-in-law, Margaret and Alfred Munson (Phyllis Calvert and Cecil Parker), and are instantly smitten. The only complication, which at first we don't know, is that Grant is a confirmed bachelor who has a habit of lying to his lovers about his marital status.

At the beginning of the film Bergman returns from Majorca to her London townhouse, which has original modern paintings (including a Picasso) and two servants, Carl and Doris Banks (David Kossoff and Megs Jenkins). When her sister and brother-in-law arrive, she laments that she no longer has enthusiasm for the theater and feels she'll never have a lasting relationship with a man. She's just broken off from her most recent lover, who, she says, has the body of a Greek statue but knows only two words: "scotch" and "soda." The sister is exasperated: "You told me he was good looking and danced beautifully—that's all one is entitled to." Bergman says that she's weary of suitors who use this year's favorite line: "I'm separated and unable to get a divorce."

The sister gives her encouragement: "You're beautiful, talented, and famous. Someone will turn up." Sure enough, someone does.

Bergman changes into a house robe, chats with her relatives, and is using tissues and cold cream to remove her makeup when suddenly Cary Grant appears in her open doorway, a hat, overcoat, and suitcase in his hands. "The door was open," he apologizes. (The film has a deliberate life-as-theater quality—we're introduced to Bergman's townhouse when the camera looks in from the front window as drapes are drawn open like a curtain, and the various entrances and exits have a theatrical effect.) In close-ups, Grant and Bergman gaze at one another for a moment, subtly conveying a *coup de foudre*. Unrealistically tan, noticeably slim, and gray at the temples, Grant says he has "fervently" admired her on the stage, but he maintains a politely straight face as he steps through the doorway. Bergman's brother-in-law, who works with NATO, introduces him as a visiting American consultant just arrived from Paris. The brother-in-law has invited him to the townhouse before going to a public function to which everyone is invited. Bergman's sister asks if Mrs. Adams has come along, and Grant, ducking into another room to change clothes, says, "There is no Mrs. Adams." The brother-in-law explains that Grant will be the speaker for the evening and that "he beat the squash champion at my club."

Bergman immediately overcomes her weariness, exchanges a significant glance with her sister, and agrees to accompany everyone to the event. In the resplendent Painted Hall at Greenwich, Grant, dressed in tails, delivers a speech about international monetary policy in boring but charmingly modest style. Bergman's sister whispers, "I can't understand one word," but Bergman is enchanted, smiling and applauding at the end as if honoring a fellow thespian. Afterward, the group returns to the townhouse, where Bergman takes a key from a majolica pot outside her door. She invites everyone in, but the relatives soon make an exit. Alone with Grant, who has an hour to wait before his return flight to Paris, she offers a drink. He asks for scotch and soda.

These early scenes are among the most quietly poised and inexpressive of Grant's film performances—amusingly so because the film is very much about the need to maintain a front of propriety and discretion. As Mark Glancy points out, "the characters are preoccupied with appearing to behave by the norms of conventional morality but have no intention of following those norms."[7] Swinging London has yet to appear, and Grant and Bergman inhabit

[7] Glancy, 352.

a world of international diplomacy, British clubs, and respectable West End theater; he's a public figure, and she needs to avoid gossipy autograph hunters and journalists. In the buildup to their affair, he treads cautiously, avoiding the appearance of a seducer. Hence, a good deal of the film has a performance-within-performance quality: Grant maintains a politely reserved initial approach to Bergman, slightly masking his interest; in contrast, Bergman is histrionic, overtly expressive, as befits her character as a professional actor.

"I've never had a better time in my life," Grant says as he enters the townhouse, but he delivers the line unsmiling, in the manner of diplomatic protocol. A hand in the pocket of his white tie and tails, he holds the scotch and soda without drinking and looks steadily at Bergman, his eyes suggesting interest; she smiles broadly, but he's low-key, speaking in undertones as she lights a fire and invites him to sit beside her on her couch. His eyes seldom leave her, and between them there's a suggestion of I-know-that-you-know-that-we-know. She smiles radiantly and wants to charm him, but his smiles are moderate. He speaks quietly, with polite seriousness and no hint of flirtation; he tells her that he's on a temporary assignment in Paris, has never enjoyed London, and is thinking of taking a job in Mexico. His hometown is San Francisco, where, he jokingly assures her, they have road-show theater and opera. He's especially fond of ballet. "Would you like to go?" she asks, toying with a plumed hat she wore at the lecture. He suddenly becomes more deadly serious. "I'm a married man," he says softly. She tosses her head back, laughing at the comedy of the situation. (Grant and Bergman probably remembered a line from *Notorious*: "The time has come when you must tell me you have a wife and two adorable children.")

Grant apologizes, explaining that when he said there is no Mrs. Adams he meant that his wife wasn't with him. Then he makes an even more authoritative-sounding speech than his evening's lecture: he can't get a divorce and wants to follow the "rules," be straightforward and honorable, and so on. She's amused because she's heard similar things before (and we later discover that he's said them before). A non-diegetic piano begins to play a sadly romantic music as her smile fades and the meeting draws to a close. He rises to go, gets his coat, shakes her hand, gazes at her intently, and lets his mask slip a little. Unsmiling, he says, "I've been sorely tempted all evening . . . I *am* a married man and I can't get a divorce." He goes to the door, pauses with a calculated dramatic hesitation, and turns to look back at her. "Thank you again," he says in a regretful tone and exits. A wide shot shows her alone in the room, the piano music rising in the manner of a melodrama. Almost despondent, she phones down to the front desk, asking the man who works there to let her speak with Grant. "Good seats at the ballet are hard to get," she tells him. "Will you come?" Grant inhales a quiet breath of relief and without smiling says, "I'd like nothing better." He'll take tomorrow afternoon's return plane from Paris.

Grant arrives in a tux at the appointed hour. Admitted by Doris, he enters a bit shyly and takes a visible, nervous breath as he surveys the room and the yellow roses he's sent Bergman. She's made dinner reservations at London's Garrick Club, a male establishment where an influential member, a Mr. Albert Whitehead, has arranged a table for her. Grant's smile fades with the idea that it will be dinner for three. In a lightly comic scene, they descend the elevator side by side, Grant deadpan and looking straight ahead as if in a police lineup, commenting on the weather to avoid giving the elevator operator fuel for gossip.

Carl drives the couple to the Garrick Club in her Rolls Royce, and outside the club Bergman is besieged by a crowd wanting her autograph. Grant stands barely visible in the background, reacting with bemused, slightly comic puzzlement as she endures a fan with a leaky pen. In the large, empty dining room, they're seated at a table for two because Albert Whitehead has a sick aunt. Grant relaxes, realizing Bergman arranged for this, and when they both order scotch and soda he smiles broadly, toasting "the *Alberts* of this world." He observes her fondly, holding his glass as she drinks. A montage shows empty bottles of wine, a close-up of Bergman laughing and talking, and a close-up of Grant laughing silently, his eyes expressing deep affection. During the after-dinner coffee and brandy, Bergman smokes and the camera lingers on her face. One of the most radiant stars in movies, she projects the personality of an open, unpretentious, yet theatrical woman who remembers how, as a chubby girl, she found her vocation after seeing a performance of *Camille*. In a close-up, we see from Grant's eyes alone that he admires her innate theatricality and feels growing desire. She talks nonstop until she realizes they're late for the ballet.

At Covent Garden they can't be seated because the performance of *Romeo and Juliet* has already begun. Grant gives their tickets to a pair of young lovers who are hoping for standing room, saying, "I know how *Romeo and Juliet* comes out—sad." They return to the Garrick Club, where over coffee he becomes talkative. Never gesturing, seated straight with hands together in his lap, he explains that as a boy his allowance was always overdrawn and his passion was music. The fairly long speech is a good example of Grant's ability to be fascinating while doing very little. He always wanted to be a violinist, he says, but during a youthful performance, "in my *new blue suit*," the audience laughed because he's left-handed. The charm of his matter-of-fact delivery has a great deal to do with the crispness of his enunciation and his comic timing, as when he imitates his teenaged self and jerks his head back with a slight, Grant-like astonishment at the reaction of the audience to his violin playing. It's her turn to look adoringly at him.

They walk back to her townhouse, strolling through nearly empty London streets, slowly followed by Carl driving her Rolls Royce. (Grant bought the Rolls when the production ended, using it whenever he was in London.) Avoiding the chance of being seen by others, they never touch or hold hands, but when they reach Cleopatra's Needle they step behind it. The high-angle camera cranes around the sculpture, and we glimpse them kissing against a wall. Back at the townhouse, they ride the elevator again. Aware of the operator, they're as straight-faced as before, but this time they look at each other, knowing that sex is in the offing.

At her door, she asks, "Would you like to come in for a drink?" Grant replies, "Yes, I would." They enter the townhouse, and in a shot reminiscent of Ernst Lubitsch's romantic comedies, they go to her bedroom and close the door, leaving the camera outside.

Grant calls next morning from his bed in Paris to her bed in London, and he begins flying back regularly for short stays and romantic evenings. During one of his visits, Bergman's servants have a day off and she cooks a meal, serving it in a small breakfast nook. Stanley Donen said that Grant and Bergman taught him something new about acting because the performers in the scene aren't in movement (movement was one of Donen's skills).[8] Bergman is somber and a bit aloof; the subtext is the unspoken question of whether Grant might be taking a job in Mexico. They do nothing more than quietly sit across from one another until in close-up Grant announces that he's decided to work with NATO in Paris. In close-up, Bergman relaxes and smiles, whereupon Grant, pleased with himself, begins eating hardily.

The long-distance calls become occasions for pillow talk, which Donen depicts inventively and amusingly, a year before Doris Day and Rock Hudson held split-screen phone conversations in *Pillow Talk* (1959). *Indiscreet* makes it look as if the lovers are in bed together with their heads on pillows. Grant calls one evening to joke about how he's just had lamb chops with the president of France, who asked him whether saccharin is preferable to sugar; he scratches his chest through his pajamas, she ruffles her hair sleepily and turns on her side. He moves his hand in her direction as if he's giving her a loving pat on the bottom.

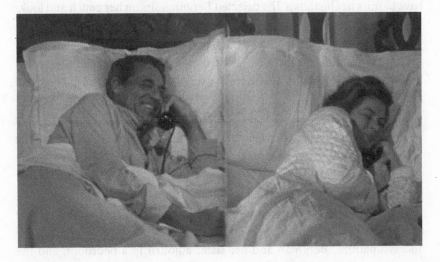

[8] Eyman, 306.

As time passes, Bergman recovers her passion for the theater, and Grant watches her rehearse and perform. When she comes out for her bow, she receives a bouquet of yellow roses from him. This leads to other gifts and celebrations. Grant buys Bergman an oil painting she's seen in a gallery window (much better than the paintings in *An Affair to Remember*); she buys him a violin, which he comically tries to play left-handed, feigning embarrassment as she watches and laughs; and he secretly buys her a yacht called *The Sea Witch*, which she planned to buy for herself. When she discovers this last extravagance and worries about it, he explains it's a good investment: "It came with a *dock!*"

The plot takes a turn on the day when they're planning to attend a dinner dance and Grant arrives early from Paris. (He now uses the key from the pot outside her door.) They embrace and sit together on the balcony outside her windows, where she dreamily leans against his chest and he puts his arm around her, nuzzling her face. She senses he has something to tell her. "You'd be surprised, Mata Hari," he says (a tossed-off remark that may have been Grant's in-joke about *Notorious*). As he speaks, their faces reflect vividly different moods. Grant is quietly serious and a bit fatherly, smiling slightly, his hand brushing her hair, his voice softly affectionate. He tells her that he needs to move to New York temporarily because of a financial negotiation only he can handle for NATO. During his speech, Bergman's face registers a series of emotions—unhappiness, trepidation, and sadness. As they rise and step inside, he says they'll be separated for three to five months, which he calmly assures her will pass quickly. Unfortunately, he sails the next day and will have to miss her birthday. The dejected Bergman sits on her couch and looks up at him. When he sits beside her, she embraces him and impulsively asks, "Could you possibly get a divorce and marry me?"

Grant's reaction is repressed surprise and silence. Ashamed, Bergman breaks into tears, begging him to forgive and forget what she said. There will be "no strings" between them, she says. Grant looks confident, paternal, and proud of her. He wipes her tears, smiles tenderly as if comforting a lovely young girl, and tells her she's beautiful. He suggests they drink a toast at the first stroke of midnight on her birthday. "Where will you *be*? I'd like to *picture* you," he asks. She replies that she'll certainly be drinking, sitting alone by the fireplace: "I did it in a play once. I was wonderful in it."

Suddenly Bergman's sister and brother-in-law arrive, preparatory to the event they'll be attending that evening; they know about the New York job and sympathize. Bergman and her sister adjourn to a bedroom, and the brother-in-law invites Grant to his club, where they can kill time with a game of snooker. In the midst of the game, as Grant is lining up a shot, the brother-in-law, who has seen Grant's security check at NATO, asks him, "Why do you pretend to be married when you're not?" Grant straightens from the table, momentarily wide-eyed, and gives a stern, calmly assured response, as if lecturing: it's all very ethical, he claims, because it frees him from having to refuse marriage and enables him to woo a woman with a clear understanding between them. He acts out the role of the average man who wants to remain single: "What do I say? *I will never marry*?" No, because that would only make the woman insist on marriage or decide to leave him. "I *love* Anna as I've never loved any woman be*fore*," he says, gesturing with his cue stick, "but I wouldn't marry *any* woman if you put a *gun* to my head."

This leads to the most theatrical, exuberant scenes of the film. In *An Affair to Remember* the male experienced a painful and touching recognition, but in *Indiscreet* the female experiences an angry and comic one. While Grant is changing for the evening event, Bergman, already dressed for the occasion, tells her sister and brother-in-law that she plans to fly to New York and surprise him when his boat docks. She thinks he hasn't asked her to accompany him because "he's too concerned about my reputation. He's the most considerate, unselfish, honorable man I've ever known!" This causes the brother-in-law to reveal that Grant isn't sailing; he plans to fly, giving him three more days to stay in London. On the evening of her birthday, he'll appear in her room at the first stroke of midnight for a surprise celebration.

Bergman breaks into tears again: "He's so wonderful!" But her sister, who knows of Grant's security check from Scotland Yard, has another revelation: "Anna, he isn't married! He's a single bachelor!" Bergman reacts with theatrical explosiveness: "I was on my knees! How dare he make love to me and not be a married man!" Screaming with anger, she exits to her bedroom, and we hear a mirror shatter. When she emerges, she's still angry but relatively calm. Slipping on a long glove, she announces that everyone should act as if nothing has happened: "That's what we're going to do."

The evening's event is a dance in the Painted Hall at Greenwich. Grant has a spring in his step. He relishes dinner and talks with his mouth full while everyone else picks at their food. Bergman smiles slyly. After the meal, the orchestra conductor announces a Scottish reel for the first dance. Stanley Donen, who began as a choreographer, co-directed *Singin' in the Rain* (1952), and later directed several other classic musicals, was in his element for this extended sequence. Grant, playing an amateur dancer who learns the reel as it goes, has great fun getting in the spirit of things. He whoops, cheers, twirls, whistles, and grins as he snaps his fingers over his head. Sometimes he turns the wrong way, and at one point almost slips and falls. When he's called upon to do an improvised solo at the center of a ring of the dancers, his comic-acrobatic skill is reminiscent of his shorter dance in *Sylvia Scarlett*. He tosses his legs wide in a balletic kick, hops in the air, jumps in a kind of plié, and imitates an old vaudeville gag of leaning back on one foot, kicking out a leg, and skipping across the floor. In the background, Bergman has her hands on her hips, looking at him scornfully.

During the evening, a waiter brings Bergman a single red rose from an admirer ("old David"), which gives her an idea. Back at the townhouse, she and Grant go through their ritual for hiding their affair from workers in the building: he telephones proposing a nightcap and she says no, after which he comes to her rooms via the service stairway. The resulting scene has the film's most ostentatious performance-within-performance, together with the rapid dialogue of Grant's screwball pictures. It's also a good instance of how the voices of Grant and Bergman play off one another: as in *Notorious*, his rhythms are quick and hers a bit languid.

Bergman is in her bedroom as he drops the key into the pot outside the door and enters, whistling and fairly dancing across the room toward the iced champagne. He pops the cork gracefully and pours a couple of glasses—"some for you, and some for me." But he enters the bedroom only to find that Bergman is wearing her housecoat, preparing for bed. He looks at the smashed mirror and wonders what happened. Bergman is smiling and brushing her hair, and he finds her mood strange. He tries to kiss her hand, but she's holding the hairbrush. Perplexed, he says, "I hope this is from a play you're in," and when he bends down to kiss her on the mouth she blocks his lips by drinking champagne. As they talk, she becomes archly amusing and mercurial. "You've been in a dozen different moods," he complains, "none of which I've seen before." He's brought a wrapped birthday gift in a small slender box and asks her to open it on the following night. In a teasing tone, she asks, "Did you give your wife many presents?" Not waiting for an answer, she smiles and adds, "I'll take it. I deserve it."

Offhandedly, she remarks that the gift must be expensive because it's so small. Crossing the room, she picks up her purse, opens it, and shows Grant another small gift—the red rose from David. "What is it?" he asks in baffled astonishment. "*Will* you get in another *mood*?" he pleads, "Something less *flippant*?" He takes off his shoes, sits in the middle of her bed with his arms on his knees, and complains that there's "nothing that makes a man more *ridiculous* than being *sentimental* when the woman is not." She can't deceive him, he says, because he knows she's only acting. She joins him in the bed lovingly and makes a speech about how fond she is of his mannerisms: "You hold your fork up, as a little boy does." It's a speech Grant has heard before, when he saw her on stage: "Now that *is* in your play!" She ruffles his hair and chucks his chin. "What character are you playing now?" he asks, and she seductively answers, "Delilah."

The telephone rings—it's Bergman's sister, but when Bergman answers she says, "Hello, David!" His hair still ruffled, Grant gets out of bed and exits, closing the door on her conversation. He returns when the call ends, his hair still on end, and walks toward Bergman with the hesitant, tentative pace of David Huxley in *Bringing Up Baby*. Gesturing with the gift he brought, he declares, "I'm not jealous," but then begins rapidly peppering her with questions about the gift of the rose: When? How? Was it when he was dancing with her every minute? Did a waiter bring it? Did David bring it himself?

She tells him David brought it to her when she was in the powder room. "*Well!*" his says in haughty disdain, "I will not *lower* myself to discussing this behavior!" He gets on his knees and reaches under the bed to retrieve his shoe, announcing, "I'm not a snob, but . . . I don't follow women into *powder rooms!*" He sits on the bed. "He *followed* you!" he says and makes an accusing gesture with his shoe.

"I'll tell him to his face," Grant declares. "He's taller than you are," Bergman says. Grant puts his shoe on and begins pacing, hands in his pockets: "What did he *say* to you on the phone?" She explains that David asked for a date and she said no. Grant visibly relaxes and smiles, trying again to give her a kiss, but she pleads a headache in transparently theatrical style. The non-diegetic piano plays a bit of romantic music. "This has turned into the most *exasperating* evening in my *whole* life," Grant says as Bergman gets under the covers to sleep. He straightens his hair in the cracked mirror, goes to the bedroom door, and pauses, trying to make a graceful exit. "I've seen plays with wonderful goodbye lines," he says gently, "but I can't think of one." Bergman feigns sleepiness. "I've heard them all," she says.

This is prelude to the night of Bergman's birthday, when she stages another scene, promising her sister that it will forever "burn" in Grant's memory. Using her theatrical experience, she plans for his surprise entrance at Big Ben's first stroke of twelve, when he will discover that she's entertaining David. She carefully arranges the *mise en scène*, filling the townhouse with large bouquets of red roses and preparing a candlelit ambiance. But David falls ill at the last minute, and Bergman has to recruit her servant, the diminutive, fearful Carl, to play the role. "I've seen many plays," Carl says, "Jealous lovers are a problem. There's always a body on the floor!" She directs him, observing his undramatic walk and opting for shadows and minimalism. Dressing him in Grant's stylish bathrobe, she instructs him to open the bedroom door exactly as Big Ben strikes twelve and stand silhouetted there for an instant. She will slam the door shut and go into a dramatic pose.

The result is more like farce than melodrama. As Big Ben strikes its first chime, Grant rushes in and announces, "Darling! I have the most *astonishing* news! We can be married . . . she's fallen in love with a *ski instructor* in *Sun Valley*! Darling, will you *marry* me?" Just then Big Ben strikes its twelfth chime and Carl appears for an instant, quickly shutting the door. Bergman breaks into relieved laughter, but Grant isn't amused at seeing a man "in a *bathrobe* in your *bedroom!*" He marches out. Alone, Bergman despairs that she's ruined her life. Grant angrily returns with the expensive diamond bracelet he bought for her birthday, tossing it on a table and telling her to consider it "payment." It's a flash of the potentially furious, psychologically wounded lover of *Notorious* and *An Affair to Remember*; the bracelet, he says, "didn't *become* our relationship," which was "something *fine* and *spiritual.*" To Grant's astonishment, she reveals Carl. Grant opens his jacket, arms akimbo, and paces. She sadly remarks that he's proposing only because of his jealousy, but he grudgingly claims he would have "*eventually* proposed." She sits on her couch, beginning to cry, and tells him they can just go on as before. "And not be *married*?" he says, "Why that's the most *improper* thing I've ever heard!" He complains that all this goes to show "*men* are the true romanticists." Then he sees her tears, reacts, and embraces her in almost the same pose as the climactic scene of *An Affair to Remember*. Romantic piano is heard again. Taking her face in his hands, he promises, "You'll *like* being married! You *will*, you'll see!" The film ends with a close-up of her tearful but smiling face over his shoulder.

5

Domestic Cary

W. C. Fields famously said that actors should never play scenes with children and dogs. Grant ignored that advice, and in his domestic-centered films was very good at sharing screen space with kids, dogs, and cats. In *Room for One More* he's the father of a house filled with children, plays midwife to a cat, and has to fight off the affections of a dog. In *Penny Serenade* he sits in the background of a shot, fondles a cat, and improvises by kissing it on the head. Even when he isn't in the same shot with kids or pets, he's convincing as a character who loves them. In *Penny Serenade* he has a lengthy scene in which he pleads with a judge to keep an adopted baby daughter he's in danger of losing due to his poor income. Director George Stevens, famous for shooting retakes in search of perfection, shot this scene many times, despite it's exhausting emotional intensity. Grant makes his speech in a couple of relatively long takes and mostly in wide shots, with his body in view. Wearing a bulky overcoat and holding his hat in his hands, he at first sits at the edge of a chair across from the judge's desk, then rises to make a couple of long speeches, then sits and speaks more quietly. He never breaks into full tears, but his emotions go through stages of begging, anger, desperation, and despair. Occasionally Stevens cuts away to the baby girl behind Grant, but most of the time Grant is the center of attention. He speaks rapidly, occasionally stumbling over a word or repeating himself as if losing control, his voice changing from an angry defense to a near whine. It's a touching performance and won Grant his first Academy Award nomination, no doubt because the Academy thought his comedy didn't require the skill of "serious" acting. The two domestic films discussed here are light comedies without highly dramatic moments—no less well acted than *Penny Serenade* but with more scenes involving children.

Mr. Blandings Builds His Dream House (1948)

Based on a popular 1946 novel by Eric Hodgins, *Mr. Blandings Builds His Dream House* concerns the misadventures of a New York advertising man

Some Versions of Cary Grant. James Naremore, Oxford University Press. © Oxford University Press 2022.
DOI: 10.1093/oso/9780197566374.003.0005

with a wife and two daughters who purchases but then then has to tear down and rebuild a large house in the countryside. It's a classic instance of post–World-War II, family-centered situation comedy, which had become a staple of radio and would soon transition to television. (In the early 1950s, Lucille Ball began a radio sitcom, *My Favorite Husband,* and Grant and Betsy Drake created a half-hour radio show called *Mr. and Mrs. Blandings,* which ran for a single season.) The project was initially developed by David Selznick, whose studio logo is imitated in the office shingle of the Blandings's architect, and produced by Dore Schary, who has a cameo appearance as a man scarfing down a hotdog in a New York sandwich shop. The screenplay was by Norman Panama and Melvin Frank, legendary comedy writers who had often worked with Bob Hope; the photographer was James Wong Howe, who contributed excellent lighting, panning, and crane shots; and the director was the critically undervalued H. C. Potter, who had previously directed Grant in *Mr. Lucky* (1943). Besides all this, the film benefited considerably from Grant's co-stars, Myrna Loy as Mrs. Blandings and Melvyn Douglas as lawyer/narrator Bill Cole, who describes himself as a "friend of the family" and Grant's "so-called best friend."

There were tensions between Loy and Grant in their previous film, *The Batchelor and the Bobby-Soxer,* in part due to schedule pressures and an ineffectual director, but on this picture they were happy together. Loy had begun her career as a dancer, and in her early films was typed as an oriental sex object ("Such quiet fires," a Turkish fan of hers says in Eric Ambler's novel *A Coffin for Dimitrios*), but in the 1940s, largely because of *The Best Years of Our Lives* (1946), she became the most likeable middle-class housewife and mother in the movies, possessed of intelligence and ineffable sweetness. (She had been a housewife in the *Thin Man* series but of a more sophisticated kind.) Her comic skills in *Blandings,* already clear in her many films with William Powell, are evident in her long, dreamy speech to a cigar-smoking foreman of house painters, in which she describes the shades of color she wants in the rooms of her new home; in a drawling, kindly, I-want-to-be-perfectly-clear manner, she orders a red resembling what she's found on a rare spool of thread—an apple red, "somewhere between a healthy Winesap and an un-ripened Jonathan." Notice also her long speech when Grant and the architect (Reginald Denny) discover an extravagant bill for an extension to a garden shed, requiring a special drainage system: Loy stands before the two seated men, realizing she should have consulted someone before ordering the job, and pleads innocence; chin up and eyes shifting to avoid direct contact, she wistfully, almost lyrically says the builder was "as nice as he could be and said well, you're the doctor and that's all anybody said to anybody!"

Douglas had suavely played Garbo's lover in *Ninotchka* (1939), a role Grant was considered for, and he almost steals this film. He's a bit taller than Grant, but the two characters are nearly twins; old school chums, they're equally dapper in three-piece suits and equally addicted to pipe smoking. Douglas uses the pipe in almost his every scene, making wisecracks when it's in his mouth and repeatedly borrowing Grant's tobacco. He's deeply cynical of Grant's increasingly expensive real estate purchase and relishes telling him what a fool he is: "You weep on my shoulder about what a terrible thing the advertising business is for a sensitive soul like yourself because you make your living out of bamboozling the American public. I would say that a small portion of this victimized group has now redressed the balance." A frequent visitor to the Blandings's household, he's adored by their daughters, who call him "Uncle Bill." Unlike his counterpart in the novel, he's a bachelor and an old boyfriend of Loy's who always gives her a kiss on the cheek when he leaves. After one of his visits, Grant puts away the tobacco holder Douglas has been borrowing from and Loy sighs, "What a wonderful friend!" Grant frowns and becomes quietly angry: "Just because a man is helpful in a *business* way doesn't give him *extra-curricular* privileges with *my wife*!" Loy is astonished: "That's a fine thing to say!" Grant, looking a bit chastened, puts his hands in his pockets, shifts weight from one foot to another, and complains that every time Douglas leaves, "He shakes my *hand* and *kisses* you. . . . Well, I just don't *like* it." Loy turns away and wryly says, "Would you prefer it the other way around?"

Although the making of the film was a happy experience, Hollywood had become a victim of the postwar Red scare, and the highly publicized House Un-American Activities Committee investigations were underway. Representatives of the Committee for the First Amendment, a group of celebrities who planned a trip to Washington to protest the public inquisition of left-wing filmmakers, were visitors to the set of *Blandings*, and both Loy and Douglas contributed money to their cause. Grant, who was sympathetic to the group, didn't give it money or public support but was responsible for writing a speech in which, as Mark Glancy has observed, he addresses one of the film's potentially awkward social issues. When Glancy

examined Grant's copy of the script, he found that Grant had rewritten several lines, calling attention to the Blandings's social class and emphasizing
the importance of home ownership for the less wealthy: "You start out to
build a home and wind up in the poor house. And if it can happen to me,
what about the fellows who aren't making $15,000 a year? What about the
kids who just got married and want a home of their own?"[1] (The film also
makes a political joke at another point, alluding to the upcoming 1948
presidential elections: Grant complains to a workman, who tells him, "the
Republicans aren't in charge yet!") But the screenplay doesn't remain completely true to the economic problem raised in Grant's speech or in the book
by Eric Hodgins. In real life, Hodgins, whose novel was autobiographical,
had to sell his dream house in order to recoup losses. Hollywood allowed
their Mr. Blandings to keep his. The studio also devised a publicity scheme
involving the construction of new homes around the country that would
be raffled off during the film's premiere, perhaps becoming the property of
"kids who just got married." The scheme was a flop, costing far more than it
was worth.

Blandings has another awkward aspect—an unconscious form of racism
typical of Hollywood in the period. One of the key characters is Gussie
(Louise Beavers), a black maid who seems to live in the Blandings's New York
apartment and moves with them when they go to their new home. (On
moving day, she rides at the rear on an open trailer, seated beside Douglas.)
Beavers plays the role skillfully; she's never condescended to or made a buf-
foon like the black servants in 1930s Hollywood, and though she's respectful,
she's sometimes assertive. She's important to the plot because in addition to
the many financial problems Grant encounters with the new home, he also
struggles to come up with an advertising slogan for Wham, a brand of ham
Gussie serves for breakfast every morning. Grant asks why they can't have
bacon or sausage occasionally, and Gussie calmly puts him in his place: "The
children like Wham. Mrs. Blandings likes it, too. I consider it very tasty!" At
the end of the film, when Grant is on the point of resigning from his job for
lack of a Wham slogan, Gussie rescues him by bringing a plate of the ham to
the family table and happily announcing, "If you ain't eatin' Wham, you ain't
eatin' ham!" Grant's eyes light up; this is his slogan, and he gives Gussie the

[1] Glancy, 292–93.

job of an Aunt Jemima figure whose image appears in the ads. Myrna Loy was right when she later wrote, "Why does every black person in the movies have to play a servant? How about a black person walking up the steps of a courthouse carrying a briefcase?"[2]

Grant nevertheless gives one of his best comic performances, filled with exasperated reactions and occasional physical gags. The key to his character is that he's frustrated, confused, angered, and foolish while everyone around him—Loy, Douglas, Gussie, and the daughters—remains rational or calm. The film often calls on his ability to react not only to other people's comic lines but also to his own errors, impediments, and mistakes.

His talent for pantomime is evident in an almost dialogue-free opening sequence illustrating a typical workday morning in the Blandings's New York apartment. The action is played realistically; its humor arising from Grant's little facial expressions and attempts to negotiate the obstacle course of the crowded rooms. He and Loy struggle over the alarm clock, and he slowly gets out of bed, putting on his slippers and stepping over furniture as he moves to a packed closet, which he opens, using one hand to keep a pile of boxes on the top shelf from falling. He searches for his robe and winds up with one of Loy's filmy gowns, which he looks at with wide-eyed frustration. He eventually finds the robe, lifting it from the closet floor with his toe, and goes down a narrow hall toward the front rooms. Howe's camera follows in a series of complex tracking and panning shots disguised to look like a long take. Half awake, Grant knocks on his daughters' doors and picks up a broom someone has left on the living room furniture. He edges around a breakfast table near the wall to remove towels covering a large birdcage, and Gussie meets him at the entrance to the kitchen, giving him an orange juice, which he quickly drinks, and a cup of coffee in a saucer. After stopping to pick up the morning paper from outside the front door, he heads back to the bedroom. He executes a twirl when his daughter comes running out the hall door of the steaming bathroom ("Father, I wish you would knock," she shouts), all the while balancing the cup and saucer, and returns to Loy. He gives her the coffee, and in a gesture he probably improvised, he reaches down and scratches the top of her head.

---

[2] Loy quoted in Simon Maier, *Inspire!* (Asia: Marshall Cavendish International, 2001), 17.

Grant goes to his bureau drawer and finds it full of Loy's underwear, which he holds up with another frustrated look. There's a muttered exchange between the two about which drawers are his. When he looks for his socks, she tells him they're in a basket on a shelf in the closet. He frowns and goes there, pulling down a basket and causing several boxes to fall. He puts the boxes back, frustration mounting, and when he closes the door they crash down again. (This would have reminded the original audience of a popular radio sitcom, *Fibber McGee and Molly*, which ran from the 1930s until the mid-1950s; a running gag in the show was a stuffed closet that, when opened, produced the lengthy sound of crashing.)

Grant then goes to the equally crowded bathroom and examines his tongue in the mirror. He removes the robe, scratches his back, weighs himself, pats his stomach (he's a bit heavier in this film), and puts a toothbrush in his mouth. Opening the medicine cabinet, he finds that somebody has squeezed the toothpaste tube in the middle. When he replaces the tube, a cascade of items falls toward the sink. Going into the Grant crouch, toothbrush still in his mouth, he desperately tries to catch various bottles and ends up tossing several in a wastebasket.

After brushing his teeth furiously, he spreads his lips to see the result, removes his pajamas, turns on the faucet of the small shower, and enters it. Recoiling from the cold water, he shouts "Ooooh," and segues into full-throated song: "Oh hooome, home on the range!" (Grant doubtless remembered Ralph Bellamy in *The Awful Truth*.) Exiting the shower, he begins shaving, but Loy enters and takes her own shower, causing him to stare deadpan at his lathered face in the steam-fogged bathroom mirror. When she finishes, she steps between him and the mirror. She examines her skin and asks why he doesn't use an electric razor like Douglas. "I'm not interested in discussing the *grain* and *texture* of *Bill Cole's hair follicles*," he replies.

Nearly all the comedy of the film has to do with Grant's repeated failures at asserting his patriarchal wisdom and authority. He gives these moments a distinctive tone: Even when he's expressing man-of-the-family irritation or anger, he never seems a threat to anybody, and we can sense an underlying gentleness. Often, the wife and daughters correct or amusingly instruct him, but he doesn't react like a henpecked male. At family breakfast, for example, he's squeezed into a place at the head of the table, his head almost touching the bird cage, so that Gussie has to edge around him when she brings him eggs and feeds the bird. As he eats breakfast, he becomes irritated by his daughters, who attend a progressive school and have opinions of their own. Betsy, the eldest (Connie Marshall), has damaged his morning paper by clipping an ad to illustrate one of her classroom assignments—an essay she's writing about the complacency of "middle-class people." Grant looks at Loy and says archly, "Just one morning I would like to have breakfast without *social signif-icance*." Loy softly tells him he should show more concern about the girls' education. Eyes widening, he points out that he not only cares about them but is also paying for their education. Joan, the youngest (Sharyn Moffett), mutters, "bicker, bicker, bicker." Grant gives her a look and says, "Drink your milk."

At Grant's invitation, Betsy gets out her notebook and stands to read her composition, which deals with "a poor honest farmer" who is selling his house and orchard in the countryside because he's "pushed to the wall by hardship." Grant thinks this is nonsense—it's just an ad by somebody who wants to sell a house—but from the way he looks at her we can see his pride in her ability. Joan chimes in, telling him she's learned from their teacher, Miss Stillwell, that advertising is "a basically parasitic profession" designed to "make people buy things they don't want with money they don't have." At this, Grant seeks help from Loy, ignoring the girls and pointing out that his work in advertising supports them. She quietly asks that he not discuss money in front of the children. He raises his eyebrows and asks, "Why not? They spend enough of it." Joan again says, "bicker, bicker, bicker." When the girls get up to leave, however, they each give him a kiss on the cheek. "Give my regards to Miss *Still*well," he says.

During one of Douglas's many visits, Grant is perturbed when Loy reveals that she's been talking with a young interior decorator named Bunny Funkhouser about remodeling their apartment in colonial style. "And where do I keep my *powdered wig*?" he asks, dismissing the idea because Funkhouser wears "open-toed sandals." But that day at work, trying to think of a slogan for Wham, he notices a full-page ad for Connecticut real estate on the back page of a slick magazine. An inducement for people to spend money they don't have, it inspires him.

The Blandings embark on a house-hunting trip out in the fresh air, and a countryfied but wily real-estate agent shows them the "old Hackett place," which has antique value because "General Gates" stopped there during the Revolutionary War. Howe's camera executes a 360-degree pan around the large property while the agent makes a sales pitch. Grant and Loy dream about their future: She sees herself in period finery, tiptoeing through her garden, and he imagines himself a country gentleman in jodhpurs, with a pipe in his mouth and a hound at his feet.

In the interest of comedy, the film tests plausibility. The house visibly leans to one side, and its shingles and boards fall off when anyone nears it. Grant is nevertheless captivated; he smiles, adopts a hearty, we're-just-looking attitude, and wonders what the price might be. When he shoves his way into the jammed front door, a flock of birds scatter from an upstairs window. He buys the place anyway, with the idea of repairing it. When Douglas sees the sales papers, he tells Grant, "You've been taken to the cleaners and you don't even know your pants are off." He recommends Joe Apollonio (Nestor Pavia), an expert construction engineer who can give advice on repairs. Apollonio travels to the site and looks at the dilapidated house. Grant rubs his hands together eagerly, saying, "Of course, any *small* changes would have to conform to the *character* of the countryside." Smiling, clasping his hands behind his back, and betraying a slight unease, he asks, "What is your *professional* opinion?" Apollonio chews a cigar and tells him to tear it down. So does a second and third engineer.

The Blandings then find themselves in the hands of an architect named Simms, who draws up plans for a new house. Loy thinks the design a bit conventional. Hands in pockets, Grant harrumphs, chuckles, and says, "Well, you know, I don't think we're ready to *commit* ourselves." Simms tells them to make suggestions. "Well, I, uh," Grant says, mumbling as he looks down at the blueprint. "Um, now if this were *my* house, for instance, now *here*, for instance." He takes a pencil and leans down to the plan. Mouth slightly open, in the attitude of an artist about to make a masterstroke, he executes his design for a playroom with a poker table.

Loy also wants improvements—more closets, and, "I refuse to en-
danger the health of my children in a house with less than four bathrooms."
Inevitably, calamities ensue. Grant runs into legal problems with the owner
of the deed for the house he's destroyed and slams his fist down in frustration: "Now just a minute," he cries, "this is *America*! A man is *guilty* until
he's proven *innocent*!" His daughter Joan overhears him and explains, "It's the
other way around, Father." The construction crew drills over a hundred feet
for a water source, then discovers water two feet under what will be the base-
ment of the house, which must be drained. As Grant proudly tours the skel-
etal structure of the house with Loy and Douglas, a carpenter (Lex Barker)
asks him, "the second floor lintels, you want we should rabbit them or not?"
Grant's reaction to the question is somewhere between fearful bafflement
and pretense that he understands. He answers, "not," and ripped-out lumber
starts falling from overhead.

Before the house is completely finished, the family must move in because
they've sold their Manhattan apartment. More problems arise, among them
a large bill for a "Zuz-Zuz water softener" and the discovery that the local
train schedule requires Grant to wake at 5 a.m. for his trips to work. When
he carries Loy over the threshold, he tramps over wet varnish on the floor,

and when he lights a fire in the fireplace, he fills the room with smoke. His daughter Joan explains to him, "The first principle of lighting a fire is to see if the flue is open. A three-year-old child knows that!"

As the daughters help unpack, Grant hears them react to a couple of things they find: a fraternity pin belonging to "Uncle Bill," and their mother's old diary, to which Betsy reacts with glee. "It's slightly torrid!" she tells her sister, who looks over her shoulder to read what Mother says about Uncle Bill. Grant shoos the girls away, lecturing them about respecting Mother's privacy, and sneaks a look for himself. That night, as he shaves in preparation for work in the morning, Loy gets between him and the mirror, just as she's always done in their New York apartment. He's uncommunicative, and she asks what's wrong. "Oh, nothing," he says but finally admits that he's read the diary. He accuses her of being in love with Douglas, and there's a brief quarrel, after which he apologizes for behaving like a child. He asks why she chose him and not Douglas, and she says, "Maybe it was those big cow eyes and that ridiculous hole in your chin." In a silhouetted close-up, they kiss and sink down out of the frame. A wide shot reveals them going to bed for the night, their twin mattresses side by side on the floor.

As summer fades into autumn, Grant still doesn't have a slogan for Wham. The head of the ham company gives him an ultimatum: Come up with something in twenty-four hours. As a result, he spends all night in his office, desperately searching for inspiration. He's aided by Mary, his secretary (nicely played by Lurene Tuttle), a sharp, experienced woman who is unafraid to tell him when his ideas are lousy. When a heavy rainstorm breaks out, he wishes he could be spending a quiet evening in his new home. A dream image shows him imagining himself in his robe and slippers, smoking a pipe and sitting in a comfy chair by the fire as Loy pours him a cup of tea. Then a clever use of optical printing breaks the illusion, showing that in reality Douglas is sitting in the chair, smoking Grant's tobacco. The heavy rainstorm has washed out a bridge, Douglas can't return to town, the Blandings children will need to spend the night with neighbors, and Douglas will need to wear Grant's bedclothes. Loy assures him he'll be pure as the driven snow in the morning.

Comes the dawn. Grant's office is littered with scraps of paper containing useless slogans, and Mary is sleeping in a chair. When he snaps his fingers to wake her and tries out a jingle about three little pigs, she wearily shakes her head in disapproval. He digs through the cigarette butts in his ashtray, finds one and lights it, getting smoke in his eye. Then he stretches out on his couch, pulls his loose tie over his nose, flips the end over his head, and tries to think.

It's useless. His life is collapsing, and he decides to resign from his job. Returning home, he finds the architect Simms conferring with Loy about expensive repairs, and in the midst of the conversation Douglas comes downstairs in Grant's pajamas and robe. Grant does an astonished double-take, stares angrily at Loy, and ignores Simms. Douglas goes upstairs to "slip into something more comfortable," and Simms exits. Loy tries to comfort Grant, but he wants to look for a job elsewhere and start their lives all over without the house. Launching into a speech about being on the "All-American sucker list," he brandishes a pile of bills and wonders how young couples without his high income can survive home ownership.

Just as everything collapses, the plot turns on a dime, ignoring the massive debt the Blandings have accrued and providing a rapid comic resolution that erases much of the satire. Mr. Tesander (Harry Shannon, whose movie debut was as Charles Foster Kane's father) appears at the door to explain about a mistake in a bill for drilling Grant's water well. It's a matter of twelve dollars and thirty-six cents, and, in Grant's view, it's the final insult. He explodes, turning his pockets inside out like a victim of a holdup. But Tesander, whose earlier dialogue has consisted mostly of "Yep" and "Nope," explains that Grant doesn't owe him—he owes Grant. He empties his small money purse to return the cash and asks Grant to count the change. As he leaves, he turns to the Blandings and tells them they sure have a pretty house.

Head down, looking apologetic, Grant says to Loy, "I just don't know any-more." When Douglas comes downstairs dressed for town and asks Tesander for a lift to the train station, Grant says to him: "Be patient with me, Bill. Maybe one of these days I'll grow up." Douglas pauses, admitting that from the start he's been the voice of doom, and that when he looks at what the Blandings have achieved he realizes "there are things you buy with your heart instead of your head." Grant and Loy exchange proud looks. Douglas kisses Loy on the cheek, says, "Goodbye, dear," and shakes Grant's hand. Grant looks at his empty hand and at Loy, and Douglas exits. Gussie has returned after the stormy night, and the excited daughters arrive in their rain gear. Breakfast is ready, and it includes Wham because "If you ain't eatin' Wham, you ain't eatin' ham!" Grant's eyes light up, and he tells Gussie she's getting a ten-dollar raise.

The last shot of the film could have served as an advertisement or a scene in the preview. In close-up, the seated Grant smokes a pipe and reads the Eric Hodgins book that inspired the movie. He looks up, smiles broadly, and in direct address to the camera says, "Drop in and see us sometime!" The camera pulls back to reveal that he and Loy are sitting outside their large new home. She also looks at us, and as she pours tea for Grant, Douglas steps into the frame to get some of Grant's tobacco, turns to face the camera, and echoes Grant's invitation: "Yes, do that!" The camera keeps pulling back to show the kids, Gussie, and the dream house shining in the background.

Room for One More (1952)

Loosely based on a 1950 memoir by Anna Perrott Rose, *Room for One More* is a sweetly comic, sometimes darkly shaded account of a married couple with three children who adopt two "problem" children. Hollywood has made several films about families crowded with children—among them *Life with Father* (1947), *Cheaper By the Dozen* (1950), and *Yours, Mine, and Ours* (1968). There was also the hit TV show *The Brady Bunch* (1969–1974). But this one is different because of its gentle social message.

The screenplay by Jack Rose and Melville Shavelson updates and fictionalizes Rose's memoir, which concerns her family's decision in the 1930s to nurture three unwanted kids with aid from foster care. Though far from wealthy, the Rose family had a home in New Jersey and a small summer cottage on the shore. Their counterparts in the film, who live at the margin of their income, have an eastern house in winter and a summer cottage on what looks a bit too much like the California coast.

The film was directed by Norman Taurog, who had won the 1931 Academy Award for directing child actor Jackie Coogan in *Skippy*. (He would later become a favored director of Martin and Lewis and Elvis Presley.) The photographer was Robert Burks, who had already begun his celebrated collaborations with Alfred Hitchcock. This was a relatively low-budget picture for Grant, who took a lesser upfront salary than usual. The shooting schedule was brief, the cast was made up of reliable but not widely known character actors, and Grant's co-star, in the role of Anna Rose, was Betsy Drake. Grant also serves as narrator, and at the beginning of the film, as the camera tracks across a long row of newborn babies in hospital cribs, his familiar voice tells the audience, "This is the story of my wife." The line had a double meaning for viewers who knew he was married to Drake, and it's likely that the two had a good deal to do with the story, finished screenplay, and direction.

The least admired of the Grant films I've concentrated on in this book, *Room for One More* deserves more attention than it's been given. It doesn't fit neatly into a generic category, it has unusual characters, and in often sugary fashion it raises important issues about child psychology, unwanted children, and the problems of parenting. Within the strict boundaries set by Hollywood's Production Code, which was only slightly liberalized in the 1950s, the film touches on issues movies usually avoided. At one point Grant explains to a boy how children are born; he doesn't go as far as describing conception, but his simple anatomy lesson raised the ire of the Catholic Legion of Decency, which gave the film a B rating on the grounds that it was "morally objectionable in parts."[3]

The most unfortunate thing about the film, especially from today's perspective, is that although it raises important issues, it's all too clearly a prisoner of the dominant social/ideological attitudes of America in the early 1950s. The adoption agency, the schools, and the public meetings are entirely white, and there's no person of color anywhere in the film. Grant and Drake adopt a girl who has been abused and abandoned by her parents and a boy who has to wear braces on his legs, raising them both to the verge of responsible adulthood, but the children's gender roles conform smoothly to conservative norms: The girl develops a maternal instinct and becomes the most popular beauty at her school prom; the boy overcomes his disability and is awarded an Eagle Scout badge symbolizing male virtues. The ritual

---

[3] Glancy, 319.

ceremonies involved in these achievements—a formal-dress New Year's prom and a patriotic event presided over by the town's mayor—are designed to elicit sentimental approval, but today they seem almost cringeworthy.

Grant's character, George Rose, is likeably unconventional and in some ways different from Grant's typical roles. Although he's a city engineer and the family's only breadwinner, he does as much cooking and cleaning as anybody in the house, and although he often objects to his wife Anna's "Lady Bountiful" instincts or is frustrated when she doesn't have time for sex (a rare problem for Cary Grant as a movie star), he eventually gets in the spirit of raising a large family. A thoroughly domestic male, he's far more engaged with his wife and children than with his job. We see him in his office only once, when he's late and has to endure an angry boss because he was purchasing a war-surplus life raft for a family vacation. A bit of an eccentric, he likes to entertain the family and show off his modicum of French, often saying *"bonsoir,"* and at one point declaring, *"Enchanté de vous voir."*

Grant is almost the entire source of the film's comedy, yet his most amusing moments seldom involve interaction with Betsy Drake, who plays an attractive, admirable, but almost drab character, a woman unwilling to buy herself new clothes because of her children's needs. At the beginning of the film, when she visits a foster care center with a local ladies' club, she's moved by the crowd of children trying their best to look adoptable, and unlike the other women in her group, she feels a need to help. "I'd like to put you out of business," she tells Miss Kenyon (Lurene Tuttle), who runs the agency, and volunteers to give a temporary home to a child. Her husband, she says, will be crazy about the idea "just as soon as I get the nerve to tell him."

The agent has in mind a girl of thirteen who has suffered "years and years of hell" from a father who beat her and a mother who didn't want her. This is more than Drake bargained for, and she starts backing out the door before finally relenting. Deeply maternal and soft-hearted, she's also intelligent and strongly committed. Drake as actor has the difficult job of keeping this character from seeming too saintly, and she succeeds largely through her moments of awkwardness and uncertainty. Grant's obvious affection for her in their rare moments of intimacy also helps reinforce her likeability.

We're introduced to the Rose home by a shaggy, soaking-wet dog, later dubbed Tramp, who passes the house on a snow-filled sidewalk and instinctively realizes he might find welcome. Inside, Grant is preparing a birthday cake for Teenie, his youngest child, who sits near him on a tall stool by the kitchen stove. Teenie is played by George Winslow, whom Grant had recommended for the film after seeing him on Art Linklater's popular TV show *People Are Funny*. The boy has a deep, gravelly voice that earned him the name "Foghorn" and a serious demeanor that made him seem a pint-size adult. Cute and unselfconscious, he's a unique comic who sometimes hardly needs to act at all. Howard Hawks would soon cast him with Grant in *Monkey Business* and with Marilyn Monroe in *Gentlemen Prefer Blondes* (1953), but his career ended when he grew a few years older. He served in the Navy during the Vietnam War and at the end of his life was working at the US Post Office.

One of the most enjoyable things about Grant's performance is that he repeatedly combines humor and unthreatening fatherly supervision with an ability to talk with children in uncondescending fashion. He enters the spirit of childhood because the clown in him lets him relate to a child's mischief, curiosity, and unpretentiousness. He also knows how to play straight man to a youngster. In his opening scene, he's wearing an apron and a white shirt, standing over a stove and tending a pot of chocolate icing for a layer cake resting on a table behind him. (As is often the case with Grant, he's improbably tanned; at one point we can see that he has polished loafers and silk socks.) It's Teenie's birthday, and Grant gives him his present, which the boy somberly unwraps to reveal a book.

Grant frowns and looks down at the disappointed Teenie, who tosses the wrapping on the floor, showing more interest in the progress of the cake.

Grant puts his spoon aside and kneels beside the boy, looking up at him with polite, instructive seriousness. The shot favors the frowning Teenie, and Grant, maintaining an adult manner, lets the child get the laughs. The book, he explains, is the collected poems of James Whitcomb Riley, which cost two dollars and ninety-five cents. It contains one hundred "masterpieces" by the celebrated Hoosier poet, "some of which rhyme." Among them are " 'What *Old Santa Said*,' 'Little *Orphant Annie*,' and 'The Lugubrious *Wing Wang*.' " The serious tone of the conversation is similar to ones that brought young George Winslow fame on the Art Linklater show, but Grant improves on the humor by maintaining a convincingly sincere, person-to-person attitude, to which Teenie replies simply, "Poppy make cake." Frustrated, Grant says, "Can't we take a few moments off for *culture*?"

Suddenly Grant's two other children—a boy and girl—rush into the kitchen, and comic chaos develops involving a good deal of complicated blocking and movement. Tim (Malcolm Cassell), who wears a Boy Scout uniform, carries a bowl of water and crouches down to push it under the stove while Grant is working. Tim is followed by Trot (Gay Gordon), carrying a laundry basket and crouching down beside her brother, who has gone part way under the stove. Somewhere beneath Grant, a litter of kittens is being born; there's hardly any room in the small kitchen, and he has to lift one foot as he stirs the icing.

"Tell that cat to limit production," he says, and then realizes a dog is scratching at the back door. Trot gleefully admits the dog, and Teenie joins her to embrace it. Grant frowns, bends down, and ushers the dog out, gently patting Teenie on the back as he does so. When he closes the door, he realizes Teenie has gone out with the dog and has to retrieve the boy. Then he rapidly returns to the stove, where more excitement develops. He stirs and smiles briefly, letting the kids take charge as the first kitten is brought forth. When more kittens follow, he reacts in straight-man style, helping put them in the basket. Teenie goes to the spoon Grant has been using and licks it. Grant goes to the sink to wash his hands, and Teenie pulls at his apron, urging him to get back to work. Just then Betsy Drake arrives from the foster care center, greets everyone, and sees the dog. "Well! Hello! Come on in!," she says, and as she pets the dog, Grant, who is still at the sink, says, "You have to control these generous impulses." She kisses him and he adds, "Well, not all of them." While all this is going on, the dog has found the unfinished cake and begun to eat it. Grant controls his anger, puts his hands on his hips in frustration, and caps the scene by sticking a small birthday candle atop the half-eaten cake.

Trouble arrives next morning when Grant, dressed in a business suit and preparing to go to work, needs to awaken the sleeping Drake. He scratches the top of her head as he did with Myrna Loy in *Mr. Blandings*, but he needs to do it a second time before she groggily gets up. Kneeling beside the bed, he tells her Miss Kenyon from the foster care center is downstairs with a young girl. "She's a disturbed adolescent," Drake says, to which Grant rapidly replies, "I'm a disturbed *husband* and I'm late for work and I want her *out* of here!" She gets her robe, and he begins stiffly reprimanding her, never raising his voice, as she backs off to the bathroom.

The scene is well played by Grant, who balances his tone between irritation and love. He stands at the bathroom doorway, and she occasionally sticks her head out as he complains that they can't afford another child: "I'm on a *fixed* income, and they fixed it *good*!" When she sits at a small vanity and begins brushing her hair, he stands behind her, straightening the collar of her bathrobe and gently holding her shoulders. "You haven't bought a thing for yourself in ages," he says, noting the bathrobe "is older than any one of the children." He reminds her, "We finally got the children old enough to take care of themselves—now we can have time for ourselves." She gets up with a weary attitude and guiltily puts her head on his shoulder as he looks down at her. He points a finger and lectures, saying, "I know we're owed one more, but not *now*, and not *this* one." Then he chucks her under the chin and tries to speak reasonably as they go downstairs.

Below is Jane (Iris Mann), a sullen, angry girl, suspicious of all adults, who accuses Grant and Drake of trying to profit from the little money foster care provides. The three other children observe from upstairs as Grant stands in the background looking angry. Late for work, he tries to kiss Drake goodbye, but Tramp, the dog, rises on his hind legs and puts grateful paws on his chest: "Not *you, her!*" he says. In a huff, he puts on his hat and scarf and marches out the front door, slamming it behind him. Then he makes a quick, undignified return because he's forgotten his overcoat.

Drake nevertheless accepts Jane for a two-week stay. That evening at dinner Grant is in a better mood, smiling and patting Tramp on the head. He puts a small piece of hamburger on the table for the dog, but Teenie eats it when Grant isn't looking. Everyone at the table silently watches the hungry Jane eat, which makes her resentful, and at the end of the meal, they clear the table and file off to wash the dishes. Jane stays put, wolfing down her hamburger patty. Two other patties are supposed to be leftovers, but she covers them with her napkin and runs upstairs to hide them in her room. Tramp licks the empty platter. When Jane returns, she takes her plate to the kitchen and slams it down on a table. Grant tries to defuse the situation by sending all the kids to the front room where Tim can read aloud from Teenie's book to "improve your minds." Jane angrily shouts that her mind doesn't need improving and slams the door as she exits.

These scenes of strife tend to be counterpointed by scenes of affection. The aproned Grant prepares to dry dishes, and when Drake gives him a kiss on the cheek, he grabs her lustily—not the typical Grant move. She smiles, struggles, and playfully sticks a piece of bread in his mouth. "Man does not live by bread alone," he says, and she kisses him again. She then brings Jane a broom and gently asks her to sweep under the dining table, but Jane flings the broom across the room, shouting, "I *won't* sweep!" She's heard Tim reading "Little Orphant Annie" from Teenie's book and furiously says, "I'm *not* an Orphan!" Drake tries to calm the girl by handing her the book and approaching the open fire in the family hearth, where she kindly tells Jane she doesn't have to do anything she doesn't want to and can burn the book if she chooses. Jane does just that.

Later that evening, Grant and Drake have a moment of rest by the fireplace. Preparing for bed, Grant extinguishes his pipe and the fire, puts an arm around Drake, and says, "I'm going to find out who her *parents* might have been. Was *John Dillinger* ever married?" In the hallway upstairs, he again tries to make a sexual move, patting Drake on the bottom, but she's concerned about Jane. Grant goes away, mumbling to himself, and Drake visits Jane's bedroom. The girl is fearful of turning out her light, and when Drake tries to kiss her goodnight, she recoils in horror.

Grant assumes a secondary role as Jane gradually becomes a full member of the family. Drake has the idea of giving the girl confidence by finding her a job as a babysitter. The plan works but not without a suspenseful moment when Grant and Drake have an evening out with the Foreman family (John Ridgely and Randy Stuart), who leave their child in Jane's care. Grant's car runs out of gas, and when everyone finally returns, they find the Foreman house in shambles. A broken shelf in the refrigerator has caused the baby's bottles to crash on the floor, and Jane has searched everywhere, eventually finding ingredients to make more formula. Exhausted, she's asleep in a chair with the sleeping baby in her arms. Drake smiles in pleasure, and Grant removes his hat, giving Drake an admiring look.

Drake adds to the girl's pride by arranging for her to open a bank account with the dollar she's earned, and on the next evening Grant and Drake visit the children in their bedrooms. Tim is practicing Boy Scout skills by wrapping Teenie in bandages: "I got a compound fracture of the left collar bone," Teenie growls, "and the tibia and fibula." Grant scratches his stomach and says, "That's the *worst* place!" Trot, almost asleep, is hiding Tramp under the bedcovers. Jane accepts a kiss goodnight and turns out her light.

Once Jane becomes a happy member of the household, Grant has another comic scene. He's in the kitchen wearing a robe and slippers (a chalk board behind him bears the reminder, "Get flea powder") and is making pancakes for the children, who sit together at the kitchen table like an audience. He goes into a kind of vaudeville routine, singing "Row, row, row your boat" in a deep, stagey voice. He hops cheerfully from one foot to another as he stirs batter. He pauses, pours batter into a pan, lets it cook, and throws his arm out like a magician demonstrating a trick: "*Regard!*" he says in his French accent and turns to his audience. He flips the pancake in the air.

He catches it in the pan, his audience cheers, and he takes an extravagant bow. This causes the pancake to slip off the pan and land on the floor, where Tramp, who has been watching, starts eating it. Grant chides the dog for not waiting for syrup and returns to the stove, pouring out more batter. "As you see," he says, "I think a *pan*cake should be the size of a *pan*. Of course, that takes more skill than the *average* human being can muster!" Turning to the audience, putting a hand on his hip and kicking out a heel in a fey attitude, he boasts, "I studied with *Escoffier!*"

Just at this point, Miss Kenyon appears from the foster care office to reclaim Jane from her short-term stay. Jane is now loved by everybody, and as they give her a sad goodbye, Grant silently retrieves the bag she's packed and takes it back upstairs to her room. They will soon adopt her, and when she sees Grant ascending the stairs she rushes to kiss him. Soon afterward, however, Drake finds another unwanted child. While the family is doing teamwork in the kitchen in preparation for their summer holiday, one of the kids mentions a "little boy we're taking to the beach." Grant, washing up at the sink, reacts wide-eyed, turns, and stiffens: "*What* little boy?"

It's Jimmy-John (Clifford Tatum, Jr.), who is nearing adolescence and burdened with leg braces as a result of polio. Grant reluctantly goes to find him in a schoolroom and discovers that he's an angry, disruptive boy with a five-minute attention span; he can't read and refuses to learn, and his teacher has forced him to sit under her desk, where he bit her ankle. Grant tells the teacher, "I'd bite *both* your ankles," and he takes the boy home.

The remainder of the film is chiefly devoted to the rehabilitation of Jimmy-John, a tough kid who talks like a would-be Cagney. When Grant drives the family and Tramp along the crowded highway to their beach house, happily singing "Row, row, row your boat," Jimmy-John starts a fight in the back seat and has to be moved to the front. At the beach, there are comic scenes—as when Grant's Army-surplus raft develops a leak and sinks him—but Jimmy-John causes trouble. He's caught peeping in the girls' bedroom window, and Grant pulls him aside for sex education, talking to him man to man and using a stick to draw the female anatomy in the sand. "I had to do it from *memory*," he later complains to Drake.

When Jimmy-John tries to ride a bicycle at night while wearing his braces, it crashes, leaving him helpless and intensifying his already considerable anger. He causes so much trouble that the other kids have a secret ballot in favor of having him leave, but when they learn he can't read the ballots, they change their minds. With Drake's care and tutelage, Jimmy-John begins to learn to read, and, partly because of Tim, he becomes interested in the Boy Scouts, who welcome him at a party for their troop in the Rose house. The party is a disappointment for Grant, who has brought home champagne and flowers for Drake; he's reduced to shaking her hand as they lie in bed and she helps Jimmy-John read. "*Bonsoir*," she says to Grant. The boy is so determined to become an Eagle Scout that he strengthens his legs and goes for a long hike in uniform on a snowy night, refusing Grant's help. (The young Archie Leach had been an avid member of the British Boy Scout troop in Bristol, and Grant must have identified with this aspect of the film.[4])

The film nears its ending with a near orgy of celebration, beginning with Christmas morning, when Grant, aided by a stunt double, slides down the family banister with all the kids. Before they can open their presents he stands in front of the tree, grins broadly, and rubs his hands together like a maestro warming up an audience. "Don't you think we should get into the *spirit* of things?" he asks, proposing they sing "Good King Wenceslaus." Teenie quietly complains to Drake that this happens every year because it's the only song Grant knows how to play. Drake tells him they all should humor their

[4] Glancy, 25.

father to keep him from sulking. The family stands behind Grant at the piano and he sings "Good King Wenceslaus" louder than any of them.

Grant's performance of the song is funny not only because he seems to be enjoying it more than the others but also because he's Cary Grant, one of Hollywood's most popular leading men. The film isn't trying to make a self-referential joke, but this is one of many instances in his later career when a scene wouldn't be as charming if it were performed by anyone other than Grant.

Jane's Christmas present is an old party dress that Drake has altered to fit her; she's being courted by one of the senior Boy Scouts, who has invited her to the New Year's prom. Everyone feels this gift is inadequate, and in the true spirit of Christmas, the other kids give up their gifts so the family can buy Jane a proper dress. But when the event arrives, Jane's suitor cancels his invitation on the orders of his mother (Mary Lou Treen), who disapproves of Jane simply because she was adopted; like Jimmy-John's schoolteacher, this woman is the film's snobbish, uncharitable representative of those in the community who differ from the Rose family. Grant confronts her, and her husband causes her to relent immediately. At the New Year's prom, Grant arrives and dances with Jane, finding that she's surrounded by admirers.

More public events include a speech Drake gives for a packed auditorium of the local PTA, entitled "Raising Foster Children Can Be Fun," which provides an opportunity to make the film's message explicit. A member of the audience asks why Drake didn't adopt younger children. Drake says, "Anyone can start from scratch," and besides, older kids are an interesting challenge. Grant rises from a back row without identifying himself, and in skeptical fashion asks what problems this might cause for the man of the house. Drake says that her husband is "deeply interested" in the children and "reasonably patient." He also has "the undying love of every member of his family, including his wife." Grant smiles.

At the film's close, a kindly neighbor invites all the family's children for a visit so that Grant and Drake can at last have an evening together. At the neighbor's doorway, Grant lines up the children and gives each a kiss on the hand, saying, "*Bonsoir, bonsoir, bonsoir, bonsoir, et bonsoir!*" As Grant and Drake take a stroll together in the moonlight, he says that he's neglected to tell her he loves her. They walk toward their door, and the film's closing title card is "*bonsoir.*"

6

Cockney Cary

As I've said at the beginning, the title of this book alludes to William Empson's *Some Versions of Pastoral* (1935), which has different concerns from mine. Here at the end, however, Empson becomes relevant. He aims to show how the pastoral convention of "putting the complex into the simple" has been used in the history of canonical English literature, but he begins with an essay on "Proletarian Literature," a topic of special concern to intellectuals in the 1930s and related both to Grant's career and the films I'm about to discuss.[1]

Empson contends that "the essential trick of the old pastoral," which had to do with shepherds or country folk and implied "a beautiful relation between rich and poor," was to "make simple people express strong feelings (felt as the most universal subject, something fundamentally true about everybody) in learned and fashionable language."[2] But he also argues that "pastoral" can be applied to any art that invites us to identify with the humanity and complexity of relatively unlettered characters, including beggars, outlaws, children, and the working class. In his view, contemporary proletarian literature is "worked from the same philosophical ideas" as pastoral, and "good proletarian art is usually Covert Pastoral."[3]

Empson questions the degree to which any art can be of, by, and for the working class. Artists, merely by becoming artists, tend to leave the class from which they come; moreover, the poor and working class lack access to social drama and are sometimes uninterested in it. When Empson looks for good proletarian art in England, the best example he finds is a film: John Grierson's *Drifters* (1929), a documentary about herring fishermen, which conveys "a pastoral feeling about the dignity of that sort of labor." Nevertheless, he observes, herring fisherman are unlikely to see *Drifters* because of its inadvertent "high-brow" quality.[4]

---

[1] William Empson, *Some Versions of Pastoral* (New York: New Directions, 1950), 22.
[2] Empson, 11.
[3] Empson, 6.
[4] Empson, 8.

Some Versions of Cary Grant. James Naremore, Oxford University Press. © Oxford University Press 2022.
DOI: 10.1093/oso/9780197566374.003.0006

For my part, if I had to choose a film that could be described as good (indeed great) proletarian art, I'd pick Charles Burnett's *Killer of Sheep* (1977), an extremely low-budget picture about a black family man in Los Angeles who works in a sheep slaughterhouse. Burnett's film isn't highbrow, but he's lamented that "if the socially oriented film is finally made, its showing will generally be limited and the very ones it is made for and about will probably never see it."[5]

There are a number of Hollywood films that deal with the working class and have covertly pastoral elements. *On the Waterfront* (1954), for example, gives Brando opportunities to express complex feeling and a kind of dignified pathos. But the cinema with the strongest proletarian association is probably Italian neo-realism, especially *Bicycle Thieves* (1948), in which a pastoral quality is expressed by means of the touching relationship between a father and son. Despite its subject matter, however, *Bicycle Thieves* wasn't a low-budget production and wasn't made by proletarians—and for all its emphasis on the working class, it was received mainly as an art film.

I mention *Bicycle Thieves* because one of the curious facts about its history is that when director Vittorio De Sica was searching for financing, he entered into discussions with David O. Selznick, who was interested on the condition that Cary Grant play the leading role. De Sica turned down the offer and explained why: "Grant is pleasant, cordial, but he is too worldly, bourgeois; his hands have no blisters on them. He carries himself like a gentleman. I needed a man who eats like a worker, is moved like a worker, who can bring himself to cry, who bats his wife around . . . Cary Grant isn't used to doing such things and he can't do them."[6]

There's no reason to regret De Sica's casting of Lamberto Maggiorani, who in real life was a machinist; but Grant was more familiar with the working class than De Sica realized (probably more familiar than De Sica) and had a fair amount of experience playing Hollywood versions of working-class characters—all of whom, in his case, were Cockneys. As I've already noted, he's a tough Cockney soldier who survives a battle in *Gunga Din* and a crooked Cockney gambler who reforms his life in *Mr. Lucky*. These and Grant's other Cockney films have what William Empson would describe as pastoral elements, in the sense that lower class characters are given dignity

---

[5] Charles Burnett, "Inner City Blues," in *Questions of Third Cinema*, ed. Jim Pines and Paul Willeman (London: British Film Institute, 1989), 224.

[6] De Sica quoted in Eric D. Snider, "11 Heart-Stealing Facts about *Bicycle Thieves*," www.metalfloss.com/article/70637/11-heart-stealing-facts-about-bicycle-thieves.

and express strong human emotions. The two most important examples, however, are *Sylvia Scarlett* and *None But the Lonely Heart*. Although both were box-office failures, the first made reviewers aware that Grant could act, and the second was a personal project related to Grant's early life.

Sylvia Scarlett (1935)

The breakthrough role of Grant's reputation as an actor was Jimmy Monkley, a Cockney thief and con man in George Cukor's *Sylvia Scarlett*. The picture was conceived by Cukor as a star vehicle for his frequent collaborator Katharine Hepburn, who helped persuade RKO to borrow Grant from Paramount. By most reports, Cukor resisted the casting, claiming he hardly knew Grant and was never "weak-kneed" over him.[7] It's difficult to believe they were strangers; they had moved in the same New York theatrical circles, and Grant's personal secretary in Hollywood, Frank Horn, was Cukor's neighbor. But at this point Grant had shown relatively little evidence that he was more than decorative and had never acted with Hepburn. Fortunately, Cukor took a chance, giving Grant an opportunity to exhibit a broad range of his talents.

The unorthodox film was loosely based on a 1918 novel *The Early Life and Adventures of Sylvia Scarlett* by Scottish author Compton Mackenzie. Screenwriting credits went to Gladys Unger, John Collier, and Mortimer Offner; but Evelyn Waugh, who was one of Mackenzie's admirers, was paid and probably also contributed. Mackenzie is almost forgotten today but was once greatly praised, not only by Waugh but also by Henry James, Scott Fitzgerald, and George Orwell. The most commercially and critically successful movie based on his work was Alexander McKendrick's *Whiskey Galore* (1947), but *Sylvia Scarlett* is in some quarters a greater favorite of today's cinephiles.

Cukor was known in Hollywood as a "woman's director." Female stars respected his talent and trusted him personally, perhaps because his homosexuality, never discussed but widely known within the industry, made them feel he wouldn't try to get them into bed. He was dismissed from *Gone with the Wind* (1939) because Clark Gable didn't want coaching from a woman's director, but he's more accurately described as an actor's director. Some of his players were irritated when he told them how to read a line or make a gesture,

---

[7] Cukor quoted in Eliot, 126.

but he was enthusiastic, supportive, and had good taste. In the early stages of his movie career he allowed photographers and editors to have their way with camera "coverage," leaving him free to evaluate details of performance. Beginning in the 1940s, however, he favored long takes, usually avoiding complex tracking or showy reframing. A late Cukor film such as *The Actress* (1953), for example, is a model of unobtrusive long takes or sequence shots in which the camera barely moves and the actors do the work. *Sylvia Scarlett* has a more conventional decoupage, but its best moments are the wide shots in which actors are artfully grouped and blocked.

Despite Cukor's skill, and despite a buoyant atmosphere among the cast during shooting, *Sylvia Scarlett* was a disaster for everybody except Grant. At a preview showing at Radio City Music Hall, the restive audience began walking out—among them, B. B. Kahane, the new president of RKO. Hepburn was dismayed, offering to make another picture free for producer Pandro Berman. When the film appeared, national box-office returns were less than half the production cost and reviews were unfavorable. The only thing on which critics agreed was that Cary Grant could act. *Variety* announced that Grant "virtually steals the picture" (January 15, 1936), and the *New York Times* said that he "turns actor in the role of the unpleasant Cockney and is surprisingly good at it" (January 10, 1936). Viewing the film retrospectively, Pauline Kael wrote that Grant's inner knock-about comic was unleashed, giving him a "boisterous energy . . . so loose and virile that he has more life than anyone in the picture" (*The New Yorker*, July 14, 1975).

There are two fairly obvious reasons why the picture was unpalatable to its original audience. The first is its wayward, picaresque plot, which shifts moods and generic expectations, jumping whimsically and without much plausibility from one adventure to another. The action begins in Marseilles, where Sylvia Snow (Hepburn) lives with her father Henry (Edmund Gwenn) in the rooms of her deceased mother's dress shop. Henry has gambling and drinking habits and to make matters worse has been discovered as an embezzler. He hopes to escape to England, smuggling a batch of expensive lace that he can sell; the only impediment is his daughter, whose gender, for reasons that aren't clear, would make travel difficult. The problem is solved when Sylvia proposes to cut her long braids and dress as a boy, changing her name to Sylvester. The two embark for London, but aboard ship they're observed by Jimmy Monkley, who flatters Henry, gets him drunk, and learns about the smuggled lace. During the customs inspection, Jimmy plays a trick and Henry's lace is impounded.

On the train to London, Jimmy confesses to Henry and Sylvester that he, too, is a smuggler, and has betrayed Henry to distract the customs officers. He pays for the lost lace and proposes that the three become jolly partners in crime with himself as the mastermind. In London, he devises a con game that goes awry because of Sylvester. He then gets an idea for a jewel theft in Buckingham Gate, where a rich family are abroad and have left their house in the care of Maudie (Dennie Moore), a Cockney serving girl who is one of Jimmy's old friends. When the group arrives at the townhouse, Henry is smitten by the flirtatious Maudie. They all get gloriously drunk on champagne, and Sylvester proposes that they make an honest income by becoming a band of traveling entertainers in the countryside.

When we next see the group, they're the "The Pink Pierrots," having somehow acquired enough money to travel through Dorset and Cornwall and put on shows in the summer moonlight. During one of their performances, Sylvester attracts the attention of Michael Fane (Brian Aherne), a handsome painter who thinks Sylvester is a boy but gets a "queer" feeling when he/she is around. Things begin to resemble the pastoral comedy in *As You Like It*. One day at the Cornish seaside (which looks a good deal like Malibu), Sylvia steals the dress of a woman bather, goes to Fane's house, and awkwardly reveals that she's not a boy. The two begin to fall in love, but their idyll is disrupted by Fane's lady friend Lily (Natalie Paley), a Russian aristocrat who "lives for one sensation after another" and who accuses Fane of stealing Sylvia from "that bad handsome Pierrot man." Meanwhile, the drunken Henry, besotted with Maudie and convinced she's unfaithful, falls from a seaside cliff and dies on the rocks. More complications ensue, until Sylvia and Fane at last pledge their love. On a train escaping Dorset, they learn that Jimmy and Lilly are aboard and to evade discovery they jump out. Seated in a train compartment, Jimmy spots them landing on the ground, puts his feet on the seat cushions, and laughs boisterously.

Everything was beautifully photographed by Joseph H. August, who photographed several Grant pictures in the 1930s. The strange plot, however, didn't engage the original audience. A second, more serious problem, never directly commented upon by reviewers, was a not-so-subtle departure from heterosexual norms, which is precisely why *Sylvia Scarlett* has become an amusing and sexy cult film for today's LBGTQ community. Cukor's fondness for theater was never so suggestive of the ways theatrical costuming and pretense spill over into the performances of everyday life. The characters need to act parts whenever they're engaged in a criminal plot, and some of their private interactions involve as much playacting as their brief appearances on stage in the travelling show. When Fane contemplates Sylvia, he wonders, "Are you a girl dressed as a boy or a boy dressed as a girl?" Amused when she wears a dress and sits with her legs spread apart, he instructs her in the arts of performing femininity and attracting men, who of course have their own performance codes. In the end, the film reassures audiences that everyone is heterosexual and makes certain that the chief characters are successfully mated; but *Sylvia Scarlett* remains an androgynous comedy that plays with the idea of gender as performance. In Molly Haskell's words, it "dared to challenge, in a lyrical stage whisper, our traditional assumptions about male-female roles."[8]

Disguised as a dashing youth in a trim suit and a rakish fedora, Hepburn vaults over barriers or through open windows (at one point she injured herself), all the while giving Fane his "queer" feeling, making Jimmy think she/he would be "a proper little hot water bottle" on cold nights, and fighting off Maudie's attempt at seduction. ("Your face is as smooth as a girl's," Maudie remarks as she paints a Ronald Colman mustache on Sylvester/Sylvia's upper lip and tries to steal a kiss.) Most of the other characters have sexually ambiguous moments. Brian Aherne has an aristocratic accent, locks of curly hair, and a dandified scarf that make him a near parody of the effete, gilded bohemian; and the "Pink Pierrots"—Henry the clown, Maudie the "sweet soubrette," Sylvester the boy poet, and Jimmy the baritone singer/piano player—have identical blousy costumes adorned with bells, collars, and wide hats that make them look vaguely feminine or non-binary.

Sylvia never gives up her androgynous quality. Throughout, she retains athleticism, love of adventure, and youthful idealism, which spoil Jimmy's inclination to crime. As Rebecca Bell-Metereau has argued in *Hollywood Androgyny*, Sylvia's moral code differs from most movie representations of women in the period because she's neither a goody-two-shoes nor a bad girl: "Although she plays with her female identity and the notion of pretense, her behavior is acknowledged as play," and although she has moral standards, she isn't "the entrapper or the civilizer, for she displays the butterfly qualities of Peter Pan, not a Pollyanna or a puritan."[9]

The least sexually ambiguous characters are Maudie and Jimmy, a pair of rowdy, stereotypical Cockneys. By far the most important is Jimmy, who serves as foil to Sylvia and provides Grant with a more complex role than he

[8] Molly Haskell, *From Reverence to Rape: The Treatment of Women in the Movies* (Baltimore: Penguin Books, 1974), 225.
[9] Rebecca Bell-Metereau, *Hollywood Androgyny* (New York: Columbia University Press, 1985), 113.

had been given previously. Like all the actors in the film, he performs in an ostentatiously theatrical style suited to Cukor's thematic aims, but compared to the other players he's an imposing figure who brings greater speed, energy, and variety to his behavior. Most of the time, he speaks with a stage-Cockney accent, dropping an initial *H* at every opportunity; but his speech is crisply enunciated, attentive to the music of the lines, and modulated in a style that makes the accent understandable to American ears.

One key to the performance is Grant's mixture of cheerfulness and potential threat. Often he exudes chipper peppiness and an air of showmanship, as when he introduces himself to Henry as "Jimmy Monkley, gentleman adventurer, one of the 'awks," then proudly explains, "Sparrers and 'awks, that's 'umanity." But he also has a mercurial personality suited to a con man. The characterization involves one change of accent, more wardrobe than anyone in the film, and a series of performances-within-performance. Equally important, it involves changes in mood, shifting from the sinister, to the farcical, and to moments that reveal Jimmy Monkley has hidden wounds and a touch of human kindness.

Our first glimpse of Grant, standing in darkness on the ship to England as he sizes up Gwenn and Hepburn, is sinister indeed. Hat turned down, overcoat collar turned up, his eyes gleam with a cold intensity.

In the ship's bar, where he strikes up a friendship with Gwenn, he leans confidently back in the corner of a booth, collar up but hat brim raised, smiling slightly as Gwenn, in the foreground, chatters and swills gin and tonic. Grant's stillness attracts attention. Conveying the attitude of a hawk who has spotted a sparrow, he observes and assesses Gwenn, making occasional polite inquiries and offering a cigarette. Cut to Hepburn on deck, coping with seasickness and hesitating to use either the women's or the men's WC. When we return to Grant and Gwenn, the atmosphere has changed. Several empty glasses are on the table, and Grant is loudly singing, waving a matchbook, leading the drunken Gwenn in a sing-along of "Who's Your Lady Friend?," a British music-hall tune made wildly popular in the early twentieth century by Harry Fragson. (It has an ironic implication here, given Gwenn's traveling companion.) Grant booms out the lyrics Cockney style: "ooo, ooo, ooose yer lady friend?"

Soon Gwenn begins boasting, one crook to another, about the smuggled lace, and reveals it by unbuttoning his vest. A close-up of Grant, not as drunk as he seemed, shows him exhaling a plume of smoke, his eyes amused and sleepy with pleasure. Hepburn enters and approaches the two men warily. Grant is silent, smiling a bit, observing her. As Hepburn helps Gwenn with his coat, Grant rises, cigarette in his mouth, and cheerily introduces himself to Hepburn: "Jimmy Monkley, that's me . . . friend of all the world, nobody's enemy but me own!" Suddenly he grabs Hepburn at the waist and begins feeling her. The tiny Hepburn struggles, angered at being touched but also anxious that her gender might be discovered. Grant makes his exit with a tough, jaunty confidence. "Ticklish, aren't you?" he says, "Just wanted to see if there's more lace in the family."

On the train to London, Grant confesses his betrayal, playing the scene with quick changes of posture and an animated, smarmy charm. "*Tai toi!*" he says to the angry Hepburn, who tries to punch him. Leaning forward with one hand casually bent on his knee as if making a deal, he asks Henry, "How much you say your lace was worth?" Without waiting for a reply, he looks up at the ceiling, squints, and calculates: "Thirty you might have got for it." Pointing a finger at Henry, he raises his brows.

He looks slyly out the side of his eye. "Am I right? Right!" Waving a hand, he tosses his head back in a gesture of noblesse oblige, swiftly reaches in his pocket, and begins dealing money from a stack of bills: "And for your inconvenience, let's make it up to a round figure." Hand to his heart, he boasts that he's a "man of public spirit." Then he sits straight, frowns, presses his lips together disapprovingly, and launches into a lecture about how to get on in the world as a "gentleman adventurer." He winks. Hepburn laughs skeptically. Grant leans back comfortably in his flashy striped suit, both hands on his knees, and evaluates Sylvester with a slightly ironic tone: "'E's got 'umor," he says. "'E's got imagination, 'e 'as."

Grant establishes Jimmy as an untrustworthy, amusing character with practiced yet undeniable charisma, but in the next three episodes he becomes a more comic figure. Grant's talent for farce comes into play when Jimmy organizes a con game on a London street; he drops the Cockney accent, changes out of his flashy suit, and acts like a posh type in a skit. Speaking clichéd King's English and sounding a good deal like Cary Grant, he brandishes a fancy walking stick and wears a high collar, cravat, and cutaway coat. Sylvester pretends to be a distraught French boy who has just been cheated of money.

As a crowd gathers, Henry introduces himself as a passerby who can act translator for the boy. Grant wanders upon them, reacting with exaggerated concern. "*Dear, dear, dear, dear,*" he says loudly, "This sounds like an *in*famous *racket,* probably the work of an *organ*ized *gang*! *I* know when I'm *needed*!" Henry praises him for helping, and Grant, adopting an imperious attitude, takes a coin from his pocket, bows down, and gives it to Sylvester. "Here is a *pound,*" he says, turning to go and tipping his hat like an actor about to leave the stage. He lingers as Henry applauds his heart of gold. "*Come, come,* old chap!," Grant says, bowing his head in modesty, "I've not *always* been what I *should* be." Standing straight, both hands atop his walking stick, he looks upward and announces, "I *welcome* this chance to put a *little item* on the *right side* of the *ledger.*"

He pauses, turns his gaze even further up to the sky, and adds, "Up above." He then arranges to pass his hat for money, and appeals to nationalism: "*Splendid, splendid*! I *say,* we'll show this boy what *English*men *really are*!" When Sylvester spoils the scheme by accidentally speaking English, Grant wipes his finger under his collar like a worried fellow in a cartoon and suddenly runs away.

The three characters return to their small room and the tempo becomes more farcical, filled with rapid action and touches of slapstick. Furious, Grant bursts into the room, hurls his walking stick violently to the bed, and hangs his coat on the door. The door suddenly opens and bumps him as Hepburn enters. He jerks her inside and pushes her across the room, where she lands on a table, smiling triumphantly. She flops on the bed as Grant, his hat cocked back, paces quickly back and forth, chewing his nails and asking himself, "Where's me ideas?" Hepburn moves next to Henry and tries to make food, but discovers the eggs are rotten. Grant continues rapid pacing, shifting his hat brim forward and back, considering possibilities. "Might snatch a bag," he says. Then he sits at the table and leans forward with his hand to his mouth in the pose of *The Thinker*. Hepburn naively asks, "Why can't we be like Robin Hood?" Grant stands, scowls, and announces to Henry, "'E's got no more sense than a girl!" This makes him think of a badger game they could pull off if only they had a girl—if you're amusing and a bit nice to them, he explains, you can get them to do whatever you want. Henry is almost at the point of revealing Sylvia's identity when she kicks him and makes him shut up. "Why don't we all get jobs and go to work?" she asks. Grant grabs her by the seat of her pants and the neck of her jacket, lifting her and pushing her across the room and out the door, which he slams behind her—a move that, due to Grant's skill, seems comic rather than dangerous. Henry sighs, "Can't [Sylvester] see what work's done to me?"

When Jimmy gets the idea of the heist at Buckingham Gate, the characters once again become actors or pretenders. Henry is without a hat, so Grant snatches the chapeau of a piano tuner from a peg in a hallway of their rooming house and gives it to him. Henry sweeps the brim up at a flamboyant angle, sticks out his chin, and relishes the idea of playing an artiste. Grant tells Henry he looks like an impresario, "and so you shall be!" They link arms and march forward like a comedy team. Sylvester, hiding in the hallway above, decides to secretly follow.

At Buckingham Gate, some of the action resembles bedroom farce. Grant rings at the door of a townhouse and acts overjoyed to see his old pal Maudie, who, we discover, has always wanted to break into show business. He grabs her from behind, lifts her off the floor, and tries to kiss her as she giggles wildly. There's always roughhouse in Jimmy Monkley's treatment of women—he simply takes what he likes—but Grant gives it a comic element, avoiding brutishness. Maudie wonders what the stranger accompanying Grant must think. "'E's broad minded," Grant says. "'E's in the theatrical line, as you can see by 'is 'at." Maudie, wide-eyed, sexy, and fluttery, becomes a demure lady. "Pleased to meet you, I'm sure," she says, offering her hand.

The scene is filled with performance-within-performance. Henry kisses Maudie's hand and adopts the trilling, polished accent of a man of the world: "It's a pleasure to meet a true English rose." Grant grabs her again and pulls her close, explaining with a sly smile that they've come in the front door because he's learned the owners of the house are "off on the briny" and he wants her to meet the distinguished Mr. Scarlett.

The movements in the wide shots are equally theatrical, as if the camera were viewing a comic stage routine in which Grant crosses left and right, striking poses. Going into a salesman act, he turns to Henry and says, "You've 'eard many beautiful singers, I'm sure, but this little girl . . ." He pats her on the bottom and pushes her forward. Then he crosses, takes her aside with a few graceful steps, and in stagy confidentiality persuades her to break out champagne, dress in the clothing and jewelry of the lady of the house, and perform a number for Henry. Maudie cheerfully complies. Grant embraces her roughly, nibbling her ear before she rushes upstairs.

As Maudie dresses, Henry knocks at the boudoir door, wearing a Napoleon costume that belongs to the man of the house. He gives her a leer and she giggles, pushing him out to finish dressing. Meanwhile, Sylvester is trying to climb in the bedroom window. The sight of Sylvester's hands on the pane causes Maudie to shriek for help, and she and Henry hide in the closet. Grant bursts in and angrily drags Sylvester inside. Once his fury subsides, Maudie sings and he accompanies her on the piano. A cigarette in his mouth, he leans back flamboyantly, one foot on the floor and the other cocked on the piano bench. Afterward, he grabs her again, gives her a long kiss, and lets her go, putting his hands in his pockets to conceal the fact that he's just purloined the "sparklers" around her neck.

This doesn't fool Hepburn, who threatens to call the police. Grant acts as if he's going to beat Sylvester, but doesn't. Champagne softens the mood, and everyone seems to agree when Sylvester suggests they become traveling players in the countryside: "A caravan! The cornfields and the sea!" They break out singing "I Like to Be Beside the Seaside," and Grant, going into a dance with Maudie, thrusts out his pelvis, spins, tips his hat, does a quickstep, swings one leg to the right and the other to the left, and kicks up his heels.

When the action moves to Dorset, we see a complete performance of "The Pink Pierrots," with Grant at the piano.

But in this half of the film. As the relation between Sylvia and Fane develops, Grant seems a bit different from the fellow we've seen until now. After spying Sylvia's transformation into a woman, he finds her walking home in humiliation from Fane's house, where she's just encountered Lily, her apparent rival. Wearing a straw boater, a sporty jacket, a white turtleneck, and white shoes, he approaches and walks along with her in a lengthy traveling shot. "Going my way, little girl?" he says, tipping his hat and smiling in lascivious amusement. He looks her up and down in frank approval and doesn't hesitate to take possession: "Well, well, well . . . From now on we're going to be a proper little foursome . . . I *like* you." He grabs her at the waist and pulls her to him, ignoring her resistance. Back at the caravan, he becomes commanding, pulling out a cigarette and ordering Maudie to pack up because "We're moving on." Everyone prepares but Henry, who is crazed with jealous imagination and seems to realize that Maudie has taken an unseen lover.

The first sign that Jimmy feels true affection for Sylvia comes that night during a storm, when he hears her calling for the missing Henry. To her surprise, he helps her search for her father. They have no success, but in the morning they notice a bit of clothing at the edge of a seaside cliff. Protectively, Grant holds Sylvia back and goes to look down, where he sees a body on the rocks—Henry has fallen to his death during his search for Maudie, who has left for good with her lover. "Poor kid," Grant says quietly when Sylvia looks down in grief.

On the next day, Grant and Sylvia return from Henry's funeral, walking in another traveling shot; she's in black, and he has a black armband on his striped suit. Hat tilted back, he smokes a cigarette with a troubled attitude. No longer the sinister thief or comic con man, he notes that Fane wasn't at the funeral: "The fellow didn't even come to give you a word of sympathy . . . Maybe we ain't good enough for some people." Then he stops and makes his version of a marriage proposal—a far cry from the sort of thing moviegoers came to expect of Cary Grant. "You and me suit," he says. Speaking for himself, he adds, "there's a little bit of warm 'eartedness, you know." Taking her by her arms, he makes an offer: "Let's you and me muck along together, eh? And let the rest of the world go to pot." He tosses his cigarette aside, removes a grain of tobacco from his lips, and kisses her despite her sorrow and reluctance.

Lily's cries are heard in the distance. She's in the ocean and is either suicidal or a poor swimmer. Without hesitation, Sylvia runs to the shore, pulls off her shoes, and swims out to rescue the drowning woman (the waves are high, and Hepburn almost drowned doing the stunt). Sylvia and Grant bring the unconscious Lily to the caravan, make a bed for her to rest, and move out to the caravan steps, where they discuss the situation. In close-up, Sylvia expresses her *chagrin d'amour* but wants to give the news to Fane because she believes he and Lily are an ideal romantic couple who should be united.

This is one of Grant's best moments. He frowns in distaste and calmly shrugs off Sylvia's suggestion: "Ain't my job to fetch and carry for mister curly-headed artist." In close-up, he looks away, frowns again, and contemplatively remarks that Lily is no romantic heroine: "If she'd met a good-looking yokel on the way to the water, she wouldn't be 'ere now." Sylvia reacts with disgust. "You've got the mind of a pig!" she says. Jimmy keeps looking away and replies in a soft but grim tone: "It's a pig's world." Grant's reading of the line is lucid and forceful yet understated. Unlike Jimmy Monkley's earlier boast that the world is made up of hawks and sparrows, it's an expression of class resentment, hinting at a history of wounds.

Sylvia takes the news to Fane, who has just heard of Henry's death. When he learns about Lily, he praises Sylvia's goodness and embraces her. They leap in his car and go to help Lily, only to find that the caravan is gone. A mad chase follows, but both Jimmy and Lily have disappeared. Jimmy Monkley's "little bit of warm 'eartedness," combined with his talent as a good-looking scoundrel, has brought Sylvia together with Fane and at the same time found himself a wealthy lover. As for Grant, he's given a performance that not only runs against the grain of his image but also shows the considerable variety of his skills.

None But the Lonely Heart (1944)

One of Grant's personal projects, this film was based on a 1943 novel by British author Richard Llewellyn, who had become a familiar name in Hollywood. His previous novel, *How Green Was My Valley*, concerning a family of Welsh coal miners, had won the 1939 National Book Award and in 1941 was filmed by John Ford, winning best-picture and best-director Oscars in the same year as *Citizen Kane*. It was proletarian in its subject, and, as its title indicated, pastoral in its spirit. In contrast, *None But the Lonely Heart* concerned characters at the fringes of the working class in London's East End—an environment less subject to the heroic nostalgia and sentiment Ford bestowed upon *How Green Was My Valley*. Grant read the new novel in galleys and was doubtless reminded of some aspects of his early life in Bristol. RKO's production chief, Charles Korner, knew of Grant's interest and purchased the rights.

Korner assigned the screen adaptation to Clifford Odets, a veteran of the Group Theater, who was famous for the working-class dramas *Waiting for Lefty*, *Golden Boy*, and *Awake and Sing*. Odets was relatively new as a screenwriter, and the task of creating a vehicle for Grant wasn't easy. Llewellyn's novel, set in the years before World War II, is told from the point of view of the young Cockney Ernie Mott, just emerging from adolescence and living with his mother in cramped East End quarters. Ernie has untutored talent as a painter, and his mother, who runs a battered second-hand shop, occasionally gives him money for paints. Plagued with acne and sexual yearning, he becomes interested in two women in the neighborhood: a bohemian type who occasionally has parties with musicians, and a beauty who works at an amusement arcade called the Fun Fair. Ernie's growth is charted through his relationship with his mother and these women, plus his eventual involvement with a criminal gang.

The result is rather like a *Bildungsroman*, but without a typical conclusion. Llewellyn wrote the novel during wartime, and it was unfinished when he joined the British military; it was nevertheless published, and in 1944, on the Italian warfront, he saw the movie adaptation, its reels out of order, with an audience of US troops. "I hadn't known that Cary Grant had bought the screen rights," he wrote in the preface to an expanded 1969 edition of the novel, "but I thought it gallant to the point of recklessness. It's an abstrusely difficult subject, to start with, and it had a beginning, middle, but no end."[10] He was overjoyed by what the film achieved.

Grant was equally overjoyed by the screenplay—so much so that he influenced RKO to assign Odets, who had plenty of experience with theater but relatively little with motion pictures, as the film's director. (At one point studio publicity announced Alfred Hitchcock would direct, which seems an odd choice, even though Hitchcock had a Cockney background.) Odets wrote to Herman Kobland, his New York secretary, noting that "Cary and I got on very well and he seems to have a real shine for me, including trust in my talents."[11] As the film neared release, he wrote again to

[10] Richard Llewellyn, *None but the Lonely Heart* (New York: Macmillan, 1969), ix.
[11] Clifford Odets correspondence, June 6, 1944, Box 3, Lilly Library, Indiana University.

Kobland: "I begin to think it will bore a small hole in some people's heads and breach the movie business a little bit, showing what can be done with simple, conventional means in the way of real and fresh result . . . Cary Grant is actually off his handsome head with delight, but I wasn't surprised, for he has taste."[12]

A lasting friendship developed between Odets and Grant. At one point Odets told Kobland of plans for another film with the star—"my Hollywood story, with a studio background."[13] This was probably the genesis of Odets's *The Big Knife*, in which, sometime later, he wanted Grant to take the lead role. It never happened, either because Grant had other obligations or because of the postwar Red scare. In 1947, Lela Rogers, mother of Ginger, testified before the House Un-American Activities Committee in her newly appointed role as RKO's official "expert" on communist infiltration of Hollywood, and branded *None But the Lonely Heart* "communist propaganda." Odets's movie career was damaged by the congressional hearings (he had been a member of the American Communist Party in the 1930s), and he would direct only one other film, *The Story on Page One* (1959).

RKO invested heavily in *None But the Lonely Heart*. It constructed what trade papers described as the largest indoor set in Hollywood—a dreary, East End street lined with tightly packed houses and storefronts covering two large sound stages. Grant's co-star, Ethel Barrymore, who plays Ernie Mott's mother, was in the midst of a successful touring company of *The Corn Is Green* and had not acted in movies for many years. Grant wanted her so much that the studio covered all the expenses of temporarily closing her play's tour. In the end, however, the film lost money. Critical reception was favorable but qualified. *None But the Lonely Heart* won Academy Awards for Barrymore, composer Hans Eisler, and editor Roland Goss; Grant was nominated for best actor but lost to Bing Crosby in *Going My Way*.

Odets made Ernie Mott a thirty-five-year old (Grant was in his forties), creating adult relationships. He also gave Ernie musical aptitude and sexual experience. He retained the novel's prewar time frame, but the shadow of impending war hangs over the film from the start, when we see Ernie

[12] Odets correspondence, September 7, 1944, Lilly Library.
[13] Odets correspondence, September 12, 1944, Lilly Library.

entering Westminster cathedral on the eve of the celebration of World War I's Armistice Day. He encounters Henry Twite (Barry Fitzgerald), a peddler who becomes one of his friends. Twite, gazing down at the tomb of the Unknown Warrior, mutters, "might have been my son." Grant looks over Twite's shoulder, frowning in baffled wonder, and quietly says, "might be my old man." As Grant exits the church and walks home, a somewhat pretentious, voice-of-God narrator tells us, "When Ernie Mott, humble citizen of London, looked down at the tomb of the Unknown Warrior, he little realized that he might be a warrior in a second world war . . . This is his story, the story of Ernie Mott, who searched for a free and whole life in the second quarter of the 20th century." At the film's end, the theme of war resurfaces when Grant and Fitzgerald look up at aircraft in the sky and make speeches about the need to fight for a better world.

Critics and audiences may have been put off by the wartime message elements, or because Grant wasn't playing "Cary Grant," or because the film makes no attempt to provide relief from the impoverished atmosphere. Even so, Grant's performance is among his best. Ernie Mott isn't a theatrical, sometimes comic personality like Jimmy Monkley in *Sylvia Scarlett*, and Grant's skill here often consists of low-key reactions to other players. It's a realistic performance in which he underplays the Cockney accent and only occasionally shows Cockney-style exuberance. (Despite this, some viewers at the film's sneak preview complained they couldn't understand what the actors were saying.)

Grant establishes certain aspects of the character at the start, in a non-comic but slightly Chaplinesque sequence. Tramp-like Ernie, wearing dirty clothes, a scarf, and a battered cap, returns late at night to a deserted street in his old neighborhood, accompanied by a bull terrier on a leash. Walking gracefully, an unlit cigar stub in his mouth, he puts his hand on a newel post and hops over it. He peeks into a familiar lighted window, frowns, and crosses to the front of a used furniture store labeled MOTT'S, where he opens the door with a key, lets the dog in, and turns with his hands in his pockets, moving toward the corner. Hitching up his baggy pants, he crouches and uses a piece of chalk to write large letters on the sidewalk: ERNIE MOTT IS HOME AGAIN. Standing with cap pushed back and stogie in his mouth, he gives a slightly contemptuous, music-hall hop, skip, and salute.

Ernie is a handsome vagabond whose air of confidence is tinged with bitterness, and the film gradually reveals his complex character. It also provides Grant with a series of recognition scenes, actorly moments of Aristotelian *anagnorisis*, in which Ernie acquires knowledge and undergoes change. We begin learning more about him through his troubled relationship with his mother, who awakens the next morning, scowls at the strange dog in her drab quarters, and silently goes about preparing breakfast for her wayward son.

Barrymore's performance as Ma, especially in the first half of the film, has a quality of intense, angry reserve. Quiet, slow moving, she's weighted down with poverty and hard work, and, as we later discover, she's terminally ill. Her infirmity is neatly balanced against Grant's energy, and both are skilled at handling subtext. Odets's dialogue has an indirect, bank-shot quality, and Ernie and his Ma, two strong presences trying to avoid an outright quarrel, seldom express their feelings openly. "Ernie, grub's ready," Barrymore calls, her face weary but showing muted anger. At breakfast, there's no gesture of affection. Barrymore stands apart, never smiling, and Grant conveys resentment masked by showy cheerfulness. When he finishes the meal, he tosses a scrap to his dog, Nipper. "Nothin' too good for that dog, Ma," he says proudly, "bought it myself." Legs crossed, smiling, he leans back and asks, "Don't like him, do you?" Barrymore parries with a question: "Where you been, Ernie?" Grant says, "Up North, all over the shop." Barrymore turns her back and Grant's smile fades. "What's up?" he asks, "You were standing there as if I jabbed you with your own hatpin or something." He frowns, strikes a match on his shoe, and lights his cigar butt. "What'd you come back home for, son?" she asks, her tone soft and flat, then derisively adds, "Miss me?"

Her question creates a beat change, making the characters' feelings more evident and leading to confrontation. Chewing a scrap of food, Grant puffs his cigar, rises from his chair, puts his foot on a piece of furniture, and ties his shoe. "Can't say I did, Ma," he says with an undercurrent of resentment. "You know me, *tramp* of the *universe!*"

As he crosses toward her, we see a framed picture of the beautiful young Ethel Barrymore on the wall. Also on the wall is a picture of Grant's father, Elias Leach. "Anything in the shop needs *mending*, Ma?" Grant asks, as if repeating a familiar ritual. "None that needs your help, Ernie sweet," Barrymore says contemptuously. Grant moves nearer and lists his services in an insinuating manner: "*Mending? Polishing?* Do you a spot of *gardening?*" Then he smiles, trying to make peace—he's used to getting by on charm. "Mean to do my best by you, Ma love," he says, and tries to embrace her. Barrymore suddenly slaps him hard.

Grant reacts with stunned surprise, his faux cheerfulness dropping away. "Happy couple aren't we?" he says. "A bit of proper respect is what's needed," Barrymore tells him. "I get no more from you than I got from your father... What right you got to go drifting around the country year in and year out like a breath of homeless wind?" Grant ties his scarf with a decisive air (it's a useful accessory he uses several times for expressive purposes). "Okey doke," he says as he exits, "I'll be off in the morning."

Ernie's day introduces us to three characters who have an effect on his life, but first, as he and his dog stroll along the street, we meet a few residents. An older woman leans out her window. "We live so close I can fairly hear you change your mind," she says. Her piano needs tuning, and Ernie, who is skilled at the job, promises to be back at teatime. An old man pokes his head out a broken window he refuses to have fixed. "You're a man after my own heart," Ernie says, smiling and crossing to the rooms he peeked into the night before. An elevated train passes in the distance. Standing in the doorway is Aggie (Jane Wyatt), who never takes her eyes off him.

Jane Wyatt, who at one time belonged to the New York social register, was usually cast as an idealized housewife; her career in movies was disrupted by her outspoken opposition to the Red Scare, but she later became famous as the mother in the long-running 1950s TV series *Father Knows Best*. This film takes advantage of her maternal quality, at the same time giving her opportunity to suggest sexual passion. An anomalous character in Ernie's neighborhood, she's a cellist for hire with no working-class accent, and her rooms are equipped with a fine piano. Ernie has been here many times, as we can sense when Grant enters, looks at the surroundings, and knowingly grins.

Like the previous scene, this one involves subtext. "It's yours whenever you want it," Aggie says, and she's talking about more than furniture. Grant smiles slyly: "Have to take you with it, do I, Aggie?" He tosses his cap aside and sits at the piano, where he plays a tune and sings parlando style: "He's the boy for me, I'm the girl for him, he's my lump of toffee cake and pudding!"

Smiling broadly, he says, "You're the biggest fool I ever met, Aggie . . . Black as the ace, I am. Don't you know it yet?" She simply nods. He reaches out, pulls her gently toward him, and tells her about Ma's ultimatum. When she asks what he plans to do, he puts her in his lap and kisses her. Fade out.

When the script of *None But the Lonely Heart* was submitted to Joseph Breen of Hollywood's Production Code Administration, Breen responded, "Aggie's attitude toward Ernie must not contain any inference that she is willing to sleep with him."[14] The film gets around the command in two ways. First, it relies more on the actors—Grant's knowing smile, Wyatt's quiet attitude of unconditional love, the passionate kiss—than on dialogue. Second, it elides time with the fade. We fade into the sound of a chiming grandfather clock in Ma's shop and look over her shoulder as she gazes out her window at Aggie's place across the street. After an indeterminate passage of time, we dissolve to Aggie, who is practicing her cello as Ernie reclines on her couch, frowning and listening with interest.

[14] Odets correspondence, February 22, 1944, Lilly Library.

Ernie notices that Aggie plays one note "a little flat" and asks if the music is Italian. "Russian," Aggie says, without identifying it as Tchaikovsky's 1869 "None But the Lonely Heart," which has Russian lyrics based on a poem by Goethe. American audiences in 1944 may well have recognized the music because Frank Sinatra had recently recorded the song with English lyrics on a V-disk. "Nice," Ernie says, and Grant's expression shows that he's hiding its effect on him. As he prepares to go, Aggie suggests they meet at nine. Teasing, he says, "All alike, you women. I don't go on no *time-table*, like a *train*! Ernie Mott, *citizen* of the *great smoke*, I don't stay put!" He raps his knuckles on a table, gets his cap and dog, and adds, "Maybe I'll see you tonight." Pausing at the door, he smiles his pleasant Cary Grant grin and says, "And maybe not." Aggie points to the cleft in Grant's chin and asks, "Who gave you that?" He tells her, "A present from me Pa."

Ernie doesn't return that night because he meets two other important characters. After cadging a pack of cigarettes at the shop of Dad Pettyjohn (Roman Bohnen), where a couple of pig-tailed girls are fascinated by an aquarium and by Ernie's handsomeness, he goes to the Fun Fair. A familiar customer, he strolls through the crowd with a confident, slightly Chaplinesque air, his feet a bit turned out, one hand in his pocket, leading his dog. Pausing at a shooting range, he greets the barker, who waves aside a group of well-dressed gangster types and makes a great show of inviting

Ernie to shoot. Grant grins broadly, pumps the rifle, and fires off a full round of bullseyes. He wins a pack of cigarettes, and because he already has a pack, he gives it away. The gangsters are disgruntled (one is played by the diminutive Skelton Knaggs, who began as a performer in London's East End and in the 1940s became a memorable character actor in Val Lewton's RKO films).

Ernie continues his stroll, examining a coin-operated music machine that's out of tune. He's followed by Jim Mordinoy (George Coulouris), boss of the small group of gangsters. Impressed with the shooting demonstration, Mordinoy offers Ernie a quid "just to be a pal," asks if the bull terrier fights, and adds that he can't understand why "a man of your talent wears them rags." Grant speaks calmly, emphasizing that he "*never*" fights his dog and describing his rags as "the *uniform* of my *independence.*" Delivering one of Ernie's more philosophical speeches, he leans an elbow on a banister, looks Coulouris in the eye, and talks as if he doesn't care who hears: "That's what it's all about—be a victim or be a *thug*. Suppose you don't want to be either, like me? Not the 'are, and not the 'ound? *Then* what?"

Shifting to a confidential tone, he asks about a luminous blond nearby who wears a tight sweater and dispenses change for the customers. Mordinoy identifies her as Ada Brantline, who is wary of men. Grant's eyes light up like a child anticipating Christmas. "Have to box carefully there," he says.

June Duprez, who plays Ada, was an English actor who had starred in Alexander Korda's *The Thief of Bagdad* (1940). Her Hollywood career was brief and this was its high point, creating pathos and lending a breathy Cockney accent to the dialogue. Ada is sad and quietly fearful. She's overheard the conversation with Mordinoy, and when Ernie approaches she guardedly asks if he's some kind of artist like the unpleasant fellow in the paperback she's reading. "Pooh!" he says and tries to seduce her with his resumé, which Grant reels off with speed and flair: "Play the *piano* by ear. *Tune* pianos, that's me. *Polish* furniture . . . Got any *bugs* in your house? Send for Ernie Mott. Know how to medicate *dogs* and *cats*, repair *clocks* and other *delicate* machinery. I invent *inventions*! I'm working on my greatest invention now. A human animal that don't look for a master." She almost whispers, "I like that kind of talk." Ernie gives her his big smile. "That brings up one question, Ada dear. What time you get off?"

They meet that evening in a dim alleyway behind the Fun Fair. Ada is fatigued, leaning against a wall, her hair glowing in the moonlight. As Ernie walks into the alley with his Chaplinesque gait, he passes a man digging in the garbage and tosses him a coin. When Ada comments on this, the unlettered Ernie, who keeps surprising us with homely wit, poetic sensibility, and ur-socialism, voices a parable: "Saw in the distance what seemed an animal, come up close and saw it was a man, come still closer and saw it was my brother." Shadowed, he walks toward Ada, his cap concealing his face as he looks down into her eyes and asks, "Tired?" They gently kiss. "Quiet as mice, ain't we," he says, "tired, ain't you?" She tells him she's always tired.

Ernie takes Ada out to dinner in a simple café, leaving his dog behind because she refuses to have an animal along. He's puzzled by her quietness, and their conversation is uneasy. She speaks almost to herself, amazed that she's never allowed a man to kiss her so immediately. Chiefly with the tone of his voice, Grant indicates his awareness of her sadness; he awkwardly compliments her painted fingernails, like "five red beetles," and taps an empty teapot with a fork, boasting in a detached, thoughtful way: "G-sharp. Perfect pitch, that's me. Not one in a million has that, don't you know? Very *unusual person*, didn't you know?" As they walk back to her place, he hitches up his pants and does the talking. "No place to go and going there tomorrow," he says and explains that his Ma is in the business of "squeezing pennies out of paupers." When they reach Ada's door, she refuses to let him in. "Black as ace, I am," he says, and leaves her. On the next morning, as he prepares to leave for good, there's another quarrel with Ma. "I'm not in the business of sweating pennies out of devils poorer than me self," he says. She tells him, "Someday you'll know I'm your only friend."

At this point Ernie's character is almost fully developed. In conflict with his mother and his environment, he's refused to become either a hare or a hound and instead become a drifter. He's more limited in knowledge and experience than most men in their mid-thirties (a vestige of Odets's reworking of Llewellyn's much younger character), but he gets by with native intelligence, a musical ear, a variety of self-taught talents, and the ability to charm women. Beneath his occasional bravado, Grant lets us feel his spiritual homelessness, frustrated idealism, and spasms of "black as ace" guilt. The remainder of the film involves his crisis of discovery and futile, tragic attempts at change.

Ernie tells Aggie that he's sick of the street where he was born and its smell. On the way out of town he stops at a greasy fish-and-chips diner run by Lew Tate (Dan Duryea), a creepy fellow with a toothpick in his mouth. Tate stands behind the bar, his mother next to him, and advises Ernie to stay home: "It's safe, that's what it is, safe!" Ernie smiles, nibbles chips, and ignores Tate. He's pleased to find nearby Ike Weber (Konstantin Shayne), a kindly Middle-European who runs a local pawn shop. (The film suggests that Ike is Jewish but never says so.) We've already met Ike in a scene with Ma. Because of her illness and concern about Ernie, she's trying to raise money by selling her valuables, and she lets Ike know that she's dying. He's long been in love with her from a distance, and his encounter with Ernie over fish and chips is no accident. He delays Ernie's departure by offering him two pounds for a quick repair of a watch in his shop.

Once Ernie's job is done, Ike says, "I want to put a flea in your ear. Your mother is a very sick woman." Grant stands from the work bench with a fed-up attitude, looks threateningly down at Ike, and holds out a big hand: "You owe me two pounds, Ike. *Pay* it. I'll be on my way." He gets his coat, cap, and scarf and heads for the door, where he pauses and turns with a frown of irritation. "What is it she's got," he asks, "pain for her *no-good son*?" Ike quietly says, "Your mother is not a superficial woman, Mr. Mott." Grant walks back into the room, standing in close-up. He begins tying his scarf with a suspicious, insolent attitude, but his eyes suggest concern. "What is it?" he wants to know. "Cancer," Ike says. Grant uses the scarf as an expressive object. The moment of recognition strikes a blow, and his hands freeze as the scarf billows from his jacket.

That night Grant sits almost Hamlet-like on a low wall by the river. Brooding and a bit drunk, he encounters Henry Twite, who takes a fatherly interest. Grant underplays much of this long-take scene, keeping signs of Ernie's drunkenness and emotion at bay. He introduces himself to Twite as Ernest Verdun Mott, the middle name a reference to his Pa's death in the war. "A friend of mine put something in my ear and I can't get it out," he says woozily, rubbing his ear and softly murmuring, "buzz, buzz, buzz." He tries to drive off the feeling: "I'm a lone wolf barking in the corner, plain disgusted with a world I never made and want none of." Then he covers his face with his hands and weeps.

The two go to a pub, where Twite sits at a table rolling cigarettes from the tobacco he picks out of butts, while Grant sits at a piano, head bent in sorrow, playing chords from "None But the Lonely Heart." Wandering homeward, they pause at an underpass, and in a shadowed, low-level shot they lean against a wall, whistling and singing to make an echo. "Echo, echo, echo," Grant mutters. "Buzz, buzz, buzz." Cut to Ma, awakened from sleep by the sound of a door opening. She finds Ernie struggling up the stairs and drunkenly stopping to sit. He looks up at her and says, "Changed my mind. Home to stay. Less said the better."

We next see Ernie painting the sign above Ma's store and exuding cheer. Descending a ladder, Grant smiles and lands on the ground with a dancing, "hop, ta-dah" gesture. He never reveals his knowledge that Ma is dying, but their relationship is transformed. She wryly smiles as she prepares to run an errand and teasingly invites him to "take charge of the shop." When she returns, she's bought him a suit. He comes downstairs wearing it and stands awkwardly in a doorway. The suit is flashy, down-market, and ill-fitting, but Ernie's uniform of independence is gone, and he looks just a bit more like Cary Grant.

The relationship with Ada also changes, leading to more discoveries. She's sorry he's returned, but they're soon in love. A long take frames the two in close-up as they smoke cigarettes, talk quietly, and kiss—it's a good example of Grant's almost unique ability to play love scenes with what Lionel Trilling, writing about Scott Fitzgerald, once described as "gentleness without softness."

Afterward, he encounters Aggie in the street as she returns from playing cello at a club dinner filled with drunks. "I get sick of it," she says. Ernie tells her he's now attached to Ada, but the main reason he's staying is Ma's illness. This does nothing to affect Aggie's feelings for him.

Ada has begged Ernie to take her dancing, but their evening in a nightclub is a disaster. Ernie isn't a good dancer, and in his suit he suffers from the heat of the crowded room; what's more troubling, Mordinoy invites him and Ada for champagne at his table. Ernie, who has never heard of champagne and doesn't like it, undergoes several humiliations, which Grant plays with a combination of discomfort, challenge, and mounting anger. Mordinoy adopts a superior attitude, amused by Ernie's hostility. He casually mentions that he's just bought the Fun Fair. When a stranger approaches and invites Ada to dance, he needs to ask Mordinoy's permission. A thoroughgoing sadist, Mordinoy begins fondly reminiscing about when he and Ada had adjoining rooms in a hotel, and he bought her clothes and gifts. Just as Ernie is ready to start a fight, Mordinoy informs him that Ada is the ex-Mrs. Mordinoy.

Ada subsequently explains that she's been divorced for two years, but on the next day, working in the shop with Ma, Ernie still feels anger. Grant expresses it indirectly, grimly sewing a button on the old sweater he's wearing. Ma tells him she'd like to see him have a "nipper" or two. "There's lots of love in you," she says, and it "wants an object." Later in the day, while managing the shop, his frustrations mount again. The customers include a little girl who tries to sell worthless items to buy winter boots and an aging woman who wants to sell a bird cage housing her dead bird. When the woman leaves, Ernie explodes with anger at the world and smashes the cage.

We've reached a turning point. In an earlier scene, Ma is visited at night by a woman who wants her to fence stolen goods; Ma refuses, but she's subsequently visited by another woman, the leader of a gang of local shoplifters and thieves, who offers her five hundred pounds. Nearing death and worried about Ernie's future, she secretly gives in to the temptation. At virtually the same time, against all his natural inclinations ("Peace, that's what I'm looking for," Grant passionately declares, "straight bones without dirt and distress!"), Ernie privately decides to travel with the hounds.

Ernie visits the auto repair garage that serves as the front for Mordinoy's gang, offering his services, and then visits Ada, who for the first time invites him into her apartment. She's looking for another job and reveals that she's the mother of a baby girl. Once again Ernie experiences discovery. Grant reacts with pleasant surprise and performs another love scene with a mingling of gentleness and strength. "What a *wallop* you give me, Ada," he says, "Put your *face* up half a mo." They kiss, and as they talk Grant lovingly manipulates an object—a child's music box that belongs to the baby. Ada wants to leave town. He tells her he's thinking of going in with Mordinoy, and she reacts with fear verging on panic.

Ernie nevertheless joins Mordinoy's gang, and Ma goes to a meeting of the thieves, among whom are Lew Tate and his mother. With advance wages, Ernie buys expensive gifts for Ma, including a radio. She suspects he's gone wrong but gives him a gift from her shoplifters' loot—a platinum cigarette case, which he thinks is silver. It makes trouble for both of them.

Ernie's first assignment from Mordinoy is to accompany him and his goons to Ike Weber's shop, where, on bogus evidence, they seize what they claim is a stolen ring and take pleasure in beating Ike. It's a tricky scene for Grant because he mostly stands in the background, registering anger and shame silently. As one of the thugs tortures Ike, Grant can stand it no longer and punches him.

The trap he's fallen into of his own making tightens further when he goes with Ada to Mordinoy's tiny office above the Fun Fair and rebelliously announces that they're going to marry. The space is claustrophobic, and Odets blocks the action skillfully. Mordinoy ignores the couple, standing with his hat on and his back turned, playing a slot machine against the wall. Ernie takes a chair and Ada sits a few feet across from him on a two-seat sofa. Mordinoy turns and sits beside Ada, who stands and crosses, standing fearfully behind Ernie. Mordinoy then stands before them and forbids them to leave or marry. "I'm a machine," he says, "I'll sink you worse than any Titanic."

One of Clifford Odets's major problems in adapting Llewelyn's novel was how to end the film. The original version of the novel was essentially unfinished, but it didn't leave Ernie in a trap. Odets chooses to shift into a short burst of melodramatic action that he soon undercuts, achieving an ambiguous closure without the escapist satisfaction of victory over evil. Without telling anyone, Ernie decides that the only way out is to kill Mordinoy. He sends Ada off in the care of Henry Twite and stands on a corner, thoughtfully taking a cigarette from his platinum case. Grant uses the cigarette to mark Ernie's decision; he flicks it angrily away without lighting it. He then borrows a short rifle from the shooting gallery in the Fun Fair, wraps it in a newspaper, and accepts a ride from two gangsters who want to take him for a meeting with Mordinoy. En route, the driver runs a light and finds himself in a high-speed chase with the police. Ernie tosses his rifle out the window and the car crashes, rolling over and breaking into flames. When the police rescue Ernie and one of the gangsters from the car, Grant has a brief man-of-action moment, punching the gangster. The other gangster is dead, and the horn of the car is stuck, blaring loudly as flames billow. Grant stands at the curb with the police and a group of onlookers and listens in quiet wonder to the sound of the horn. "E-flat!" he says.

Ernie and the surviving gangster are taken to the police station, where the arresting officer is intrigued by Ernie's platinum cigarette case. Hours later, Ike Weber, his face still showing signs of the beating he received, arrives at the station to bail Ernie out. "You're frying yourself in your own fat," he tells the chastened Ernie. When Ernie returns to Ma's shop, he finds Aggie, Dad Pettyjohn, and Henry Twite anxiously waiting. Ma has been arrested. The police have traced the stolen cigarette case to her and found other items from the gang of shoplifters.

Grant's face freezes in horror, and unfortunately Odets resorts to emotional cliché. It's raining outside, and Grant stands looking through a window, where streaming rivulets of water run down the pane like tears. But a more effectively emotional scene follows when Ernie visits his dying mother in prison. Grant kneels beside her narrow bed and tries to console her by announcing that he's going to get married. With what seems her last breath, Barrymore moans, "Disgraced you son!" Grant embraces her. "Disgraced me, Ma?" he says, his voice denying that possibility and carrying the full weight of his anguished love. Given what we know of Cary Grant's own relation to his mother, the scene must have had personal resonance for him.

Ernie's life further unravels when Henry Twite informs him that out of fear Ada has returned to Mordinoy. She leaves Ernie a letter and her child's music box, which Grant holds expressively while Twite reads what she's written. He and Twite have the philosophical conversation I've already described—an awkward attempt at uplifting preachment, eschewing patriotic rhetoric but alluding to a coming war that might bring social justice.

The last shot of the film is more interesting: we see Ernie returning to his old neighborhood at night, just as he did at the beginning, but on the opposite side of the street. As he passes Aggie's window, he pauses and listens to her cello playing "None But the Lonely Heart." He opens the door. A special effect, probably accomplished with an optical printer, looks as if the camera were slowly zooming back, making Grant a bit fuzzy and indistinct, a distant figure as he walks inside.

Some viewers may think this is a happy ending. Ernie is joining a woman who loves him and wants to marry him without conditions. She's the kind of woman Ma has hoped Ernie might find—a woman with "a head on her shoulders." But Ernie has never been in love with Aggie; in effect, she's his second choice, and given the off-screen narration at the beginning of the film, he may soon be off to war. The ending has an emotional ambiguity, giving Ernie and Aggie only a shadowed, qualified relief from their loneliness. It's an appropriate mood for the most unusual film of Grant's long and varied career—a film almost devoid of his comic talent but filled with an ability to render anguish, tender emotion, and social anger.

Cary Grant Filmography

Full credits are given for films that are emphasized in this book.

This Is the Night (1932) Paramount, dir. Frank Tuttle
Sinners in the Sun (1932) Paramount, dir. Alexander Hall
Merrily We Go to Hell (1932) Paramount, dir. Dorothy Arzner
Devil and the Deep (1932) Paramount, dir. Marion Gering
Blonde Venus (1932) Paramount, dir. Josef von Sternberg
Hot Saturday (1932) Paramount, dir. William Seiter
Madame Butterfly (1932) Paramount, dir. Marion Gering
She Done Him Wrong (1933) Paramount, dir. Lowell Sherman
The Woman Accused (1933) Paramount, dir. Paul Sloane
The Eagle and the Hawk (1933) Paramount, dir. Stuart Walker
I'm No Angel (1933) Paramount, dir. Wesley Ruggles
Born to Be Bad (1934) Twentieth-Century Pictures, dir. Lowell Sherman
Alice in Wonderland (1933) Paramount, dir. Norman McLeod
Thirty Day Princess (1934) Paramount, dir. Marion Gering
Kiss and Make-Up (1934) Paramount, dir. Harlan Thompson
Ladies Should Listen (1934) Paramount, dir. Frank Tuttle
Enter Madame! (1934) Paramount, dir. Elliot Nugent
Wings in the Dark (1935) Paramount, dir. James Flood
The Last Outpost (1935) Paramount, dir. Louis Gasnier and Charles Barton
***Sylvia Scarlett* (1935) RKO Radio Pictures**
    Producer: Pandro S. Berman
    Director: George Cukor
    Screenplay: Gladys Unger, John Collier, and Mortimer Offner
    Based on *The Early Life and Adventures of Sylvia Scarlett*, by Compton
        Mackenzie
    Photography: Joseph H. August
    Cast: Katharine Hepburn (Sylvia), Cary Grant (Jimmy Monkley), Brian
        Aherne (Michael Fane), Edmund Gwenn (Henry Scarlett), Natalie
        Paley (Lily), Dennie Moore (Maudie Tilt)

The Amazing Quest (1936) Garrett-Klement Pictures (UK), dir. John
   L. Balderston
Big Brown Eyes (1936) Paramount, dir. Raoul Walsh
Suzy (1936) Metro-Goldwyn-Mayer, dir. George Fitzmaurice
Wedding Present (1936) Paramount, dir. Richard Wallace
When You're in Love (1937) Columbia Pictures, dir. Robert Riskin
The Toast of New York (1937) RKO Radio Pictures, dir. Rowland V. Lee
Topper (1937) Hal Roach Studios, dir. Norman Z. McLeod
The Awful Truth (1937), Columbia Pictures
   Producer-Director: Leo McCarey
   Associate Producer: Everett Riskin
   Screenplay: Viña Delmar
   Based on a play by Arthur Richman
   Photography: Joseph Walker
   Cast: Irene Dunne (Lucy Warriner), Cary Grant (Jerry Warriner), Ralph
           Bellamy (Daniel Leeson), Alexander Darcy (Armand Duvalle),
           Cecil Cunningham (Aunt Patsy), Molly Lamont (Barbara Vance),
           Esther Dale (Mrs. Leeson), Joyce Compton (Dixie Belle Lee),
           Robert Allen (Frank Randall), Robert Warwick (Mr. Vance), Mary
           Forbes (Mrs. Vance)
Bringing Up Baby (1938), RKO Radio Pictures
   Producer-Director: Howard Hawks
   Screenplay: Dudley Nichols and Hagar Wilde
   Based on the short story by Hagar Wilde
   Photography: Russell Metty
   Editor: George Hively
   Cast: Cary Grant (David Huxley), Katharine Hepburn (Susan Vance),
           Charles Ruggles (Major Applegate), May Robson (Aunt Elizabeth),
           Walter Catlett (Constable Slocum), Fritz Feld (Dr. Lehman), Barry
           Fitzgerald (Gogarty), Leona Roberts (Hanna Gogarty), George
           Irving (Mr. Peabody), Virginia Walker (Alice Swallow), John Kelly
           (Elmer)
Holiday (1938), Columbia Pictures, dir. George Cukor
Gunga Din (1939), RKO Radio Pictures, dir. George Stevens
Only Angels Have Wings (1939), Columbia Pictures, dir. Howard Hawks
In Name Only (1939), RKO Radio Pictures, dir. John Cromwell

His Girl Friday (1940), **Columbia Pictures**
  Producer-Director: Howard Hawks
  Screenplay: Charles Lederer
  Based on the play *The Front Page*, by Ben Hecht and Charles MacArthur
  Photography: Joseph Walker
  Editor: Gene Havlick
  Cast: Cary Grant (Walter Burns), Rosalind Russell (Hildy Johnson),
      Ralph Bellamy (Bruce Baldwin), Gene Lockhart (Sheriff
      Hartwell), Helen Mack (Mollie Malloy), Porter Hall (Murphy),
      Ernest Truex (Bensinger), Cliff Edwards (Endicott), Clarence Kolb
      (Mayor), Roscoe Karns (McCue), Frank Jenks (Wilson), Regis
      Toomey (Sanders), Abner Biberman (Louie), Frank Orth (Duffy),
      John Qualen (Earl Williams), Alma Kruger (Mrs. Baldwin),
      Billy Gilbert, (Joe Pettibone), Pat West (Warden Cooley), Edwin
      Maxwell (Dr. Egelhoffer)

My Favorite Wife (1940), RKO Radio Pictures, dir. Garson Kanin
The Howards of Virginia (1940), Columbia Pictures, dir. Frank Lloyd
The Philadelphia Story (1940), Metro-Goldwyn-Mayer, dir. George Cukor
Penny Serenade (1941), Columbia Pictures, dir. George Stevens
Suspicion (1941), **RKO Radio Pictures**
  Producer-Director: Alfred Hitchcock
  Screenplay: Samson Raphaelson, Joan Harrison, and Alma Reville
  Based on *Before the Fact*, by Francis Iles
  Photography: Harry Stradling
  Music: Franz Waxman
  Editor: William Hamilton
  Cast: Cary Grant (Johnnie Aysgarth), Joan Fontaine (Lina Aysgarth),
      Sir Cedric Hardwicke (General McLaidlaw), Nigel Bruce (Beaky),
      Dame May Whitty (Mrs. McLaidlaw), Isabel Jeans (Mrs. Newsham),
      Heather Angel (Ethel), Auriol Lee (Isobel Sedbusk), Reginald
      Sheffield (Reggie Weatherby), Leo G. Carroll (Captain Melbeck)

The Talk of the Town (1942), Columbia Pictures, dir. George Stevens
Once Upon a Honeymoon (1942), RKO Radio Pictures, dir. Leo McCarey
Mr. Lucky (1943), RKO Radio Pictures, dir. H. C. Potter
Destination Tokyo (1943), Warner Bros., dir. Delmer Daves
Arsenic and Old Lace (1944), Warner Bros., dir. Frank Capra
Once Upon a Time (1944), Columbia Pictures, dir. Alexander Hall

None But the Lonely Heart (1944), RKO Radio Pictures
    Producer: David Hempstead
    Director-Screenplay: Clifford Odets
    Based on the novel by Richard Llewellyn
    Photography: George Barnes
    Music: Hans Eisler
    Editor: Roland Gross
    Cast: Cary Grant (Ernie Mott), Ethel Barrymore (Ma), Barry Fitzgerald
            (Twite), June Duprez (Ada), Jane Wyatt (Aggie), George Coulouris
            (Jim Mordinoy), Dan Duryea (Lew Tate), Roman Bohnen (Dad
            Pettyjohn), Konstantin Shayne (Ike Webber)
Night and Day (1946), Warner Bros., dir. Michael Curtiz
Notorious (1946), RKO Radio Pictures
    Producer-Director: Alfred Hitchcock
    Screenplay: Ben Hecht
    Photography: Ted Tetzlaff
    Editor: Theron Warth
    Music: Roy Webb
    Costumes: Edith Head
    Cast: Cary Grant (Devlin), Ingrid Bergman (Alicia Huberman), Claude
            Rains (Alexander Sebastian), Louis Calhern (Paul Prescott),
            Leopoldine Konstantine (Madame Sebastian), Reinhold Schunzel
            (Dr. Anderson), Moroni Olsen (Walter Beardsley), Ivan Triesault
            (Eric Mathis), Alex Minotis (Joseph), Wally Brown (Mr. Hopkins),
            Eberhard Krumschmidt (Kupka), Fay Baker (Ethel)
The Batchelor and the Bobby-Soxer (1947), RKO Radio Pictures, dir. Irving Reis
The Bishop's Wife (1947), Samuel Goldwyn Productions, dir. Henry Koster
Mr. Blandings Builds His Dream House (1948), RKO Radio Pictures
    Producers-Screenplay: Norman Panama and Melvin Frank
    Director: H. C. Potter
    Based on the novel by Eric Hodgins
    Photography: James Wong Howe
    Cast: Cary Grant (Jim Blandings), Myrna Loy (Muriel Blandings),
            Melvyn Douglas (Bill Cole), Reginald Denny (Simms), Sharyn
            Moffett (Joan Blandings), Connie Marshall (Betsy Blandings),
            Louise Beavers (Gussie), Ian Wolfe (Smith), Harry Shannon
            (Tesander), Tito Vuolo (Mr. Zucco), Nestor Pavia (Joe Apollonio),
            Jason Robards (John Retch), Lurene Tuttle (Mary), Lex Barker
            (carpenter), Emory Parnell (Mr. Pedelford)

Every Girl Should Be Married (1948), RKO Radio Pictures, dir. Don
    Hartman
I Was a Male War Bride (1949), Twentieth-Century Fox, dir. Howard Hawks
Crisis (1950), Metro-Goldwyn-Mayer, dir. Richard Brooks
People Will Talk (1951), Twentieth-Century Fox, dir. Joseph L. Mankiewicz
Room for One More (1952), Warner Bros.
    Producer: Henry Blanke
    Director: Norman Taurog
    Screenplay: Jack Rose and Melville Shavelson
    Based on the book by Ana Perrott Rose
    Photography: Robert Burks
    Cast: Cary Grant (George Rose), Betsy Drake (Anna Rose), Lurene
        Tuttle (Miss Kenyon), Randy Stuart (Mrs. Foreman), John Ridgley
        (Harry Foreman), Irving Bacon (Mayor), Mary Lou Treen (Mrs.
        Roberts), Iris Mann (Jane), George Winslow (Teenie), Gay Gordon
        (Trot), Malcolm Cassell (Tim), Clifford Tatum, Jr. (Jimmy-John),
        Larry Olsen (Ben)
Monkey Business (1952), Twentieth-Century Fox, dir. Howard Hawks
Dream Wife (1953), Metro-Goldwyn-Mayer, dir. Sidney Sheldon
To Catch a Thief (1955), Paramount, dir. Alfred Hitchcock
The Pride and the Passion (1957), Metro-Goldwyn-Mayer, dir. Stanley Kramer
An Affair to Remember (1957), Twentieth-Century Fox
    Producer: Jerry Wald
    Director: Leo McCarey
    Screenplay: Delmer Daves and Leo McCarey
    Photography: Milton Krasna
    Editor: James B. Clark
    Music: Hugo Friedhofer
    Cast: Cary Grant (Nickie Ferrante), Deborah Kerr (Terry McKay),
        Richard Denning (Kenneth), Neva Patterson (Lois Clark), Cathleen
        Nesbitt (Grandmother), Robert Q. Lewis (himself), Charles Watts
        (Ned Hathaway), Fortunio Bonanova (Courbet)
Kiss Them for Me (1957), Twentieth-Century Fox, dir. Stanley Donen
Houseboat (1958), Paramount, dir. Melville Shavelson

Indiscreet (1958), Grandon Productions
  Producer-Director: Stanley Donen
  Screenplay: Norman Krasna
  Based on *Kind Sir*, by Norman Krasna and Joshua Logan
  Photography: Freddie Young
  Editor: Jack Harris
  Music: Richard Bennett
  Cast: Cary Grant (Philip Adams), Ingrid Bergman (Anna Kalman), Cecil
        Parker (Alfred Munson), Phyllis Calvert (Margaret Munson),
        David Kossoff (Carl Banks) Megs Jenkins (Doris Banks)

North by Northwest (1959), Metro-Goldwyn-Mayer, dir. Alfred Hitchcock
Operation Petticoat (1959), Granart Company, dir. Blake Edwards
The Grass is Greener (1960), Grandon Productions, dir. Stanley Donen
That Touch of Mink (1962), Granley Company, Arwin Productions, Nob Hill
        Productions, dir. Delbert Mann
Charade (1963), Universal, dir. Stanley Donen
Father Goose (1964), Granox Company, dir. Ralph Nelson
Walk, Don't Run (1966), Granley Company, Sol C. Siegel, dir. Charles Walters

Selected Bibliography

(In addition to the published sources listed here, see the Grant fan website at www.carygrant. net and Mark Kidel's informative documentary film, *Becoming Cary Grant* [2017].)

Bell-Metereau, Rebecca. *Hollywood Androgyny*. New York: Columbia University Press, 1985.
Bogdanovich, Peter. *The Cinema of Howard Hawks*. New York: Museum of Modern Art, 1962.
Bogdanovich, Peter. *Who the Hell's in It?* New York: Alfred A. Knopf, 2004.
Britton, Andrew. *Cary Grant: Comedy and Male Desire*. Newcastle upon Tyne: Tyneside Cinema, 1984.
Callahan, Dan. *The Camera Lies: Acting for Hitchcock*. New York: Oxford, 2020.
Cavell, Stanley. *Pursuits of Happiness: The Hollywood Comedy of Remarriage*. Cambridge, MA: Harvard University Press, 1981.
Chandler, Raymond. *Selected Letters of Raymond Chandler*, ed. Frank MacShane. New York: Delta, 1987.
Cole, Toby, and Helen Krich Chinoy, eds. *Actors on Acting*. New York: Crown, 1970.
Crowe, Cameron. *Conversations with Wilder*. New York: Alfred A. Knopf, 2001.
Dyer, Richard. *Stars*. London: BFI, 1979.
Eliot, Marc. *Cary Grant: A Biography*. New York: Harmony Books, 2004.
Empson, William. *Some Versions of Pastoral*. New York: New Directions, 1950.
Empson, William. *Some Versions of Pastoral*, ed. Seamus Perry. London: Oxford University Press, 2020.
Eyman, Scott. *Cary Grant: A Brilliant Disguise*. New York: Simon & Schuster, 2020.
Glancy, Mark. *Cary Grant: The Making of a Hollywood Legend*. New York: Oxford University Press, 2020.
Goffman, Erving. *The Presentation of Self in Everyday Life*. Garden City, NY: Doubleday, 1959.
Harvey, James. *Romantic Comedy in Hollywood*. New York: Da Capo Press, 1998.
Haskell, Molly. *From Reverence to Rape: The Treatment of Women in the Movies*. Baltimore: Penguin Books, 1974.
Hecht, Ben. *A Child of the Century*. New York: Ballantine Books, 1970.
Hillier, Jim, and Peter Wollen, eds. *Howard Hawks: American Artist*. London: British Film Institute, 1996.
Kael, Pauline. *When the Lights Go Down*. New York: Holt Rinehart & Winston, 1977.
Kanin, Garson. *Hollywood*. New York: Viking Press, 1974.
Kozloff, Sarah. *Overhearing Film Dialog*. Berkeley: University of California Press, 2000.
Krohn, Bill. *Hitchcock at Work*. London: Phaidon Press, 2000.
Kuleshov, Lev. *Kuleshov on Film*, trans. and ed. Ronald Levaco. Berkeley: University of California Press, 1974.
Lane, Christina. *Phantom Lady: Hollywood Producer Joan Harrison*. Chicago: Chicago Review Press, 2020.
LaValley, Albert J., ed. *Focus on Hitchcock*. Englewood Cliffs, NJ: Prentice-Hall, 1972.

Leitch, Thomas, and Leland Pogue, eds. *A Companion to Alfred Hitchcock*. Chichester: Wiley- Blackwell, 2011.

Maier, Simon. *Inspire!* Asia: Martin Cavendish International, 2001.

McBride, Joseph. *Hawks on Hawks*. Berkeley: University of California Press, 1982.

McCarthy, Todd. *Howard Hawks: The Grey Fox of Hollywood*. New York: Grove Press, 1997.

McElhaney, Joe. "Medium-Shot Gestures: Vincente Minnelli and *Some Came Running*." In *Vincente Minnelli: The Art of Entertainment*, ed. Joe McElhaney. Detroit: Wayne State University Press, 2009, 322–35.

Miller, Mark Crispin. *Boxed In: The Culture of TV*. Evanston: Northwestern University Press, 1988.

Morrison, James. *Auteur Theory and My Son John*. New York: Bloomsbury Academic, 2018.

Naremore, James. *Acting in the Cinema*. Berkeley: University of California Press, 1988.

Nelson, Nancy. *Evenings with Cary Grant: A Biography*. Lanham, MD: Applause Books, 2012.

Palmer, R. Barton, and David Boyd. *Hitchcock at the Source*. Albany: State University of New York Press, 2011.

Shipman, David. *The Great Movie Stars*. London: Hamlyn, 1970.

Shumway, David. *Modern Love: Romance, Intimacy, and the Marriage Crisis*. New York: NYU Press, 2003.

Spoto, Donald. *The Dark Side of Genius: The Life of Alfred Hitchcock*. Boston: Little, Brown, 1963.

Thomson, David. *A Biographical Dictionary of Film*. 3rd ed. New York: Alfred A. Knopf, 2004.

Truffaut, François. *Hitchcock/Truffaut*. Rev. ed. New York: Simon and Schuster, 1985.

Walker, Michael. "*Suspicion* Revisited." *Hitchcock Annual*, no. 20 (2020): 1–38.

Wood, Robin. *Howard Hawks*. London: British Film Institute, 1983.

Index